THE POLICEMAN
IN THE COMMUNITY

THE POLICEMAN
IN THE
COMMUNITY

Michael Banton

New York
BASIC BOOKS, INC., PUBLISHERS

Contents

Preface

The idea that a sociologist should study the police is one that catches popular attention. When they heard that I was doing this many people in the United States assumed that I must be primarily interested in police corruption and brutality. Though people in Britain were less inclined to make this sort of assumption, they also generally believed that I must be examining defects in police organization and conduct. The tradition of research into social problems is now so firmly established that the public takes it for granted that sociologists study social institutions that are not working satisfactorily. The idea that it can be instructive to analyse institutions that are working well in order to see if anything can be learned from their success has not yet taken hold. Yet obviously the science of social relations cannot be advanced very far unless people study all sorts of institutions to see how they function. Some will say that we understand quite enough about how the police, the church, the civil service, and the shipbuilding industry work. The same sort of people four hundred years ago would have asserted that we knew quite well how our bodies functioned and that to bother about how blood got from one part of the body to another was a waste of time. Humanity managed for many centuries without any knowledge of the circulation of the blood and with very little understanding of how most of its social institutions really worked. But in recent years more and more people have come to appreciate that research into our social organizations may prove as rewarding as research into our physical organisms. This study of the police is intended as a small contribution to the understanding of a very important institution in modern life; one which has not hitherto attracted sufficient attention in the analysis of society; and one which, given the continuance of present trends, is going to become more important still. I have tried not to pass judgement upon how well policemen do their job; though, inevitably,

vii

many of the incidents and practices I describe here will seem to merit commendation or condemnation. Of what occupation could not the same be said? I ask the reader, therefore, to try – as I have tried – to lay aside moral judgements and seek simply to understand the policeman's occupation in its social context.

Between 1956 and 1958 I was engaged in a study of British behaviour towards coloured immigrants. At the beginning of this period there seemed to be a dialogue between two opposed points of view. One school argued that British people were strongly prejudiced against the immigrants and that in every sphere one found social discrimination if one only looked hard enough. The other school maintained that the public was remarkably tolerant of the newcomers, who were, after all, rather tiresome, and that there was no colour bar in Britain. To exaggerate somewhat, the dialogue was between those who claimed that the British people were devils and those who thought them angels. A more detached examination of the evidence suggested that Britons were sometimes devils and sometimes angels. The interesting sociological questions were: in what situations were they the one rather than the other? What factors in these various situations called forth the different kinds of behaviour? My analysis produced some tentative answers to these questions and I sought to follow them up by studying intergroup relations in a different sphere. At that time (1958) I thought I detected signs of a similar dialogue concerning police-public relations. One school, complaining about the way the Metropolitan Police had treated political demonstrators, was inclined to view the police as having fascist leanings and as being the enemy of the working class. The other school, represented by the organs of the establishment, asserted that the British police were the best in the world, and was inclined to place them above criticism. It was the devils or angels argument again. It seemed to me that the situational factors were once again the interesting ones. I knew that in the East End of London the police often adopted a different approach to the public from the one they used in middle-class suburbs and I could see why such differences might be expected. It seemed that this might offer an opportunity for testing and elaborating upon the ideas I had developed earlier.

There were other reasons for attempting such a study. Very many people indeed seem to be interested in the police, and the fascination of this occupation must reflect its very central position in our way of life. One author, Mr Geoffrey Gorer, has even suggested that the orderliness of the British population since the middle of the last century is owing to our having adopted the policeman as a model of the ideal male character. Then in 1958 there were already signs which led me to believe that social tensions associated with police-public relations might well be on the increase. To some extent this opinion was justified by later events, for in January 1960 a Royal Commission was set up to review police organization, pay, and 'the relationship of the police with the public and the means of ensuring that complaints by the public against the police are effectively dealt with'. In more recent months, other incidents have kept the questions of police organization and public relations in the spotlight of popular attention.

The appointment of this Royal Commission, the memoranda submitted to it, and the final report, all gave rise to much argument about whether relations between the police and the public had deteriorated, remained the same, or improved. These arguments proved quite inconclusive. Why? The fundamental difficulty, I would hold, lay in the attempt to come to a quick and simple judgement about a complex and only partially analysed phenomenon. There can be no question that police-public relations have changed since the end of the second world war, and are continuing to change. It is difficult to think of a single major social change which has not affected the police in some way: the expansion in road traffic; the National Assistance Acts; the growing concentration of population in London and the South-East; commonwealth immigration; television; nuclear defence policy; hire purchase; the improved chances for educational mobility (which affect the pool of police recruits); the changing structure of social class – all these and many others have been of significance. The same influences bear upon members of the public and bring them into contact with the police in varying ways. The increasing rate of technological progress moves more and more of the population out of the smaller communities in which people have an active sense of the communal good and are able to forward it in their own ways, into larger industrial communities in which people seem to be more oriented to private ends and where the solitary individual can do little to influence the society in which he lives. If this is the case, it may well make the individual member of the public less inclined to go out of his way to help the police, but the source of the change lies outside the police-public relationship. Anyone who seeks to discuss these issues in a meaningful and constructive fashion must address himself to this complexity: simple statements are bound to be misleading. Anyone who hopes to render the problem less complex must also concentrate upon statements of fact rather than upon the judgements of value which permeate questions of 'deterioration' and 'improvement'.

My first approach to the police regarding the possibility of conducting research on these lines was made early in 1958. Some of my colleagues at the university thought that the approach would be futile, and that the police would be unwilling to have an outsider interview their personnel. They were mistaken. The police officials with whom I discussed the project were at first a little surprised by its novelty, but they pointed out that they had nothing to hide, and, on my offering not to publish any information gained as a result of their support that had not first been agreed with them, they gave me every assistance. It was my opinion at the time, and I am more than ever convinced of its correctness, that it would be difficult to study police-public relations without first learning more about the nature of the policeman's job and the pressures that bear upon him. It also seemed only sensible to try to assemble evidence on the relatively accessible aspects of the occupation before attempting to study the more sensitive ones. Before the social scientist can discern the problems that he can fruitfully study, he often needs a fair amount of basic descriptive material concerning the field. For the police these data were nowhere available – neither in the training manuals nor in the reminiscences of former policemen – and it seemed advisable first of all to clarify what the ordinary policemen did most of his time and how he did it. I felt, with George C. Homans, that first of all we needed more systematic examination of the commonplace events of everyday behaviour.

Owing to other commitments I was not able to start my research until early in 1960, when I began by conducting a series of eight group discussions, of about one and a half hours' duration, with sergeants attending the Scottish Police College. These discussions were recorded. Their object was to explore differences in the social position of policemen working in country districts and in the cities, and to see what effect these differences had upon their satisfaction with the job. Later that year I began interviewing recruits in order to get some impression of what they expected, with a view to finding out later, by means of more group discussions, how the reality measured up to the expectation. The third phase, which started at the beginning of 1961, was a study of the organization of an urban division and the nature of patrol work.

In February 1962 I went to the Massachusetts Institute of Technology for twelve months as Visiting Professor of Political Science and as a staff member of the Center for International Studies. This offered me an excellent opportunity to extend my police studies and to benefit from a comparative perspective on my Scottish data. I talked with officers from a number of Massachusetts police departments and approached two particular departments for permission to make a closer study of their work. One was unable to give me any research facilities (it had been subjected to considerable criticism in past months and was generally suspected of corruption) but the other department was most helpful. To gain experience of police work in another region of the United States I travelled to the South during the summer vacation and spent four full weeks with one police department and two weeks with another. On other occasions I also discussed the questions that interested me with police officers from different parts of the country. Furthermore, in both 1961 and 1963, I was able to make some brief inquiries into police work in Sweden, where local forces will shortly be integrated into a national police service.

As I had hoped, my American experience did allow me to see Scottish police work in a new light. The research as a whole has not enabled me to follow up the ideas about intergroup relations in the way I had wanted, but it has uncovered some unexpected and equally interesting questions. Interest in the sociological study of police work has grown considerably of late. Several political scientists, sociologists, and social psychologists have projects on hand in the United States and some other sociologists are working on this question in Britain. I have had a great advantage in being able to compare patrol work in these two countries, in which the conception of the police officer's role remains fundamentally similar, although social conditions show considerable differences. It may therefore be of help if I attempt a general comparison and a sketch of what seem to me the chief dimensions of the role. The study is not as well balanced as could be wished, for on some points it takes a long time to collect evidence. Were I to aim at a really complete description and analysis of the policeman's role I fear that I should commit myself to a lifetime's labour. One of the difficulties is that the police service is a little world of its own in which almost everything is related to everything else and it is impossible to isolate a single aspect for separate examination (some indication of this may be seen in the way the separate chapters of this book sometimes have to consider the same topic from different standpoints). But a start has to be made, and others may rectify my omissions. My research has been based chiefly on observation of police conduct in a relatively law-abiding Scottish city and among above-average American police departments. I have not been able to study what happens in situations where policemen are subject to strain and provocation, and can say little about the sorts of incident that attract newspaper publicity. My work provides no answer to questions whether police-public relations are good or bad, better or worse, but it may convey some understanding of what constitutes police-public relations and how the culture of the police occupation affects these relations. Because of the approach adopted it tends to reflect the police view of public relations and does not adequately explore the attitudes and experiences of different groups within the public. This latter question is something I plan shortly to investigate in a separate study.

It may be advisable to emphasize once again that this is a study in occupational sociology. To study the way in which an occupation is organized is not to explain away its purpose. A police administrator faced with the task of how to allocate his men, how to ensure that they do their job and that none of the less-estimable old hands has a bad influence upon the recruits, has the same problem as a works manager, a hospital administrator, or a bishop, though so far as I know the managerial aspects of the bishop's role in the twentieth century have not been studied. Many investigations have demonstrated that in certain kinds of factory the workers attempt to set their own level of production: they put pressure upon any of their number who works too little or too hard. This reaction is one that seems to us very natural and we might expect it to operate in other occupations. Do old-time policemen induce enthusiastic recruits to slow down a bit? What do clergymen feel about the extra-hard-working young man from Oxford, who has obviously got an eye on a deanery and is not above flattering the bishop or making the sort of marriage that will help his career? Factory workers with a griev-ance often 'work to rule' or reduce output. Do policemen? Do clergymen? If not, why not? Such questions seem slightly facetious at first, but there is no reason to doubt that the comparative study of occupations may reveal many relationships of theoretical interest and of practical significance. A man's occupation is coming to be the role which most determines his other roles and his position in society. It is often of particular consequence for his wife – indeed a study of police wives might prove very rewarding. Though it would be idle to claim that we have yet developed any very satisfactory framework for analysing occupations or even for studying particular roles, this is likely to become an important sphere for social science research in the near future.

Many individuals and organizations have contributed to this study by giving me facilities for the research, by advising me on questions of substance, and by vetting portions of the manuscript – though none of them is to be held responsible for any interpretations or mistakes in this book. It is impossible to mention as many of my helpers as I would wish, but so far as the Scottish research is con-cerned I must acknowledge the support of the Committee for Co-operation and Research in the Social Sciences of the University of Edinburgh, and the assistance of the police associations of Scotland. At a variety of points I have received generous help from: S. A. Kin-near CBE, Commandant of the Scottish Police College; Chief Con-stable John R. Inch, CBE; Superintendent Ian McLaren; Constable Robert McClement (of the Scottish Police Federation); Constable A. McCreadie; and officers of the Scottish Home and Health Department.
For help with my inquiries in the United States I am particularly indebted to the Center for International Studies of the Massachusetts Institute of Technology, which financed my work during the vaca-tion; to Lieut.-Colonel D. A. McCandless, Director of the Southern

Police Institute; to Police Chiefs Herbert T. Jenkins, J. J. Hord, and John J. Buckley; to Captain W. A. McCall, Lieut. D. H. Riley, and Mr T. B. Francis. I shall long remember the warmth and friendly reception accorded me by officers of all ranks in the American departments I visited.

MICHAEL BANTON

Department of Social Anthropology
October 1963   University of Edinburgh

CHAPTER 1

Social Control

A cardinal principle for the understanding of police organization and activity is that the police are only one among many agencies of social control. This is generally appreciated by police administrators, even though their public statements sometimes fail to recognize it. One American police chief, for example, writes:

'A condition precedent to the establishment of efficient, professional law enforcement in a community is a desire and a demand on the part of the residents for that type of service. In this respect, law enforcement does not differ greatly from private industry. The one factor which predetermines the success of any business is the market. . . . A second lesson the police administrator can draw from industry is that markets are created. . . . The vital elements of civilized life, including our most sacred institutions, at one time or another have been laboriously *sold* to the people' (Parker, 1954, p. 6).

One of his captains echoes him:

'. . . not only do we have a product to sell (law enforcement) which often meets with strong sales resistance. . . .' (Gourley, 1954, p. 136).

And another police chief declares in similar vein:

'We have a pretty good product to sell in the protection of life and property and with 300 officers selling police efficiency 24 hours a day. . . .' (Carolina City Police Department, Information Bulletin No. 1).

Though the police are concerned to a very important extent with law

1

enforcement it is not a product, nor is it to be attributed to the police. Indeed the police are relatively unimportant in the enforcement of law.

Consider, for example, some of the variations in criminality. In the average United States city of 500,000 people there were, in 1962, thirty-six cases of murder and non-negligent manslaughter, and sixty of forcible rape; whereas in Edinburgh in the same year there were two of murder, two of culpable homicide, and eight of rape. The Edinburgh figures are lower not because the police are more efficient or meet less 'sales resistance' but because the community is more orderly. Social control – as Homans demonstrated so well in *The Human Group* (1950) – is a property of states of social relations, not something imposed from outside. The level of control, be it high or low, is determined by the kinds of social relationship that exist among the individuals who make up the society, and their effectiveness in getting people to follow prescribed patterns of behaviour. The number of people who obey the law and follow such patterns without ever a thought for police efficiency is striking testimony to the power of social norms and humanity's methods of training children to observe them: most people grow up so well conditioned that they cannot feel happy if they infringe the more important norms. Thus control is maintained by the rewards and punishments which are built into every relationship, and which are evident in the conferring and withholding of esteem, the sanctions of gossip, and the institutional, economic, and moral pressures that underlie behavioural patterns. Law and law-enforcement agencies, important though they are, appear puny compared with the extensiveness and intricacy of these other modes of regulating behaviour.

The communities with the highest level of social control are small, homogeneous, and stable – like small tribal societies in out-of-the-way regions, or the more remote villages in industrial nations. In such communities social order is maintained to a very large extent by informal controls of public opinion, and there is little resort to formal controls such as legislation or the full-time appointment of people to law-enforcement duties. Most tribal societies have no police forces, prisons, or mental hospitals: they are small enough to be able to look after their own deviants. The small society with a simple technology can afford to have its 'village idiot'; the large and complex one cannot, for many people would not recognize him and he might easily injure himself or create havoc in the affairs of others. Village societies are usually tightly knit communities because everyone is so dependent upon everyone else. If there is only one shop, everyone has to go there at some time or other, and the shopkeeper has to keep on reasonably friendly terms with all the local inhabitants. If there are two grocers, people may feel obliged to patronize the one who attends the same church as they do. Residents cannot disregard the opinion of their neighbours because there may come a situation in which they will need their cooperation. In these circumstances the job of the policeman is to oil the machinery of society, not to provide the motive power of law enforcement.

The orderliness of the small homogeneous society is not simply a matter of economics and social organization; as in any other kind of society it has moral qualities. In the village society, the rich are under greater obligation than their city counterparts to recognize responsibilities to the unfortunate; village people are involved in one another's affairs at work and in leisure whereas, in urban districts, social contacts and the sense of mutual commitment are more restricted. In homogeneous societies girls and boys grow up attuned to the social order, accepting their place in it and believing the distribution of rewards to be reasonably just. People who live together like this are agreed in what they consider right and wrong, so it can be said that the highly integrated society is characterized by a high level of consensus, or agreement on fundamental values. These moral judgements pervade social life and do not stop short when business relations are in question. The policeman obtains public cooperation, and enjoys public esteem, because he enforces standards accepted by the community. This gives his role considerable moral authority and sets him apart from the crowd socially, much as does the role of minister of religion.

Life in a small highly integrated society has many attractions, but most people find the rewards of economic progress even more attractive, and the two sets of values do not go well together. In the traditional kind of society the various social institutions are so interrelated that an alteration in one affects all the others and it is difficult to introduce changes. In an economically developing society, however, people and resources have to be moved around. Individuals have to

B

pursue their private benefit and to fight the community controls that put a brake on change. Some people receive great rewards, greater than their moral deserts; others, who are scarcely less worthy, are much less fortunate. In a developing economy rewards are distributed according to economic criteria: the successful businessman is honoured because he has been successful – money comes itself to have a moral value. At many points economic values clash with community values and frequently break them. For instance, a man may have had an exemplary career for the first forty-five or fifty years of his life and hold an honoured if not particularly distinguished position in the community; then suddenly technological discoveries affect the industry in which he works. His skills become obsolete, the plant is reorganized, and he has to begin again. He may have to take a lower-paid job or to work under people who were previously his juniors, and this inevitably undermines his position in the community. In numerous sectors of industrial society, people appear to take many of their criteria for community ranking from the economic order and the occupational hierarchy. In one way and another industry is continually imposing on the community its own criteria of economic rewards.

Another example which makes the same point in a different way can be drawn from the effect of the introduction of the automobile upon the social structure of the Southern States of America. These were communities in which Negroes were expected to defer to Whites and to allow them precedence. When Negroes acquired automobiles the question arose whether precedence should be determined by the rule-of-the-road or by local custom. For a time the answer depended on the speed of the vehicle: below 25 mph the white driver, especially if it was a woman, expected the Negro driver to give way; above that speed no one took risks (Myrdal *et al.*, 1944, p. 1,368). Nowadays there is hardly any of this. Driving rules cannot be based upon particularistic criteria of skin colour: they must be the same for every driver, otherwise the confusion would be interminable. Thus new technical developments impose their own logic and upset community values of deference to older persons, to women, and, in some situations, to persons of superior social class or race.

Community life cannot be organized upon purely economic or technological principles because many important factors, like mother-love, neighbourliness, sympathy, and so on, cannot be valued in a market. They have a different logic. Industrial life can take place only within the larger context of society which creates the demand for various kinds of product, and if, in seeking to maximize its own goal of productivity, industry overturns these social values, it can destroy the context within which it seeks to operate. Major strikes – especially in towns dominated by a particular industry – sometimes illustrate how people can feel when deep-set community values are disturbed and notions of justice wounded. Perhaps the most extreme example of what happens when economic ends are unregulated is the gold-mining or prospecting camp, in which everything is subordinated to individual greed for gold, and community life is at its most tenuous. Yet even in the residential suburbs of Europe and North America the effect of increasing industrialization upon community values can be observed. People move house or employment as opportunity offers, and they seek less the rewards of community approval; their goals are the financial rewards of occupational success and they know that social approval will follow when these have been attained. In these circumstances there is less feeling that the social order is a just one, and less agreement upon moral standards. The majority, however, seem to feel that the lower sense of community is more than offset by the rewards of economic advance.

No social changes are without their costs, and one of the principal costs of making the social structure more flexible is the decline in social integration. An index of this is the crime rate. In 1962 the number of crimes known to the police in England and Wales rose by 11 per cent over the previous year, and in Scotland by 8 per cent. Between 1938 and 1960 the incidence of larceny, breaking and entering, receiving, fraud and false pretences, sexual offences, violence against the person, and a small residue of other offences increased by 225 per cent. In the United States the crime rate for 1962 was 5 per cent above that for the previous year and 19 per cent above that for 1958, after adjustment for population growth.

As the problem of maintaining order becomes more severe, societies increasingly adopt formal controls, summarized by an anthropologist as 'courts, codes, constables, and central authority'. In the early days the parish constable was simply a citizen on duty. All able-bodied men were expected to give their services in turn, being elected for a

5

year and serving without payment. By the eighteenth century this system had broken down completely in London and, after serious disorders, a permanent constabulary was created in 1829. But the authority that the new police exercised was still that of the citizen constable. Under English law every citizen is still technically bound to arrest anyone who commits a felony in his presence; this is his civic duty and he can be punished if he fails to perform it, though admittedly there is no record of anyone's being prosecuted for such a failure in recent times. Under both English and Scottish law a citizen must go to the assistance of a constable if called upon to do so. The policeman does have certain common law powers as acknowledged by judicial authorities, and he has since been given others by express direction of Acts of Parliament, but the core of his authority stems from his responsibilities as a citizen and the representative of citizens. Judicial decisions of both English and Scottish courts make it clear that the constable is not the employee of the local authority: he exercises his powers and discharges his duties as the independent holder of a public office. If he wrongly arrests and detains someone, then he is personally liable for his actions should the aggrieved party open civil proceedings against him. Nor would it be completely correct to regard the constable as a servant of the Crown: he does not have the immunities of the Crown servant and he cannot shelter behind the orders of a superior – as, for example, a soldier sometimes can. In this sense the constable is a professional citizen: he is paid to discharge obligations which fall upon all citizens, and his obligations are to the community as a whole.

With the changes in police methods necessitated by the increase in crime this conception of the police officer is becoming somewhat anachronistic though it retains a sentimental appeal. Some years ago a Home Secretary observed: 'The British policeman is a civilian discharging civilian duties and merely put into uniform so that those who need his help know exactly where to look for assistance.' Today, especially in connection with the traffic laws, this description is not accurate: the policeman is increasingly seen as an official exercising authority and power over citizens. A division is becoming apparent between specialist departments within police forces (detectives, traffic officers, vice and fraud squads, etc.) and the ordinary patrolman.

The former are 'law officers' whose contacts with the public tend to be of a punitive or inquisitory character, whereas the patrolmen – as later chapters will show – are principally 'peace officers' operating within the moral consensus of the community. Whereas the former have occasion to speak chiefly to offenders or to persons who can supply information about an offence, the patrolmen interact with all sorts of people and more of their contacts centre upon assisting citizens than upon offences.

In contrasting village society with the big industrial nation it is difficult not to convey a false impression. Even in the small-scale stable society consensus is never perfect; it is only relatively high. An even greater mistake would be to imply that consensus is absent under urban conditions. Certainly in some urban situations the moral controls are weak and the formal organization has to impose strict penalties, but there are many basic issues – such as ideas of duty to kinsfolk, work-mates, and neighbours – where popular morality remains powerful. In many urban residential neighbourhoods there is a very real sense of community even if informal social controls are less extensive than in the village. Policemen, being subconsciously aware of their dependence upon these other mechanisms of control, prefer to work as peace officers and to see their role in these terms. There is in Britain a current of opposition to specialization in police work and to the employment of civilian auxiliaries, which cannot easily be explained but which seems to rest upon this ideal of the policeman as a peace officer.

These same considerations apply to a considerable extent in the United States as well, for the Americans inherited the British conception of the civilian constable. In the United States, as in Britain, the police officer is legally responsible for his actions and an aggrieved party may take out a civil suit against him. American police standards have in many places been depressed by local political control – in some municipalities the chief of police is still an elected official – but these arguments about changes in the policeman's role are nevertheless quite relevant to the American experience. The same contrast obtains between rural and urban areas in respect of social control, but, as might be expected with the volume of relatively recent immigration and the continuing internal population movement, social integration is lower than it would be in British communities of comparable size.

When the police officer's role is viewed, not from the standpoint of public order, but simply as an occupation, another major characteristic appears which is common to Britain and the United States, and, indeed, perhaps to all the industrial democracies. The policeman is a member of the society whose laws and norms he is required to enforce. This simple proposition is in fact fundamental, for on the one hand his membership of the society has an important effect upon the way he performs his job (see Chapter 5) and, on the other hand, his having to police his own community has a profound effect upon his off-duty role as a member of that community (see Chapter 7). Moreover, there is a basic inconsistency in his role in that he is called upon to be both the master and the servant of the public. The implications of this situation are particularly worthy of examination. Any analysis of the policeman's role must also be concerned with the likely impact upon it of future social changes. The ideal of the policeman as a peace officer is based upon conditions which are becoming less prevalent. When the average British household has a telephone and a motor car, the patrolman's pattern of activity will be significantly different.

The first task must therefore be to study closely the nature of the relationships in which police and public meet one another. The Royal Commission on the Police (which reported in 1962) failed to give due weight to this aspect of the matter and relied excessively upon the public opinion poll which they had commissioned. Opinion polls are of the greatest value when there is a close association between a subject's attitude and his behaviour – as, for example, in voting studies – but they are of much more limited utility when the attitudinal factor in behaviour is weak compared with situational determinants. The Commission did not consider the obvious limitations of their evidence concerning public opinion, apparently out of an anxiety to acquit the police of criticisms that they felt were unjustified. They stated:

'The findings of the survey constitute an overwhelming vote of confidence in the police, and a striking indication of the good sense and discrimination of the bulk of the population in their assessment of the tasks that policemen have to carry out. It is clear that such change as there has been in public opinion in recent years has

8

been mainly in favour of the police. We therefore assert confidently, on the basis of this survey, that relations between the police and the public are on the whole very good, and we have no reason to suppose that they have ever, in recent times, been otherwise. This is a finding which we believe will give great satisfaction to Your Majesty, to the police and to the public' (*Royal Commission on the Police 1962, Final Report*, pp. 102–3).

But there is no reason to think that the state of relations between police and public is adequately assessed by people's responses to some such question as 'What do you think of the police?' After asking members of the public if they thought that the manner of the police had improved or deteriorated, interviewers went on to ask if they thought that the behaviour of the public had changed: 43·9 per cent answered that the public in general behaved worse than they did ten years ago (ibid., Appendix IV to the *Minutes of Evidence*). If responses to this question are to be taken at face value (which is how the Commission took the answers to the previous question) then they suggest that, in the eyes of many members of the public, relations with the police must have deteriorated independently of what they as individuals may say they think about the police. Even more striking is the Commission's view – based principally on the fact that 82·7 per cent of those questioned said that they had 'great respect for the police' – that relations between the police and the public were very good, although 68·8 per cent of the police respondents – who had far more experience of the matter – asserted that relations had changed for the worse.[1] The difference in the responses derives from the fact that the people were stating here what their attitudes were, whereas the police were inferring public opinion from the degree of cooperation they actually received. Obviously, the latter judgement reflected the more important social problem and was the one that required closer consideration.

Similar confusion is apparent at the opening of the Commission's section on police-public relations where they ask,

'whether there is a peculiar quality in the relationship between the

[1] This criticism was expressed strongly in an article in *The Times Literary Supplement*, 14 September 1962, which was reprinted in the *Police Review*, 26 October 1962.

police and the public of this country, in terms of which we can make assessments of improvement or deterioration from time to time. We believe that there is. It is attested by the foreign visitor whose favourable comments on our police are well known, and it is demonstrated in the common every-day instances in which people instinctively consult a policeman when in difficulty or perplexity even of a minor kind. Perhaps it is a fact of little objective importance that the British consider their police to be the best in the world; but it is not generally disputed that there is a kind of relationship between the policeman and the man in the street in this country which is of the greatest value.'

It is difficult to follow the reasoning of this passage. Is the 'peculiar quality' which is referred to simply a matter of measuring social changes in the same country over time? – in which case it is a fairly simple question of social research techniques. If so, why cloud the issue with references to the opinion of foreigners and the notion of the British police as the best in the world? Or can it be that the Commission see the 'peculiar quality' in police-public relations as something distinguishing Britain from all other countries? In the nineteenth century the Metropolitan Police were probably the best in the world, but others have learned from British experience. It is extremely difficult today to see any reason for considering the British police better than their counterparts in Sweden (and probably in the other Scandinavian countries) and it may be doubted if their reputation is any higher than that of the Royal Canadian Mounted Police. There are police departments in the United States and probably in many other industrial countries with standards little different from those in Britain. To attempt a comparison of police forces as if this were a bathing beauty contest is to display a warped sense of what is important in these matters. It would have been more to the point had the Commission investigated the practice of the police in other countries to see whether they had experienced similar difficulties to those which have arisen in Britain, and whether anything could be learned from their policies, instead of regarding these problems as peculiarly British.

To discover what sorts of activity constitute police-public relations it is necessary first to establish in what situations police anp public interact, and the relative frequency, for example, of 'service' contacts compared with arrests or authoritative contacts. In Chapter 2 a close descriptive account is given of the organization of a patrol division in a Scottish city and the tasks of the man on the beat. Some readers may find Chapter 2 excessively detailed and prefer to skim through parts of it, but it is essential, I would maintain, to have at the outset some idea of how in fact most policemen spend most of their time. This chapter is followed by shorter comparative studies of three American police departments and then by a general discussion of the problems of police organization in Britain and the United States. In the second half of the book the factual content is lower and I have attempted to interpret police actions rather than to describe them. These later passages all start, however, from the discussion of social control in this introductory chapter; they take up some of its assertions and state a more reasoned case for their acceptance.

CHAPTER 2

Police Work in a Scottish City

The following is an account of the organization and activities of police officers serving in one division of a Scottish city's police force. It is based principally upon records kept by all officers on duty for two days (a Thursday and a Friday) of June 1961.

THE DIVISION AND ITS PERSONNEL

The division has an area of approximately 17,000 acres or forty square miles, and a population of 170,000. With 203 police officers, this means that there is one policeman to every 832 inhabitants. The perimeter of the division totals twenty-seven miles. Most of the area is urban in character but there are some farms on the outskirts of the city which fall within the division's boundaries. There are also some fifty stockholders whose records of animal movements have to be inspected by the police. The land rises from sea level on the coast to a height of over 1,600 feet inland; this high land is not built over and needs little policing except for the occasional patrol to keep an eye on youngsters who may break into a reservoir there or damage young trees. These patrols are often undertaken by the mounted section (on horseback). Altogether a total of 440 miles of roadway within the division is patrolled; every one of these miles is at some time patrolled by foot but the regular patrols in the outskirts may be by cycle or mobile patrol van.

A feature of the division is the large number of centres of entertainment within its area, which give rise to considerable crowds and create special problems. There are two major football grounds. For important fixtures the larger one may draw an attendance of 80,000 and create severe problems of parking and traffic control. On such occasions over 200 police are required: one chief superintendent, one chief inspector, eight inspectors, sixteen sergeants, and 190 police constables. Additional police have then to be drafted in from other divisions. At the other ground, police strength may have to rise to one chief superintendent, one chief inspector, three inspectors, eleven sergeants, and 124 police constables. Minor fixtures require fewer men but they are a constant drain on the division's resources of manpower. The recent installation of floodlighting, permitting major fixtures to be played at one of the grounds in the evening, has entailed a further demand upon manpower.

In addition there are six cinemas, four theatres, three dance halls, an ice rink, a zoo, an aerodrome, and a cattle market. One dance hall attracts 2,000 clients on some Friday and Saturday evenings, and up to ten policemen may have to stand by part of the time. Other events create special demands. For example, at the time of the Co-operative Wholesale Society's dividend distribution, two police constables are put onto supervision of queues, etc. for ten days. Then, in the summer season, crowds gather along part of the foreshore, and extra patrols have to be arranged there. The city is also the scene for an unusually large number of special functions; these create corresponding police problems which affect the division directly.

This particular division is one of the four into which the city force is divided. In addition, the city force has three other special departments which relieve the ordinary divisions of certain more specialized duties. These specialist departments are: (i) traffic, including motor patrols, mounted constabulary, communications, police dogs, taxi-cabs, and road safety; (ii) headquarters, including licensing, recruiting, court work, aliens, firearms, dangerous drugs, lost property, pay and records, clothing, information room, and central charge office; (iii) criminal investigation department, including photography, fingerprinting, criminal records, etc.

Divisional police organization is focused upon the uniformed patrol of the entire division. This is carried out in three shifts: the early shift from 6 a.m. to 2 p.m.; the late or 'back' shift from 2 p.m. to 10 p.m.; and the night shift from 10 p.m. to 6 a.m. Each shift is in the charge of an inspector, who, in the division under consideration, will have at his disposal four sergeants and about thirty police constables as well as charge office staff, etc. Apart from the men on shifts, certain officers are on duty principally during the day: these include the senior officers (chief superintendent, chief inspector, and the senior inspector), certain clerical staff, traffic inquiry officers, pointsmen, and drivers. In addition there are some plain-clothes officers who work a different rota of shifts and have special duties in connection with the control of vice, inquiries into applications for firearms licences, etc. The work of these more specialist officers will be described after the account of patrol work. But it may be emphasized here that, apart from the station sergeant and his clerk, all the officers of the division are on duty in the streets some part of the day, or are liable to be called out for duty.

On the two days which were the subject of special study the active strength of the division was very slightly above average. Taking an average of the two days the distribution of personnel was as follows:

Rank	On duty	Absent	Total strength
Chief superintendent	1	0	1
Chief inspector	1	0	1
Inspectors	4	0	4
Sergeants	12	8	20
Constables	112	65	177
Women police constables	2	3	5
Police female assistants (typists)	4	0	4
Cadets	2	0	2
Telephonist (civilian)	1	0	1

The absentees were to be accounted for in this fashion:

Weekly rest day	3 Sgts	27 PCs	1 WPC
Additional rest day	1 Sgt	11 PCs	
Annual leave	2 Sgts	10 PCs	1 WPC
Leave because of extra duty	1 Sgt	2 PCs	
Special duty (e.g. attending training course at College)	1 Sgt	12 PCs	1 WPC
Sick		3 PCs	

The allocation to duties on the Thursday was:

	SHIFT				
Section	6 a.m.		2 p.m.		10 p.m.
1	1 A/Sgt	9 PCs 1 WPC	1 Sgt	9 PCs	1 Sgt	6 PCs
2	1 Sgt	6 PCs	1 Sgt	6 PCs	1 A/Sgt	6 PCs

Section	6 a.m.		2 p.m.		10 p.m.	
3	1 Sgt	7 PCs 1 WPC	1 Sgt	8 PCs	1 A/Sgt	7 PCs
4	1 Sgt	8 PCs 1 WPC	1 A/Sgt	6 PCs	1 Sgt	7 PCs
Total (per shift)	37		33		30	

Total: 100

(A/Sgt = PC acting as Sgt)

In addition, 5 PCs were on plain-clothes duty; 1 man was relieving the telephonist; 2 men together with 2 cadets were compiling the duty variations list and attending to pay and records; 3 men each did duty for a shift as station sergeant and 4 as station clerk.

Beat Boxes

When a new shift comes on duty each officer, apart from station sergeant, clerk, and driver, goes straight to his beat. Somewhere on each beat there is a beat box, which is a grey structure, resembling a telephone kiosk though slightly larger, and with a smaller number of windows in frosted and smoked glass. He 'parades' at the beat box where he meets the constable coming off duty and receives from him any relevant information. For the late and night shifts the officer coming on duty is required to report fifteen minutes before his shift officially starts in order to facilitate this take-over. In the beat box there is a telephone, a desk containing the log book and report forms, a stool, a small bench seat, a wash-hand basin, an electric kettle, a small electric fire, and a dog-catcher (a pole with a loop of rope attached). This is the beat man's headquarters, and he may not need to visit the divisional police station for several months on end.

The division is divided into four sections, each of which is in the charge of a sergeant. Each section contains six to eight beats. Section 1 is the smallest section: it lies nearest the centre of the city and contains some very busy streets and traffic junctions. Section 2 lies a little further out. Both these sections are policed entirely by foot. Their section sergeants use the station as their headquarters and go out from there to supervise their constables. Sections 3 and 4 are much larger in area and cover the residential districts out to the city boundary. They are policed by a combination of motor, cycle, and foot patrols. The sergeant taking over a shift reports to the section

15

beat box, where he and his driver relieve officers who have finished their shift. He supervises his constables with the aid of the mobile patrol van which is on the radio network.

It is important that the whereabouts of all officers on patrol should be known so that messages can be passed to them and due supervision can be exercised. The patrol vans present no problem, but communication with the man on the beat is less easy. The difficulty is dealt with by having every constable telephone the operator at the station once every hour. For each day of the week he has a special time at which to ring in, say, nine minutes past the hour, or twelve minutes to the hour. He arranges his patrol so that he is back at the box just at this time, and when he rings in he has only to state his number. When he leaves the box he makes an entry in the box journal to say where he is going. Each beat has a number of 'turns' or specified patrol routes, so the constable has only to write that he is taking a particular turn. If his sergeant arrives while he is away, a glance at the book and at the time he started the patrol is sufficient to indicate his approximate position. In Sections 3 and 4 it is more difficult for the constable to time his patrol, and less stress is laid upon telephoning at the exact time. In the outlying districts the system of beat boxes is supplemented by a number of telephones mounted in a special pillar on the pavement, from which the constable can ring in. When he returns to the beat box the constable is supposed to spend only two minutes there before setting out on his next turn, but the volume of paper work (reading reports and instructions, filling in forms, etc.) is now such that a longer delay is common. In the middle of the shift the constable is allowed a 45-minute refreshment period, when he rests in the box, makes himself a cup of tea, and eats his sandwiches. The beat man may also leave his raincoat or overcoat in his box while he is on patrol, and should the weather become inclement he may return for it.[1]

EARLY SHIFT

6 a.m. to 10 a.m.

At 6 a.m. the new shift takes over. I will describe first what happens

---

[1] In some Scottish forces the relieving shift parade at the station to be inspected and then march to their beats. The men take their meals communally in mess rooms fitted out for this purpose.

in the four hours up to 10 a.m., taking each of the sections in turn and using the survey forms completed by the officers themselves. Between 9 and 11 a.m. each member of the shift is allowed a 45-minute refreshment period, but the timing is staggered to avoid having all the men in their boxes simultaneously.

The divisional inspector is first engaged in reading daily information and force orders, and in going through correspondence. He then checks reports prepared after 5 p.m. when the senior inspector left the office; some of these will be filed and others forwarded through the divisional chief superintendent to the chief constable at city headquarters. By 8 a.m. on the Thursday he is free to patrol No. 1 section, visiting all constables, examining journals, and watching traffic in the streets most liable to congestion. At 9.15 a.m. he returns to the station and takes his refreshments. On the Friday he has instructed a number of new recruits (probationary constables) to parade at the station at 6 a.m., and he spends the first hour instructing them on procedure for dealing with various incidents liable to arise on patrol, and allocating them to beats. From 8.30 to 9.30 a.m. he is out supervising constables on duty in No. 2 section.

The station sergeant (a stationhouse keeper, to use the correct, if archaic, terminology) arrives on the days of the survey at 5.40 a.m. and is first engaged in checking and amending reports. On the Thursday he has also to check the station equipment and fittings, and to submit a report regarding the extra duty he had performed earlier in the week in attending court as a witness. He complains of needless time spent holding the telephone while intending holiday-makers ascertain the address of their 'reference'. After refreshments he takes a wireless message concerning a stolen car and circulates it to beat officers. Then he turns to the distribution of incoming mail, and records in the letter book reports which have been approved by the chief constable. The station sergeant also has to check 'lost and found property' before its transmission to headquarters. In all these duties he is assisted by the station clerk who helps with answering the phone, typing reports, etc.

The divisional driver starts work at 5.35 a.m., delivering information to beat boxes and collecting reports for submission. He is back at the station about 7 a.m., and on the Thursday is put onto general office duties (answering the telephone and attending to complaints and inquiries at the public counter). After refreshments he carries out a patrol in the car from 8.30 to 9.10 a.m. At 9.14 a.m., while in the station helping the charge office staff, he takes details of a 999 emergency call and has the 3rd section mobile patrol van attend to it. Between 9.40 and 10.05 a.m. he is away taking reports to the chief constable's office, after which he returns to office duties. On the Friday his routine is much the same except that he has to go out from 7 to 7.30 a.m. to collect some bulky found property, and on his return he has to bring up-to-date the files of shop references and unoccupied dwelling houses. (The tenant of every shop is requested to leave his address with the police so that they can get in touch with him if the premises are found unsecured or if they are broken into; people going on holiday are similarly requested to leave with the police details of their absence and of any person having a reserve key to the house – these persons and their addresses constitute a 'reference'.)

In No. 1 section the sergeant parades at a beat box together with a recruit at 6 a.m.; he notes the daily information, makes a routine examination of the box journal, and signs it to show that he has done so. He rings in for duty. From 6.25 to 6.40 a.m. he is at the divisional station (DHQ) to study the special instructions for his section. Then he patrols the section, supervising the beat constables and pointsmen. He attends to the build-up of traffic at a busy junction between 8.30 and 9.25 a.m., helping a lady motorist whose car has broken down. Then he goes to the station to take his refreshments. On the Friday it is much the same, except that from 6.10 to 6.46 a.m. the sergeant is engaged in briefing constables with regard to suspected trouble at a shop in their area.

The sergeant has ten constables to supervise. Certain duties are common to them all: they all have to read daily information and then watch the rush-hour traffic; some are detailed to stand by particular sets of traffic lights so that they can take charge if any difficulty arises. Those of them who have beats in the central area have to visit shops which hold a brokers' licence to buy second-hand goods (many of them are antique shops, jewellers, etc.; they are licensed so that trade in stolen goods may be checked). The policeman takes them daily lists of stolen articles; he checks their registers of purchases and, if all is in order, signs them. In many of the central beats policemen have to put out 'No Parking' or 'No Waiting' bollards. Many cities have permanent signs attached to the lamp-posts, or have coloured kerb stones to serve this purpose, but in the area under study the local council is as yet unwilling to make such provision. The police regard this duty as menial and unnecessary. On the Friday morning all beat constables throughout the division are engaged in a special search for stolen motor vehicles. Every street is checked, starting at 6 a.m., and the registration numbers of parked cars are examined. This search takes longer in the outlying districts. Another regular duty which is heavier at this time of the year is the check on unoccupied dwelling houses. Each beat man has a list of such houses which he has to inspect.

The following specimen is a reasonably representative account for No. 1 section at this time:

a.m.

5.55	Paraded for duty.
6.00–6.20	Noted general, crime, and beat information.
6.20	Rang in.
6.21–6.45	Set out twelve bollards at places specified.
6.45–7.10	Delivered daily notices of stolen property to cycle agents and jeweller on beat.
7.10–7.20	Returned to beat box and rang in.
7.20–8.20	Patrolled beat, keeping an eye open for stolen and abandoned vehicles.
8.20	Rang in.
8.21–8.40	Attended Donald's brewery. They had telephoned 999 for an ambulance because a man had been scalded.[1]
8.40–9.20	Stood by traffic lights at junction and cleared congestion as necessary.
9.20–9.35	Returned to box. Rang in. Informed station sergeant of result of 999 call and entered same in journal.
9.35–10.20	Refreshments in box.

[1] In some forces 999 calls for an ambulance or a fire are not communicated to the police. The ambulance or fire services notify the police if their attendance is desired. In this city the police are notified of all 999 calls and a policeman is always sent to the scene. It is considered desirable that if there has been an incident requiring an ambulance a policeman should check that no offence has been committed. But there will be no police visit if a doctor or a member of the public has requested an ambulance direct from the ambulance service.

There cannot be any properly representative specimen because policemen can sometimes have an extremely busy period of duty and at other times hardly anything may happen. A two-day sample of the activities of 132 police officers is not sufficiently extended to be a completely reliable measure, and this limitation must be borne in mind throughout this discussion.

The activities mentioned by policemen from this section between 6 and 10 a.m. included a motor accident, reporting on an attempted housebreaking, checking on a car which had been left for several days in a particular spot, serving notice of a complaint that had been made before the courts against someone resident in the beat area, and a matrimonial dispute. In the last case, a policeman had just put out his bollards at 6.30 a.m. when he was approached by a woman who complained that a man was preventing her from opening a shop for business. It turned out that a divorce was pending between a man and his wife who was the owner of the shop. There was some dispute over the shop and the wife had instructed a friend to look after it for her. It took the constable forty minutes to find out the nature of the trouble and to persuade the husband to see a solicitor instead. Later he reported the incident to the information room at the City HQ.

Section 1 includes a beat for which a woman police constable is usually responsible. Women police on early shift parade for duty at 7 instead of 6 a.m., and for the first hour the constable in charge of the adjoining beat assumes responsibility for this one also.

The work of Section 2 during this period is not very different. The constable on one beat keeps watch on both mornings from 6.05 to 6.45 a.m. over a shop doorway from which milk thefts have been reported. Other constables attend to complaints of malicious mischief in a mineral depot and of youths congregating on a stairway.

In Section 3 (mobile patrol) the sergeant has first to check the papers awaiting him when he takes over the shift and it will probably be 6.15 a.m. before he starts his patrol in the van. He has a driver, seven constables, and one woman constable at his disposition. Usually he takes up two men from their beats for a time to join him in the van. This means that if he is notified of an incident he can go straight there, leave two constables to deal with it, and then continue his own patrol. Sometimes he is continually ferrying men from one place to another while attending to routine business in between.

The sergeant and his driver report to the section box at 6 a.m. to take over from the men who have been on night shift. The section box is of similar size and appearance to a beat box. Other constables report to their beat boxes.

On the Thursday the section sergeant is engaged in checking correspondence until 6.15 a.m. when he sets off patrolling his area, visiting the constables and inspecting their journals. He takes up one constable immediately and a second fifteen minutes later. From the vehicle they check outlying streets in search of stolen cars. At 8 a.m. they drive to the central police garage to fill up with petrol and oil. As they leave the section, the sergeant reports this by radio. By 8.30 a.m. they are back on patrol.

At 9 a.m. they are told to go to an open space where a man has been seen who resembles someone wanted for assault. Ten minutes later the sergeant drops two men to search the area and then goes to see the man who had reported seeing the person in question in order to obtain further details. On returning he finds that the constables have found and apprehended the man, who is then driven to the central CID office where he is later charged with the offence. At 10.20 a.m. they return to DHQ for refreshments.

The Friday turn of duty is not very different. While taking refreshments at 9.25 a.m. the sergeant is informed that a damaged safe has been found on a building site. He sends his driver with two men to look at it. As it has obviously been broken into they notify the CID, arrange for fingerprint experts to attend, and see if anyone in the locality can give further information.

The constables on the section are occupied from 6.10 a.m. with routine foot and cycle patrols, with the inspection of unoccupied houses, and, on the Friday, with the special search for stolen cars. They have a number of minor duties, including watching a school crossing, serving a summons, delivering a daily information sheet to a scrap merchant, receiving a wallet that someone has found, delivering a hospital message, and collecting particulars about a motor accident. One constable gives the following details:

21

a.m.

8.10   Continued special search, calling at garages to check cars. Looked after schoolchildren, answering their questions about the swans on the river; tied a child's shoe-lace; took a wee lad home who always tries to follow his sisters to school; posted a letter for an old lady as I passed the postbox. Also called on a 'friend' who keeps me up-to-date on the movements of a known thief; the man is wanted on a warrant and I was able to get the number of the car he is now using.

9.15–10   Taking refreshments in box. Had to answer phone three times regarding, first, a complaint from a woman resident; second, a query about a report I had submitted earlier in the week; third, a query from the CID concerning the movements of the thief just referred to.

The sergeant in charge of the 4th section also works from a mobile patrol van. Like his colleague on No. 3 section he comments that both days were quieter than usual and that, since the sections were fully manned, fewer demands were made on his vehicle. One of them observes: 'Some days the patrol is overworked owing to the lack of personnel and the number of calls. Many of them could be dealt with at a later date but they are received on the emergency system.'

The sergeant of the 4th section has a new policewoman who is still learning the beats, and he moves her around the section. When he calls on probationers he also discusses with them the proper action to be taken in particular circumstances. A lot of the recruits' training is received on the spot like this. Among the constables' activities we find that one has received a note from the night constable that a wall behind an inn has been damaged and should be inspected, since it might indicate an attempted housebreaking. Other men have to serve court citations; to attend to a burst water main; to deal with found property; to do points duty during rush hour; to investigate a milk theft; to look into a complaint about a neighbour who left the wireless blaring; and to deliver a death message from the hospital; in addition to checking houses and searching for stolen cars. A policeman who reports on a motor accident has to give details of injuries sustained, the results of tests applied to the car, etc. So we find one constable in the section noting the receipt of a test report about a car's faulty steering and accident notes from the infirmary.

10 a.m. to 2 p.m.

The next four pages continue the account of the early shift's activities for the second half of its period of duty.

On Thursday the inspector has to go over correspondence passed to him by the superintendent, which relates to a function to be held shortly. Then he interviews a complainer. At 10.15 a.m. he goes out to the 4th mobile patrol, visiting all constables and police boxes to examine the journals. He gets back at 1.45 p.m. in time to confer with the inspector who is relieving him. On Friday he is with No. 1 section from 10.40 a.m. to 12.30 p.m., when he attends to clerical work. He prepares sections of a local instruction book designed for the use of constables and as an aid for training. He completes a visiting sheet, detailing his inspection of the sections.

The station sergeant's log reads as follows:

a.m.

10   Received mail from chief constable's department. Numbering and indexing reports in correspondence book, for attention of superintendent (15 minutes).

Received wireless message about a stolen car. Arranged for make and number to be circulated to beat officers (5 minutes).

Received reports and letters from superintendent for transmission to divisional officers (20 minutes).

Checking letters from typists before submission to superintendent (15 minutes).

Examined and certified Police Pensioner's Life certificate (5 minutes).

Interviewed former Lord Provost of city and conducted him to appointment with superintendent (10 minutes).

Miscellaneous telephone calls from beat constables (10 minutes).

Telephone call from motorist who witnessed vehicular accident this morning but did not inform PC at locus.

Particulars noted and passed to officer concerned (10 minutes).

Interviewed representative from city architect's department and showed him fittings requiring repair (25 minutes).

Telephone message from Coventry City Police cancelling court appearance of a divisional PC, since accused is pleading guilty (10 minutes).

Telephone calls from beat PCs (10 minutes).

Typed report for attention of beat PC to call on complainer regarding theft of purse (5 minutes).

Noted wireless message re motor cycle stolen in Glasgow; circulated make and number to beat PCs (5 minutes).

Engaged at inquiry counter with Gas Board employee regarding a street to be opened up on Sunday. Passed information to beat PC (5 minutes).

Taking evidence, cautioning, and charging man arrested for contravening Street Betting Act (30 minutes).

The station clerk is similarly involved with clerical work: maintaining the register of empty dwellings, checking a driver's licence, noting complaints, preparing reports, and dealing with a prisoner brought in drunk.

The divisional driver is mostly employed on clerical duties during this period, apart from going out on one occasion to collect a drunk and on another for a stray dog.

In Section 1 the sergeant continues his visits to the beat men, checking reports and so on. His men are largely occupied with routine business, too. Apart from checking empty houses, finishing off the car search, and inspecting brokers' books, they now have to make regular visits to banks and watch out for parking offences. Their chief concern is not to charge motorists for offences but to keep particular sections of roadway clear of waiting vehicles: they warn off anyone who stops in these places, or fetch shoppers out of shops, and they use their official powers only if persuasion fails or the offender is unusually truculent. If a beat man has to make an arrest – like the drunk and incapable apprehended at 1.15 p.m. on the Friday – he tries first to secure a witness to the offence, since Scots law requires two witnesses. If he can, the constable will make contact with his colleague on the adjoining beat for this purpose.

Among the tasks reported by the constables of No. 1 section are: checking newsvendors stances; reporting a subsidence on the roadway;[1] attending to parking complaints; returning a found key; holding up traffic for a lorry to reverse into a narrow street; cautioning and charging a motorist for failing to obey a 'Halt' sign; attending to complaints about a broken drain pipe, nuisance in a common stair, and noise; serving written citations; inquiring into a report about a night prowler; dealing with traffic and with inquiries from members of the public; and entering most of the above actions in their box journals. The policeman on duty at the main road junctions near the city centre has to spend much of his time directing people who want to know the way to particular places and answering varied questions.

In Section 2 from 10 a.m. to 2 p.m. the beat constables are occupied in much the same way. Additional jobs on which they report include a complaint about a dog barking at nights; a hospital message; communication with the railway police about a damaged canal barge; an abandoned motor cycle; a chimney fire; a complaint about motor cyclists; watching a known thief; notifying garages of stolen vehicles; an inquiry at a radio shop where there had been an attempted break in; following up a vehicular accident inquiry; and standing by the automatic traffic signals during the rush hour in case traffic jams should develop.

In the 3rd section the mobile patrol van was not particularly busy after 10 a.m. Routine patrol and visits were carried out, and the only incidents were a complaint that someone was searching refuse bins and a message to attend an ambulance call. In the latter case the patient was already dead but since it had been a normal illness no inquiries were necessary. The sergeant had to leave the van at one

---

[1] A policeman who sees a blocked drain, a dark street light, a missing toby cover, or some fault to which a burgh department has to attend, will telephone that department immediately. In this division – but not in some others – he then submits a written report. Should the department in question subsequently say that it was never notified, the police can refer to their records. In some forces no written record is kept of such matters.

point to visit the clothing store and have a new issue of uniform fitted. Apart from the activities of routine character already listed, the constables in this section had some new tasks, including warning the residents in one road that there would be a heavy increase of traffic there for four days in the next week owing to a diversion; reprimanding schoolboys for riding two on one cycle; reporting a damaged lamp standard; attending to a complaint about dogs fouling the footway; reporting a defect in a pavement; warning motorists for dangerous parking; and interviewing a witness to an accident.

Section 4 was also quiet. On the Thursday the sergeant had the inspector with him in the van for a while. He had to pick up a constable and take him to stand by a burst main; the man he was relieving was required at DHQ for a precognition (preliminary examination of a witness by a lawyer). Then he had to drive to the garage for petrol and have a broken clutch return-spring renewed.

The constables on this section had a variety of tasks, which, in addition to some routine duties of the kind already listed, included: charging two soldiers with the theft of a goose and a duck from a public park (the constable took a colleague with him for this job); making an appointment with a witness for a constable from another division (this proved a long job because insufficient details were available – the constable checked the voters' roll and visited everyone in the area who had the surname in question); writing a summonsing report; telephoning a joiner's to ascertain the value of a plate-glass window broken by a drunk (information needed for a report); taking a recruit round the beat and showing him the parking arrangements for a large football match. One entry should be quoted in full:

'1 to 1.10 p.m. Talking to local eccentric who reports to the beat constable and telephones the divisional station at least three times every day – for this reason alone deserves to figure prominently in any analysis of police time.'

Several of the men who completed forms added at the end that the early shift on the two days surveyed was quieter than usual. The records kept tend inevitably to underestimate minor duties. One constable, for example, reports being asked by passers-by what was being done about a complaint made just before, how badly people involved in a recent accident had been injured, when the prefabs were going to be pulled down, etc. Another adds:

'I make a point of speaking to as many people as possible during my tour of duty. This usually involves a greeting in passing or a few minutes' conversation, often about matters which have no direct bearing on police work, but are invaluable in assessing the background, habits, friends, etc. of people living and working on the beat. This will probably apply to the majority of PCs, particularly those working the same beat regularly.'

LATE SHIFT

2 p.m. to 6 p.m.

The inspector taking over the late shift arrives at 1.45 p.m. to confer with the man he is relieving. On the Thursday he is able to get through his clerical work much quicker than usual because there are no letters to attend to from outside bodies. He passes instructions by telephone to section sergeants, consults the superintendent over a matter of policy, and by 2.30 p.m. is out on patrol visiting the men. As the traffic builds up in the late afternoon he pays special attention to its flow, and returns to the station for refreshments at 5.30 p.m. On the Friday a sergeant is acting inspector; his log runs as follows:

p.m.

1.45–2   Conferring with early duty inspector.

2–2.15   Dealing with correspondence and shift administration.

2.15   To ABC in car, picked up PC 99; and to XYZ school to interview three boys concerned in fight on 15th.

2.25   Interviewing headmaster and three boys.

2.55   To MNO school.

3.5   Interviewing headmaster, and one boy, under caution, alleged to have been carrying a bicycle chain at fight on 15th. Also questioning three other boys outside school.

3.35   Returned PC 99 to ABC; returned to DHQ.

3.55   Clerical duties.

4.05   Patrolled division, Section 1.

4.25   Found Number 1 pointsman off point, having arrested two men for being in possession of a quantity of nylon

27

	stockings and unable to give an account of them.
	Wirelessed 4th mobile patrol to bring in a PC to take over points duty.
4.35	Dispatched 6 beat PC to central station (CID) with pointsman and two prisoners.
4.40	Noted complaint of urinating in common stair, and left it for attention by beat PC.
4.45	Supervised flow of traffic at PQR junction (in the absence of 6 beat PC).
5.25	Patrolled M Road and J Street, visited PCs 100 and 101 on traffic duty.
5.40	Returned to DHQ. Refreshments.

The station sergeant coming on duty at 1.40 p.m. on the Thursday takes over the prisoner (charged under the Street Betting Act) and types the charge sheet. He then spends one hour twenty-five minutes checking reports submitted by beat officers, and ten minutes checking crime reports typed by office staff. He sends the divisional driver off to investigate a complaint of indecent exposure; searches the files for information on a theft required by another division; checks the telephone account; receives a 999 call about an accident and radios the patrol van to attend; sorts out an inquiry at the public counter about a heavy load being delivered within the division; receives and sorts evening dispatches from HQ; checks the voters' roll for another division; deals with found property; and attends to four more inquiries at the public counter. During these four hours he answers twenty-eight telephone calls, makes seven himself, and either receives or sends seven wireless messages. After 5 o'clock he takes his refreshment period but this is persistently interrupted by various inquiries. The Friday is much the same.

The station clerk has also given a fairly detailed account of how he spends his time on the Thursday. From 1.45 to 5.57 p.m. he spends seventy-two minutes on the 'phone receiving, and in many cases passing on, messages, and giving advice; sixty-two minutes at the public counter giving information, noting complaints, checking drivers' insurance certificates, etc.; thirteen minutes posting the index of unoccupied houses; forty minutes typing memoranda; fifteen minutes typing a crime report; ten minutes reading the daily information; two minutes issuing pay to a constable; and twenty minutes taking his refreshments.

The divisional driver takes over his car at 1.30 p.m. and goes to the boxes for Nos. 3 and 4 sections, delivering and collecting reports and messages. Later he goes on a similar errand to the City HQ, and at 5.10 p.m. takes the chief superintendent and the chief inspector round the various main traffic junctions in the division. In between he is employed chiefly on clerical duties, on transporting prisoners, and on attending to minor incidents that require immediate attention.

The sergeant in charge of No. 1 section comes to his box at 1.30 p.m., reads the information and correspondence, gives orders to the beat PC, and telephones the other constables in his section. He then patrols the section, studying box journals and complaint books, and discussing their work with the beat constables. Part of the time he visits a cinema to check on observance of the safety regulations, and at another time he keeps a known thief under observation. Between 2 and 4 p.m. he may receive a good two dozen inquiries from members of the public. In the later afternoon traffic is a major preoccupation, but by about 5.30 p.m. he returns to DHQ, attends to any new clerical jobs, and takes his refreshments.

The beat constables on this section do not have any particularly novel duties during this period. They attend to the usual tasks such as accidents, theft, and housebreaking inquiries; complaints; and parking. One constable has to come into the station to see the chief inspector over a welfare matter; another has to take over points duty for a spell; and a third to relieve the telephone switchboard operator. From 4 to 6 p.m. on the Thursday seven probationers from the shift attend a recruits' instruction class at DHQ. Between 4.30 and 6 p.m. most of the constables on this section are fully engaged supervising the traffic flow. Sometimes this means only that a constable stands at a road junction controlled by automatic traffic signals for an hour and a half, just in case a traffic jam should develop.

In Section 2 the sergeant's routine is very similar, since his section also includes a number of important road junctions. On one afternoon he takes a PC with him to deal with a 999 call reporting that there is a disturbance in a public house, but when he arrives he finds that the three men who had been arguing have finally gone away at the request of the management. One of his probationer constables has to deal with an accident to a parked car: he marks the vehicles for road measurements and goes off to contact the owner of the damaged car. Another vehicular accident report has to be submitted, concerning a motor cyclist who fell off at a crossing. Other constables spend part of their time completing reports concerning incidents which occurred when they were on shift the day before or even earlier (this is very common, because it frequently takes some time to obtain all the details required); in this section two constables complete reports on a malicious mischief case and a fire report; others collect further information or arrange interviews to allow themselves to complete outstanding reports. A constable on duty near the employment exchange receives a complaint that a group of men have gathered at the rear of the exchange, are drinking cheap wine, begging, and urinating in a common stair; he fetches over his colleague from the neighbouring beat; they question two men but do not themselves see any offence being committed. Similarly, a constable who apprehends two suspected thieves takes them to his box and then rings the station to get them to send over a constable from an adjoining beat. When arrangements have been made for someone else to take responsibility for their beats the two PCs take the suspects to the central charge office. There is another vehicular accident in the section. While standing by the traffic signals, one PC receives information from a local woman that her sister had seen two youths acting suspiciously near parked cars three days ago when a wireless set and a tape recorder had been stolen from one of them; he passes this on to CID. On another beat the constable takes details of a housebreaking, which he passes on similarly. Elsewhere a constable delivers a witness citation and then stands by a traffic crossing outside the Deaf School for fifteen minutes. There is also a Blind Institute in this section, and constables keep an eye on persons entering and leaving both places for their own safety. One constable charges a motorist for a parking offence, and then later deals with a drunk but does not have to charge him.

At 4 p.m. the children come out of school. This is reflected in the policemen's schedules. Two men separately have to warn boys who are climbing walls near the railway line. Others speak to a fourteen-year-old who is smoking a cigarette and to a youth cycling on the pavement.

The sergeant in charge of No. 3 section on the Thursday is patrolling his section, when at 2.55 p.m. he gets a radio message to telephone DHQ. The headmaster of a school has reported that some of his boys have stolen biscuits from a nearby bread company. He takes two PCs to the school and leaves them there to investigate while he goes on to the bread company. Then he comes back, picks up the men, and they go to the biscuit factory. It would seem that some stale jam rolls had been set out for the pig swill and some of these had been taken, presumably by boys again. The factory did not wish the incident to be treated as a theft but wanted it investigated in order to prevent any recurrence. At 3 p.m. he goes on to inquire into another complaint of a theft, this time from a quarry. On arriving he finds that he has been misinformed as to the quarry in question. When he reaches the right quarry he finds that an electric motor has been smashed, that boards have been forced off the side of the compressor house, and copper and brass stolen. He telephones DHQ and writes a crime report form. At 3.40 p.m. he returns to collect the constables from the factory and resumes patrol.

At 4.18 p.m. there is a radio call about a car's having run off the road near the airport. He reaches the scene at 4.25 p.m. to find no one was injured. One constable takes particulars, another controls the road traffic while the breakdown personnel get the car back on the road. The sergeant then tells the farmer what has happened (damage to crops, hedge, etc.) and gives him particulars of the driver. By 4.50 p.m. he is back on patrol. Visiting one beat, he gives the constable advice about how he should act on a complaint about a dog who has bitten a pedestrian. At 5.45 p.m. he goes into the station to deal with any paper work and to take his refreshments.

The sergeant in charge of the section on the Friday has no emergency calls to attend to. He is able to spend more time with his beat men, and can attend to less pressing matters such as an application for a newsvendor's stance and 'phoning another police force concerning a case of malicious damage.

Among the tasks reported by the beat constables the following may

31

be noted: a cycle theft to be investigated; a man, suspected drunk, reported lying on the road, who, when seen, was found to be capable of making his own way home; 400 schoolchildren to be escorted from the zoo to the railway station; three witness citations and two copy complaints to be served; youths who were skylarking in a telephone kiosk to be reprimanded; more youths to be dealt with for pestering a swan sitting on eggs in a nest; other youths to be reproved for breaking into a private wood and teasing the keeper of an adjacent bowling green; then an old lady who comes up and says that her window has been cracked – when the policeman inquires he finds that a five-year-old has accidentally hit it with a stick, so he takes the lad with him to explain and the lady decides to take no further action; a lost brooch to be reported; a message about a woman missing from hospital to be followed up; a child who has been found wandering to be looked after, and its parents contacted; a car with an expired road fund licence seen – the name and address of its owner ascertained from the taxation department; five young boys who were throwing stones to be spoken to, and their addresses obtained so that the constable can speak to their parents later; another youth to be warned for cycling on the pavement; a complaint about a pedlar to be investigated; movement licences to be collected from a pig farm; and a dozen or more routine minor tasks.

The sergeant in charge of No. 4 section comes on duty at 1.45 p.m. He examines correspondence and finds it consists chiefly of forms about empty houses, cattle movement licences, a brake test statement, an inquiry about a motorist who has failed to produce his certificate of insurance, and copy complaints. He enters them in the section journal and starts his patrol at 2.15 p.m. After visiting two PCs he receives – at 2.55 p.m. – a wireless call to go to a chimney fire. On reaching the address he sees no sign of a fire but, looking round, discovers a roll of new copper piping at the back of the stair; he inquires about this and the reported fire from the neighbours, but learns nothing. The owner of the piping then arrives and is able to account satisfactorily for his possession of it. The sergeant resumes patrol and telephones the fire brigade. Later he has an address to verify. Then a complaint of a milk theft comes in and is passed on to the beat man. At 4.24 p.m. he gets a call to an accident but on arriving at the scene finds nothing. He makes inquiries in the vicinity and sees a twelve-year-old boy leaving a telephone kiosk. A page from the telephone directory has been stuffed into the returned coins slot and the sergeant suspects the same boy may have made the bogus accident call. He gets the beat constable to verify the boy's address while he inquires from the central information room if the call came from this particular kiosk. When his address has been verified the boy is free to go home. The sergeant then continues his patrol.

On the following day the sergeant advises a constable on procedure with a hit-and-run driver; has a dog-biting complaint investigated and details concerning a road accident obtained; he also attends to a radio call about a handbag theft.

The constables in this section are mostly employed on routine matters between 2 and 6 p.m. on the two days in question. One investigates a complaint that people are dumping garden refuse in a dell beside a road, but cannot find anything that requires police action. Another goes to the cattle market to check movement licences. Yet another deals with an accident involving three motor vehicles. One PC has to obtain particulars of a missing person; another to inspect pigs in detention at a farm; a third attends to a complaint of malicious mischief, speaks to some schoolchildren about their 'kerb drill' and to others who have been dropping litter, and sees to a complaint about dogs fouling the footway. This is apart from serving citations and copy complaints, verifying addresses for constables in other divisions, and the regular task of arranging interviews with witnesses and with people involved in incidents on which they have to report.

6 p.m. to 10 p.m.

The inspector on the Thursday resumes patrol at 7.30 p.m., attending a few minutes later to a 999 call about a burglar alarm ringing; it proves a false alarm. He watches a public meeting in the street, which breaks up after 9 p.m., then he goes back to DHQ and checks through the arrangements for the shift on the next day.

On the Friday the inspector finishes his refreshments at 6.25 p.m., and then discusses two complaints and a report with one of the plain-clothes constables. At 6.55 p.m. he starts some clerical work, resuming patrol at 7.15 p.m. He visits the policeman on duty outside a dance hall which is a recognized trouble spot. At 8 p.m. he investigates a ringing burglar alarm, which proves false, and then drives to the outer section. At 9.10 p.m. he collects one of his PCs, and together they go to interview a boy in front of his parents, under caution, concerning his carrying an offensive weapon (the bicycle chain incident referred to earlier). Twenty minutes later he resumes patrol, returning to DHQ at 9.45 p.m. to hand over.

The station sergeant on the Thursday has a number of 999 calls to deal with; he receives a variety of offiical messages for different members of the division. He attends to the public counter. He advises a PC about what should be done when a court citation is issued with the wrong address. A message comes in about some cattle that have got loose: he directs No. 3 mobile patrol van to investigate; they find nothing. Later, another report comes in that the cattle have strayed onto a golf course. As No. 3 section is busy on something else he sends the divisional driver and a traffic inquiry officer to go and round them up. Then towards the end of the shift he takes evidence from witnesses in the case of a man charged with breach of the peace and assault. (This takes in all $1\frac{1}{2}$ hours and the sergeant has to work forty-five minutes' overtime.) He adds: 'This could be considered a normal day's work though the clerical work was slightly less than usual.' It will be seen that telephone and wireless calls are fairly numerous (there were forty-six to answer). They punctuate all activities, disturb concentration, especially during the examination of reports, and generally retard the clearance of clerical work. It should also be noted that the services of a police cadet were available from 2 p.m. until 5.30 p.m. He assisted generally, answering telephone and public counter inquiries, typing minor reports, indexing reports of unoccupied dwelling houses, etc., and materially eased the burden of work during the busy afternoon period.

On the Friday evening at 6 p.m. the sergeant has first to type a summonsing report regarding a road traffic offence. Then at 6.40 p.m. he attends to another offence – contravention of Sections 3 (1) and 6 (1) of the Road Traffic Act, 1960 (these sections cover careless and drunken driving respectively). The prisoner has to be charged and detained. A doctor has to attend. Witnesses have to be interviewed. It is a long and complicated job, and though the sergeant has called in a beat PC to help him he is not finished until 9 p.m., when he has to take statements from witnesses and detain a prisoner charged with being drunk and incapable. Then from 9.25 to 10 p.m. he clears outstanding clerical work. Afterwards he composes and types the charge sheet for a second road traffic offence. This requires 1¾ hours' overtime. He adds: 'Apart from the overtime worked, this was a normal Friday late shift.'

The station clerk is fully occupied with clerical duties of the same kind as those described on the afternoon shift, and with counter inquiries about a variety of matters – from investigating a missing car to advising someone to contact the Public Health Department to present a complaint about an industrial noise nuisance.

The divisional driver at 5.51 p.m. has to drive out and collect a found child, trace its home, and return it; he is back at DHQ by 6.30 p.m., when he has to take a stray dog off to the Cat and Dog Home. Later he has to go and find a 'reference' to come and open a property where the burglar alarm is ringing, and to call at the hospital on an inquiry. Afterwards he collects three other PCs, and together they herd the straying cattle and secure them in the field from which they have escaped. This takes forty minutes, so he gets back to the station by 9.30 p.m., and in ten minutes his relief arrives. The Friday is similar – except for the cattle.

The sergeant in charge of Section 1 has a fairly quiet spell of duty after 6 p.m. on both nights. He gets round to all his constables, attends to two burglar alarms that are sounding off, and has a half-hour discussion with two plain-clothes constables who ask him about circumstances affecting two offences – one a contravention of the licensing laws, the other a case of indecent exposure.

Among the tasks reported by the beat constables may be mentioned: writing a vehicular accident report; making two inquiries for constables in other divisions and, contrariwise, requesting another division to check something; receiving information from a member of the public for transmission to plain-clothes officers; chasing children from the canal basin; serving warrants; attending to a parking complaint; inquiring into an allegation of theft; following up reports about a man drunk and incapable; supervising parking outside a theatre; inquiring into a theft from a car, notifying CID of this, and submitting a report; relieving the telephone switchboard operator;

D

completing a crime report about a housebreaking; and herding cattle (the incident referred to above). The big dance hall is in this section, and constables on the two adjoining beats keep an eye on the queue while patrons are assembling, though it is not until later that the place may become a trouble spot. Another item is that after 7 p.m. constables on some of the central beats have to collect the 'No Parking' and 'No Waiting' bollards and put them in store until the morning. The bollards are often dirty.

The sergeant in charge of No. 2 section continues his visits to constables and pays particular attention to several cinemas in his area. His men are engaged on much the same tasks as those in the first section, but they also have to inquire after a deserter from the army and a patient missing from a mental hospital; a woman who alleges that someone is doping and injecting her (she suffers from hallucinations) has to be reassured. One constable reports:

p.m.

8.35   Theft by housebreaking – means at present unknown (may be false keys) – at youth club. Noting particulars of stolen property for circulation to brokers, radio dealers, etc. Noting also description of youth found sleeping on premises and identification of same – believed identical with youth of 19 years arrested re theft of car last week.

9.15   Returned to box.

9.25–9.55   Wrote report re above theft.

Several constables in this section reported that things were a little quieter than usual during these two shifts. Some added that a number of known thieves live in the area and that they keep a continuous watch for them (one beat box at least contains a register of thieves, with their portraits, histories, and specialities listed).

In No. 3 section on the Thursday the sergeant gets a 999 call that many boys are fighting outside a billiards saloon; he drives there and detains twelve for questioning. In the middle of this job he hears about the stray cattle, so sends the van off with two men to help. A little later there is another 999 call: a youth has assaulted his father. The sergeant goes to the scene, arrests the youth for assault and breach of the peace, takes them both to the police station, and then sends the father to hospital in the patrol van so that he may receive medical attention. On the Friday there is a complaint to investigate concerning some men who have apparently called at a house under false pretences; and there is more trouble outside the billiards hall. A garden fête has to be supervised, and, among other things, a lost child has to be looked after. The driver of the van and two PCs who are patrolling in it work on the same tasks as the sergeant. They also have to complete their crime report on the theft from the bakery investigated during the afternoon.

One of the beat constables takes a colleague with him to call at a house to deliver an official caution about keeping a dangerous dog. The two of them then go to two other houses to caution boys, in their parents' presence, for malicious damage to property. Some constables in this section have to give a great deal of attention in the evenings to admonishing youths for minor misdemeanours, and occasionally visiting their parents, and to dealing with the complaints of shopkeepers and householders about the conduct of young people who foregather in particular places. They also remonstrate with adults for thoughtless conduct such as bad parking, jay-walking at a crossing, and allowing a dog to soil the footway. Other tasks reported include a minor fire, found money, delivering a death message from the hospital, and checking the permit of someone fishing in the river.

In No. 4 section on the Thursday the sergeant continues his inquiries into the bogus 'phone message about a road accident; he warns the mother of the twelve-year-old of his suspicions. Then he gets a message about a burglar alarm ringing; within four minutes he is there. All exits are watched while the staff contact the key holder; it turns out that an electrical fault had occurred. He attends to a complaint of malicious mischief at the hospital and then resumes patrol. While he is completing his reports on the day's activities a passer-by tells him that water is running to waste at a nearby electricity sub-station; on investigation it is found that electricity board staff are in charge. On the Friday there are a fair number of routine tasks, including a drunk, a missing child, a theft, etc., but the sergeant considers it a quiet day.

The beat constables are engaged on tasks similar to those that occurred in Section 3. The later part of the evening is one of the best times for constables to call on people to obtain information in connection with their inquiries; to see witnesses; to arrange interviews; and to serve court citations and copies of complaints that have been lodged by aggrieved parties. Frequently, of course, the person in question is not at home and the policeman has to call several times.

NIGHT SHIFT

10 p.m. to 6 a.m.[1]

The night-shift inspector arrives at the station at 9.30 to 9.35 p.m. As the section sergeants ring in from the boxes he confers with them about arrangements for the night. At 10.15 p.m. on the Thursday he starts patrolling No. 1 section, visiting the beat constables, but breaking off from 11 to 11.30 p.m. to watch the dispersal of patrons from the dance hall. He returns to DHQ at 1.15 a.m. for his refreshments, after which an hour goes on various clerical duties, including arrangements for night-shift patrols over the weekend. From 3 to 5 a.m. he visits No. 3 section, and at 5 a.m. visits No. 4 section sergeant and one of his constables. He returns to DHQ at 5.35 a.m., signs a variety of forms including the telephone operator's duty sheet, and hands over to his successor at 6 a.m.

On the Friday night the inspector's first concern is with the dance hall. He drives there in the divisional car at 10 p.m. and meets No. 1 section sergeant outside. The inspector stays there until 11.20 p.m. with the divisional driver. At 10 p.m. the queue for admission usually lengthens considerably, and as many of the people come to the hall from the bars there is a fair amount of rowdiness. If the queue is not kept moving the crowd can be troublesome. The section sergeant is at the hall until 11.15 p.m., and three of the constables from the adjoining beats stay until 11.30 p.m., by which time everyone is safely inside and the constables can take the first turn round their beats. The No. 4 section sergeant is also on the spot with his mobile patrol van in case it should be necessary to bundle any offenders away

[1] The description of activities on this shift is not split into two halves as with the early and late shifts.

quickly; he has three of his men with him. The police strength outside the dance hall is therefore one inspector, two sergeants, six constables, and two motor vehicles with constable drivers.

At 11.20 p.m. the inspector patrols the first section. He questions a suspicious-looking character standing in a shop doorway. At 11.50 p.m. he attends a 999 call from a hotel where a man has been found attempting to break into the manager's private suite. From midnight to 12.30 a.m. he searches the area round the hotel for the culprit, then from 12.30 to 1 a.m. he searches the adjoining area for a man seen stealing golf clubs from a car. At 1 a.m. he goes back to the dance hall to watch the dispersal of patrons. The sergeant and three men of No. 1 section are also there, but not the patrol van from No. 4 section. Tonight the dispersal is over quietly in twenty minutes. The inspector returns to his station. At 3.30 a.m. he helps take home a constable who has a minor injury; then from 3.45 to 4.05 a.m. he is engaged in connection with a door found open at a cinema: the police call the key holder and investigate to see if anyone has been trying to enter. The inspector continues his visits, returning at 5.35 a.m.

The station sergeant on the Thursday has the usual flow of in-coming calls requiring action, which he transmits to members of the division. He has two prisoners, one for assault, and the other a drunk; because the latter is a naval rating he has on this occasion to arrange for an officer from the man's ship to attend court on the Monday morning, though in normal circumstances this would not be one of his duties. Apart from dealing with a man 'found wandering' the remaining duties are clerical – checking reports, distributing orders, etc. The Friday is similar. At 10.30 p.m. a man is brought in who has broken the window of a public house; the sergeant hears the evidence, checks the man's property, detains him in the cells (which takes half an hour), and then types a report on the incident (which also takes half an hour).

On Friday nights, two PCs are usually on duty as station clerks. They assist in dealing with the prisoners, take and send messages, attend the counter, see to found property (handbag and dog), fetch in a prisoner from a nearby beat box, help the mobile patrol to search the canal bank for a man reported seen lying there, take the divisional car to the garage for refuelling, take a constable who has injured his hand on duty to the hospital, etc. The Thursday night was quieter than usual and one entry reads: 'Office very quiet; reading old reports and notices' – but this only relates to a quarter of an hour from 2 to 2.15 a.m. If a number of prisoners are brought in on complicated charges the station staff can easily get behind with their work.

The divisional driver is with the inspector much of the time on these two shifts, but he has messages to collect and is sent out by himself to search an area where someone has reported seeing a drunken driver.

The sergeant in charge of No. 1 section is chiefly engaged visiting his constables. On the Thursday night there is a disturbance as people are leaving the dance hall, and one man is arrested for a breach of the peace; otherwise there is little of note. The constables' tasks include cases of attempted housebreaking, troublesome drunks (no action is taken if a man causes no trouble and gets himself out of the way), taking a prisoner to the hospital for treatment before escorting him to the central police station, attending at a fire, standing by the dispersal of patrons from a theatre, etc.

But the most important concern of a constable on duty at night in an urban area is the checking of property. He has a series of 'turns' to do (in varied order so that someone who kept watch on him would not be able to predict his route in any reliable manner). On these turns there are particular doors – especially of warehouses and offices – which he is required to check: he tries the handle or pulls the padlock, and shines his torch along the edge of the door to see if it has been tampered with. He has a bunch of keys for entering builders' yards and similar places. At certain points he climbs a common stair, or goes through an entry and shines his torch along the back of a building. This search is quite thorough, considering the conditions; if properly performed it can have a powerful effect in preventing crime, though some officers are inclined to doubt its value in modern circumstances. A constable who notes that a ladder has been moved from its usual place checks to see if it might have been used for an illegal entry. Or he observes that the light in a photographer's display window – where there are a number of expensive cameras – is not on: he telephones the shopkeeper to inquire about it.

These and similar activities depend largely upon having a man on patrol who knows the district and the usual arrangements, so that any departure from the normal is immediately noticed.

One constable comments as follows upon night-shift work: 'The activities of night-shift personnel are normally restricted owing to the fact that 80 per cent of one's time is taken up with checking property, and one is unlikely to come into contact with the public in the early hours of the morning. A stranger, reading this account overleaf, would probably form the impression that the officer concerned was having a very easy time of it; but in fact the night-shift constable is, more often than not, busier than the day-shift constable as he checks an average of sixty shops and vulnerable premises each hour. His duties never alter very much.'

In No. 2 section there are two thefts, one from a car, the other from a tobacconist's shop where the window has been broken; a 'Keep Left' sign has been found demolished; particulars are taken of a car seen in suspicious circumstances; a man (who is himself drunk) reports that his son is missing from home; a girl reported missing is found hiding in a common stair; a matrimonial dispute (which seems to have arisen at a party after the wedding of the wife's cousin) is reported at 1.50 a.m., and the police are also summoned to another domestic dispute (a woman – whose husband is in prison – is being ejected from her mother-in-law's home), but they take no official action in either case.

No. 3 section attend to a burglar alarm that is sounding; the patrol van keeps watch for a car that has been reported stolen and is said to be entering the city along a particular road, but the police see nothing; there is a disturbance in a dance hall and complaints from nearby residents; an address of a man charged with being drunk and incapable has to be verified; a 999 call is received about a domestic disturbance but the sergeant notes: 'House quiet on arrival – previous knowledge of this house so did not disturb'; inquiries are made about missing boys; some youths are warned for loitering; a drunk is removed from a bus; a cyclist is warned for riding without lamps, etc. They were quiet shifts considering that the section was two men short and that this usually creates more work for the others.

No. 4 section searched the bank of a canal where a body had been seen, and found a drunken sailor who had fallen asleep. They examined the explosives store at a quarry. They attended to a report of an assault in a café and removed an injured man to hospital, but could not catch his assailant. Constables moved a motor van which collided with a wall shortly after 4 a.m.; assisted No. 1 section outside the dance hall; found another sleeping drunk by the canal and sent him home; took charge of some keys that had been found; went to a dwelling house where youths had thrown a stone through the window; warned two youths in the presence of their parents for cycling in the park; attended to a complaint about a 'prowler'; kept observation on a grocery doorway from which milk bottles had frequently been stolen; notified key holders of insecure doors; searched for a drunken driver. Complaints are regularly received of men urinating in stairs and other inappropriate places; quite a lot of police time has to be given to such matters and to the enforcement of elementary decencies.

COMMENTS ON SHIFT DUTIES

How far may the foregoing account be taken as representative of police work in this area? Several officers thought the days in question quieter than might be expected, but since Friday is a relatively busy day the account probably conveys a fair impression of routine police patrolling in the city.

Two other reservations were expressed. First, that periods of intense activity may be followed by a lull, and no one knows in advance when he is going to be fully stretched. One man commented: 'Note the amount of work encountered in the first four hours, and yet the latter four mainly passed in patrolling. This, I think, shows quite faithfully the general pattern of police work.' It will be recognized that police organization cannot gamble on a period of time or a district of the town being quiet; administration must be geared to the demands of the busy spells. The second reservation was that a statement such as 'a constable patrolled a particular street' has many implications that are not hinted at in so bald an observation. He is there to take action should it be necessary, and his presence is important both for crime prevention and for reminding the public of the law's requirements.

It is also perhaps worth quoting another comment: 'I find that when one is busy with a summons or a court case one cannot think of it during the normal duty. Most work done during our duty falls to be considered during one's off-duty period: e.g. if one has a trial the next day one finds it advisable to consult one's notes the night before whether on or off duty.' But this, of course, applies in many other occupations.

The shifts change over every fourth Tuesday, and the men know by the previous Saturday if there is to be any change in the duty to which they will be posted. They can plan when their weekly rest days will fall due for a period of twelve months ahead – though these are sometimes upset by special demands. If a man is promoted he is normally transferred to another division.

STATION STAFF AND MEN ON OTHER SHIFTS

Supervision of the division is the responsibility of the chief superintendent. When the chief superintendent is on leave or unavailable, his deputy, the chief inspector, acts for him. The chief inspector has therefore to work very closely with the superintendent and to be fully informed of current developments so that he can deputize satisfactorily.

The chief superintendent's duties must vary considerably from day to day. The way he allocated his time on the two days of the survey was probably not a fair sample, but it does point out some features of interest. Of the thirteen hours forty minutes on which he reported, 53 per cent were spent on routine divisional administration, 19 per cent. on making arrangements with the city authorities, and 28 per cent on preparing for special functions.

The biggest items in the routine administration were checking and editing reports for the chief constable, and examining incoming correspondence (29 per cent); next, patrolling the division and visiting the departments in the station building (10 per cent); then came conferences with the chief inspector and shift inspectors regarding the state of the division and reports to be submitted about recruits (9 per cent); telephone communications (4 per cent); and drafting divisional instructions (1 per cent).

Local authority business included meetings with the deputy transport manager and a city councillor about the siting of bus stops, and

43

with someone from the city engineer's department about road works and traffic diversions (8 per cent.); drafting reports and memoranda concerning the above (7 per cent); visiting the places in question (4 per cent); and telephoning (1 per cent).

Special functions – which are always numerous in this division – included preparations for an army recruiting march, an air force display, an agricultural show, a garden fête, and a royal visit. These entailed a lot of work drafting instructions (18 per cent), interviewing people (7 per cent), and telephoning (3 per cent).

The chief inspector's time was spent in a similar fashion: 34 per cent went on the preparation of reports (a big item at this time being recruits' progress reports); 17 per cent on conferring with the plain-clothes, traffic inquiry, variations, and other headquarters staff responsible to the chief inspector; 16 per cent on conferring with the superintendent on divisional affairs; 6 per cent on visiting the departments answerable to him; 15 per cent on consulting with air force officers about the proposed display; and 12 per cent on preparing some of the consequent arrangements.

Working in association with the two senior officers is the senior inspector. He checks reports before they go to the superintendent, prepares memoranda and divisional instructions, and, if necessary, takes charge of a shift or relieves the chief inspector in the central charge office. On the days of the survey he was concerned with studying the situation at an industrial estate to see what methods of policing were most suitable; examining arrangements for a traffic survey which would have to be covered by the police; lecturing to recruits; accompanying the chief inspector to the air force station for consultations; calculating the extra police strength needed for the special functions (men from other divisions would be sent in to assist); and visiting a factory to discuss lighting and traffic complaints. As the shift inspectors are mostly out on patrol, the senior inspector deals with many of the telephone inquiries and complaints that come in from members of the public and from firms.

In addition to the men on the early and late shifts it is often convenient to have extra constables working a different routine. On the Friday three new recruits accompanied beat constables from 10 a.m. to 4 p.m. before going to the instructional class. Three members of the City Police pipe band worked from 10 a.m. to 3.45 p.m. on one of the days before going to a band practice. One constable was on duty at the Sheriff Court. Six constables were on points duty, several of them going over to patrol work in off-peak periods.

Two constables were on parking patrol. This patrol consists of two officers working together because of the need for corroboration. They check vehicles waiting in the more crowded streets to see that the 'No Parking' and 'No Waiting' signs are observed. They keep a log of all the vehicles regularly parked in these districts so that they know where to fetch the driver should a car have to be moved. They advise motorists about the best places to leave their cars. The object of this patrol is to reduce the necessity for prosecutions by making maximum use of persuasion. By specializing in this work the constables became acquainted with a surprising proportion of motorists. They also stand by at functions such as weddings at the fashionable churches, where crowds are apt to gather.

The variations department normally consists of one constable and one cadet. It is responsible for drawing up the daily 'variations list', allocating men to beats and special duties. With many special functions and men in short supply, this can be a complex task. The department also keeps the sickness records and arranges the distribution of pay. On occasion, the staff are called on for other duties.

Constables may also be brought into the station to help with clerical duties. The annual check of property references (key holders for shops, offices, etc.) requires four constables working on it for several weeks.

The traffic inquiry department consists of four constables who work a day shift or a late shift. They investigate cases reported by the beat men and report on them to the chief inspector. If court action seems desirable the cases are passed on with supporting documents to the Procurator Fiscal. The inquiry officers get in touch with witnesses and parties to motor accidents, and take statements from them either at their homes or in the police station. They also deal with inquiries of a like nature coming from other forces. Traffic inquiry officers have perforce to attend court fairly frequently to give evidence. A lot of time is wasted waiting at court.

These officers are also on call during their period of duty to attend any serious road accident. An example of this may be taken from an incident reported when the schedule was being pre-tested:

p.m.

7.15	Returned to DHQ. Detailed to attend locus of vehicular accident.
7.20	Arrived at scene. Found other PCs in attendance. Learned that a motor van had collided with, and knocked down, six pedestrians who had all been removed to hospital. The van had failed to stop but its registration number had been noted. From this point I took charge of the inquiry.
7.30	Drove to garage where van may have been kept – no success. Left PC there in case van returned.
8	Drove to hospital to discover extent of injuries to pedestrians. Found they were still being examined. Left PC there to obtain their names and addresses. Returned to DHQ. Informed that the manager of the firm owning the vehicle resided in ABCD (a village outside the city boundary). Drove there with colleague in case he turned out to be the driver of the van. He, however, gave me the address of the person in charge of the van. Went to address.
9.10	On arrival found the driver had left for another address. Went there and found him in the house. He admitted being the person in charge and that no other person had been driving the van that evening. I formed the opinion that he was drunk, and at 9.25 p.m. arrested him for being drunk in charge of a motor vehicle. Prisoner conveyed to DHQ where he was charged with the above offence. After examination by a doctor he was allowed away. Before leaving, he came across with a story that another man (name and address unknown to him) had been driving at the time of the accident and that he had been a passenger. All he knew of this man was that he stayed in a particular small town outside the city.
10.50	Contacted police at this town as during my inquiry I had been given the name and address of a 'drinking friend' of the accused. I asked them to interview this man immediately and ascertain whether he had been

in the vehicle. Reply later received that a statement had been obtained, that the man denied being in the vehicle, but admitted to having been in the company of the accused earlier that evening. As no further inquiry could be made at that moment I went off duty at 11.40 p.m.

Remarks: The hit-and-run case is fortunately relatively uncommon. Although some extra duty was worked this is not usual for traffic inquiry officers and was mainly caused by waiting for the reply. The 'drinking friend' had to be seen immediately. Had the accused contacted him first he might have fabricated an alibi for him.

Another officer working on this inquiry noted: 'I was required to work $1\frac{1}{2}$ hours' overtime (in my case, as with many other PCs, I do not claim reimbursement when the time is spent on interesting work and making inquiries).'

One note may perhaps be inserted at this point from a member of the station staff; it is interesting for the light it throws on an aspect of patrol work. It runs: 'I would conclude by saying that I enjoy my work now; while on beat duties I sometimes suffered a feeling of frustration that, unlike a craftsman, there was no 'end product' to show at the end of the day, and the satisfaction of having done a job well was missing.'

The remaining department is that of the plain-clothes constables who are responsible for licensing (including clubs), firearms, and vice. Aliens, lotteries, and the supervision of restaurants which remain open after 11 p.m. are also their responsibility. They work a slightly different shift routine because normally there is little work for them between 2 and 9 a.m. On each of the survey days five officers were working: three from 9 a.m. to 5 p.m. and two from 6 p.m. to 2 a.m.

Plain-clothes constables normally work in pairs. On the Thursday the first pair read the daily information and reports from the night shift before attending the morning conference with the chief inspector, at which they discuss action in respect of betting offices, street bookmakers, bingo clubs, etc. At 10 a.m. they go off to investigate an application for a firearms licence. They walk there and back. As

47

police officers on the streets in civilian clothes, they also have a crime prevention and detection function. During the lunch hour they keep watch on a street bookmaker, and when they have secured the necessary evidence, arrest him and take him to the station. In the afternoon they inspect a bingo club (having checked on the various legal requirements beforehand), and note information from a beat constable regarding a suspected prostitute residing in a local street. They have much less typing and report writing to do than is usual. The pair on the Friday have a similar routine: they deal with a firearms application, arrest a street bookmaker in the lunch hour (this was shortly after licensed betting shops were opened, and unlicensed bookmakers were being driven from the streets), inspect betting offices, and attend a conference of plain-clothes officers at the central office. Owing to leave arrangements one man was on duty by himself. He was engaged on firearms inquiries, clerical work, and local patrolling.

The pair who come on at 6 p.m. on the Thursday have a summonsing report to prepare about late drinking (in this city it is the plain-clothes men who see that the bars close on time) and an address to verify; they also receive a firearms application, and a report concerning 'a male person persistently soliciting other male persons'. Then at 8 p.m. they go on foot patrol, visiting public houses en route and spending a quarter of an hour watching a woman suspected of importuning male passers-by. In the public houses they look out for any drinkers younger than 18, or any people whose movements and associations they like to keep an eye on. A licensee might be advised that a particular woman is a notorious prostitute and a suggestion made to him that he refuse her admission. At 9.10 p.m. they stop a youth carrying a portable typewriter; he agrees to accompany them to the nearest beat box, where his story is investigated and found credible, and the youth is sent on his way. They continue their patrol, speaking with local residents to pick up information and keeping known thieves and prostitutes under observation. At 10.40 p.m. they meet a man who offers them information about a housebreaking. He comes to the station and peruses photographs of known thieves with partial success. This information is passed on to the CID at 11.15 p.m. At midnight, after they have taken their refreshments, one officer starts compiling a report on a common-law charge of wasting police time, and collects information by telephone from police witnesses. The other officer types a firearms report and studies the new Betting and Gaming Act. From 1 a.m. to 2.20 a.m. they keep watch (from the back green) upon a suspected brothel.

The next evening the same two officers visit a golf club which has applied for a renewal of club registration. Then they go to a billiard saloon and public houses. In one locality they are looking out for a man suspected of a recent housebreaking. They question a 17-year-old girl who had earlier been reported missing but has now returned home. Next they patrol a street where cars are parked, watching for men who might attempt to steal from them. At 9.55 p.m. they apprehend a youth who has been drinking and is interfering with the cars. They check the CID reports to see if he has been in trouble before. As there is insufficient evidence to substantiate a charge they take him to his home but find that his parents are not there. They plan to call the following evening. Then at 11 p.m. they return to the central area to watch for women importuning passers-by. From 12.30 a.m. they keep watch on a suspected brothel for half an hour, before going on to the big dance hall where many of the patrons are now coming onto the streets. Afterwards they return to the station and complete the correspondence books.

IN CONCLUSION

One of the most striking features of this account is the great variety of tasks performed by policemen. Another illustration of their range is that on top of a cupboard in the charge office stands a bird cage. In the streets near the station there are many tenement buildings, and in the summer months budgerigars (called parakeets in America) regularly escape from them; when found they are brought into the station. The cage is often in use.

CHAPTER 3

Patrol Work in Some American Cities

CAROLINA CITY

Carolina City is a middle-sized city located in the south-east of the United States, with a population of some 200,000; it had a police department of 310 officers, thirty-nine civilian employees, and forty-three reservists at the time, July 1962, of the author's visit. About 30 per cent of the population are Negroes. The organization of patrol work in Carolina City is described first, and then, for comparison, shorter accounts are given of the organization of a larger department in Georgia City, policing a population of roughly 500,000, and of a smaller one in Felsmere City, Massachusetts, which has a population of 60,000.

The chief of police is appointed by the Carolina City Council and is directly responsible to the city manager for the operation of the department. The present chief, recently appointed, is the seventh holder of this office since 1939. The chief's staff includes: (i) a major who is in charge of the traffic, detective, and juvenile bureaux; (ii) another major who is responsible for the records, identification, communications, and special services bureaux; (iii) an assistant chief who commands the patrol division; (iv) an inspector (holding the rank of captain) who, among other duties, takes charge of recruitment, training, and promotion examinations; (v) a lieutenant who acts as planning officer; and (vi) a sergeant with a small squad of special investigators.

The patrol division consists of 159 men, of whom nine are detailed as gaolers, one as a court officer, and seven for selective enforcement duties, leaving 142 men. These are divided among the three shifts: morning (7 a.m. to 3 p.m.); afternoon (3 p.m. to 11 p.m.); and night (11 p.m. to 7 a.m.) – roughly in the proportions thirty-two, fifty, and sixty respectively. However, actual numbers are always appreciably lower, because some men will be absent on leave, through sickness, on training, etc. A representative line-up of personnel for a twenty-four-hour period would be as follows:

Morning Shift: 1 Lieutenant
                  2 Sergeants
                  4 Patrolmen in 2-man patrol cars
                 12 Patrolmen in 1-man patrol cars
                  5 Patrolmen on foot beats

                 24

Afternoon Shift: 1 Captain
                  1 Lieutenant
                  3 Sergeants
                 26 Patrolmen in 2-man patrol cars
                  2 Patrolmen in 1-man patrol cars
                  2 Patrolmen in a wagon ('Paddy-wagon' or 'Black Maria')

                 35

Night Shift: 1 Captain
                  2 Lieutenants
                  2 Sergeants
                 28 Patrolmen in 2-men patrol cars
                  3 Patrolmen in 1-man patrol cars
                  5 Patrolmen on motor scooters
                  2 Patrolmen on foot beats
                  4 Patrolmen in wagons

                 47

In the daytime, the assistant chief is himself on duty; this means that, since there is in any case a lower incidence of serious crime during this period, the morning shift can be commanded by a lieutenant instead of a captain. After 5 p.m. the officer commanding the shift is in charge of the entire police department; consequently the afternoon-shift commander needs to spend much of his time in the divisional office; but the night-shift commander is out on patrol for most of his shift, for there are few calls or callers that require his presence at headquarters. Each supervising officer – captain, lieutenant,

E   51 and sergeant – has a patrol car available for his use. All told, the department has sixty-five patrol cars.

For purposes of patrol work the city is divided into two districts – A and B, covering the western and eastern sides. Each district is divided into seven zones, making fourteen in all. The zones were established on the basis of calculations concerning population, numbers of business and other establishments, numbers of calls for police attention and of arrests, etc. These factors are presented in *Table 1* though the figures relate to the time when the zones were originally demarcated, some two years before my study was undertaken. It needs to be borne in mind, too, that foot patrolmen will also be working in zone 2 and part of 4, though during the daytime these officers would have to give much of their attention to traffic control. From the department's survey, it was found that it took an average of 4·7 minutes for a patrol car to arrive at the scene of a call from the time of dispatch; that the answering of a call took an average of twenty-eight minutes, the making of an arrest two hours, the serving of legal papers one hour,[1] and the investigation of an accident two hours. As a result of these findings, some of the zones were deemed overloaded and additional personnel were requested.

The patrol division shifts change over at 7 a.m., 3 p.m., and 11 p.m., but the traffic division personnel – for whom there would be little work in the middle of the night – work a different routine, so they are on the streets while the patrol division changes over. As the patrol cars all have to come into police headquarters near the centre of the city for the change-over, there is a danger that insufficient cars may be out on patrol at the change-over hours; each shift is therefore divided into two, one-half changing at a quarter to the hour, and the other on the hour.

Carolina City police officers almost all come to the headquarters in civilian clothes, and change into uniform in the locker room. They may arrive half an hour or more early, and sit with their colleagues watching television or playing cards. At the time for roll call, they go over to the side of the locker room where they sit in desks. The captain appears with a lieutenant or sergeant who calls the roll, allocating men to cars or beats as he does so. Papers are distributed with details

[1] Many of the persons on whom papers have to be served are 'job-jumpers' of uncertain address, which explains the high average time taken.

TABLE 1 CAROLINA CITY – PATROL ZONES

							Zones								Totals
	1	2	3	4	5	6	7	8	9	10	11	12	13	14	
Area in sq. miles	2·14	0·68	5·34	0·81	6·75	3·68	2·33	7·33	7·62	6·19	3·46	3·45	4·43	7·31	61·52
Population	14,397	2,701	19,072	11,256	14,301	19,888	8,059	11,227	15,001	11,635	12,684	19,198	18,635	10,593	188,647
Dwelling units	4,377	1,174	5,448	3,208	3,933	6,040	2,442	3,155	4,278	3,222	2,899	6,458	6,121	2,859	55,614
Business establishments	519	1,200	370	226	326	459	420	153	440	181	146	450	350	55	5,295
Schools	1	1	3	4	5	6	3	4	3	4	4	5	3	5	51
Banks	4	11	4	1	0	3	5	0	0	0	0	2	4	0	34
Pool-rooms	2	6	6	6	2	4	6	2	2	1	2	1	2	0	42
Beer stores	19	56	15	26	15	21	18	7	20	11	9	15	38	4	274
Whiskey stores	0	3	0	0	1	1	0	2	1	1	0	1	2	0	12
Clubs	4	7	3	5	7	12	9	8	15	7	19	4	24	2	126
Drive-in restaurants	7	1	6	0	5	5	8	13	10	7	7	2	5	0	76
No. of calls per month															
Morning shift	76	134	58	113	75	76	97	50	47	24	33	72	73	32	960
Afternoon shift	127	170	33	129	51	120	80	68	72	53	89	68	122	26	1,208
Night shift	69	127	33	42	44	77	61	43	56	34	58	67	72	23	806
No. of arrests per month															
Morning shift	6	15	3	46	7	8	32	12	9	2	6	9	10	3	168
Afternoon shift	23	38	7	58	13	34	28	19	18	6	20	18	21	1	304
Night shift	14	58	4	28	11	23	16	14	15	8	21	25	17	4	258

of stolen cars and other daily information. The men then go outside to the yard, where the patrol cars have just come in; they take over from the men going off duty, check the gasoline and log book, then drive to their zones. There is no formal parade or inspection. However, Carolina City officers are much smarter in appearance than officers in many northern cities: their summer uniform consists of dark blue trousers, a light blue short-sleeved shirt, open at the neck, and an eight-sided, flat-topped cap with a white cover. Each officer wears a chromium name-plate over his pocket on the right breast of his shirt, bearing his initials and name. Officers of the rank of lieutenant and above wear a white, long-sleeved shirt with a black tie; the name-plate, police badge, and buttons are in gilt instead of chromium.

One of the Carolina City sergeants and seven of the policemen are Negroes. They have a separate locker room, but attend the same roll call and sit in with the other officers. The car patrolling zone 4 – where the population is almost entirely Negro – is manned by Negro officers on the afternoon and night shifts, and a Negro officer is generally there on foot patrol. Zone 13 is also patrolled by Negro officers at times. Negro officers are allocated to cars in pairs, and a white officer is never detailed to partner a Negro officer. The Negro sergeant is mostly engaged in liaison work with the Negro schools, and another Negro officer is a detective in the juvenile bureau. One Negro reservist holds the rank of lieutenant.

Apart from traffic offences and the like, a very high proportion of the 'calls' which patrolmen have to attend are initiated by members of the public who telephone headquarters. They are received at headquarters, and if they require patrol action they are passed on to the dispatcher, who calls the number of the car he wants over the radio. The car responds. Then the dispatcher gives the men in the car the code number for the kind of call, together with the address; the car acknowledges these. When the call has been dealt with, the car notifies the dispatcher that it has resumed patrol and is consequently available for new calls. In the event of an emergency, of course, routine tasks are interrupted. As the radios of the patrol cars and of the supervisors are all on the same frequency, men in a car have a good idea of what is happening all over the city.

When legal papers are sent over to police headquarters to be served on people, the dispatcher may call in some cars that are not busy and have them distribute the papers to cars in neighbouring zones. Two cars may fix a rendezvous over the radio for this purpose or in order to transmit information.

Comparisons of British and American patrol work have, as far as possible, been reserved for the next chapter, but because the reliance upon motorized patrol is so much greater in Carolina City than in the Scottish city, it may be as well to draw attention to some circumstantial differences at this juncture. In the first place, as can be seen from *Table 2*, the Scottish city is much more compact geographically.

TABLE 2 CHARACTERISTICS OF FOUR CITIES

	Georgia City	Carolina City	Felsmere City	Scottish city
Population	500,000	200,000	60,000	474,000
Area in sq. miles	128·0	61·5	4	54·3
Size of police force	708	310	120	1,030
Police per 1000 of population	1·4	1·5	2·0	2·2
Civilians (excl. school crossing-guards, meter checkers, mechanics, and police cadets) as percentage of total employees of police department	11·2	8·6	1·2	8·2
No. of registered motor vehicles in area	204,850	132,000	24,000	70,000
Crime, 1961				
Murder	74	31	1	0
Robbery	374	118	7	90
Burglary	4,025	1,402	143	6,335
Larceny	11,626	3,716	431	6,668
Drunkenness	49,867	6,058	529	1,431
Driving: hazardous violations	123,717	18,900	168	3,081[a]
Drunken driving	3,640	354	58	271

[a] Includes non-hazardous violations.

Note: Owing to the many differences in the definition and reporting of offences it is dangerous to conclude that differences in such figures reflect variations in public conduct accurately; they do, however, reflect police activity – which is what we are concerned with here.

American cities, as might be expected in a country which is so much less densely populated, and where land is so much less scarce than the other factors of production, are spread out. Many American cities have grown up since the adoption of the automobile, so that restaurants, shopping centres, etc., have been planned with parking-space provision. Distances, accordingly, are greater, and the policeman on foot could not serve the same number of residents or business establishments. In the second place, the population is itself motorized to a high degree, so the policeman is only operating in the same way as nearly everyone else. In Britain, a constable in a motor car cannot make contact with citizens as easily as a foot patrolman can, but this does not apply to the same extent in the United States – both because the citizens are themselves often in automobiles, and because social relations are less formal and people can get onto a friendly basis more quickly. In the third place, most of the United States is subject to greater extremes of climate (at one or both ends of the thermometer) than Scotland. At times of severe cold or exhausting heat, the foot patrolman, unless he is a real enthusiast, is likely to spend as much of his time as he possibly can in a place which offers shelter, and will neglect his beat.

While visiting Carolina City, I spent most time with the afternoon shift, because it produces more representative public contacts and a better reflection of the whole spectrum of police activity than either of the other shifts. In all, sixty hours were spent with the afternoon shift, mostly at the end of the week and in the busier zones. Brief accounts follow of the activities of the officers I accompanied on two occasions.

On a Wednesday in August, car 12 had no special duties allocated at roll call or received from the outgoing shift; so, as everything seemed to be quiet, the officers drove to a drive-in restaurant and got a drink of coca-cola. They explained to me that the drinks were 'on the house' because the management liked to have police vehicles call – their presence kept roughnecks away and gave the place an additional security which was cheap at the price. After this they patrolled their zone systematically. They stopped to talk with a youth they knew who was serving a sentence in a work camp but was allowed to visit his home during the day; the officers commented that he was the sort who would never tell them anything. They went on to speak of another youth whom they had once treated leniently and who had promised to give them information about what was going on among a group of young men. Instead, he had continually misled them, so, by way of retaliation, the officers had led the members of the group to believe that one of their number, who had been sentenced, had been caught as a result of information supplied by this man. The group had responded by ostracizing him, and would not have him on their corner again. The police, the officers said, had really done him a good turn in keeping him out of such bad company.

In the early evening a Negro pedestrian was seen crossing the road in a shaky fashion against the traffic light (a jay-walking ordinance enforced closely in the city centre requires pedestrians also to wait for a green light). His speech was slurred and his breath smelt of liquor, so he was arrested, put in the back seat of the car, conveyed to the city gaol (adjoining police headquarters), searched, and put in a cell under the charge of the gaoler. The officers then resumed patrol. Another intoxicated Negro was seen almost immediately, but since he was almost home and was walking fairly straight, he was allowed to continue. When asked what he had been drinking, the man replied, 'A couple of beers', which was so obviously untrue that it only irritated the officer and made him the more inclined to make an arrest. He commented to me afterwards that he had once stopped a man who agreed that he was drunk, and he had been so surprised by this unusual honesty that he had let the man go. He went on to say that he and his colleague had once been instructed that if every drunk were arrested, crime could be cut by a half, because drunks, being defenceless, were so often robbed. (This viewpoint would be contested by many contemporary authorities on the relation between alcoholism and crime. In New York City, drunks who cause no disturbance are ignored by the police. In Scotland, men who would be arrested in Carolina City are often left alone, because they are less dangerous in British traffic conditions, and less likely to be robbed.)

The time had then arrived for the men to take their 30-minute meal break; they returned to the restaurant, where they were again served 'on the house'. At this point some comment for readers unacquainted with American conditions is called for. Patrolmen have to be allowed some break for refreshments; they have no beat boxes, and it would be inconvenient to have them return to the headquarters

57

to eat. The American public's expectations of the police officer do not require him to keep aloof from such everyday matters as eating in a restaurant, so there is nothing which of itself makes such a practice undesirable. The problem comes with what is called 'mooching' – the obtaining of free or cheap job perquisites. To try and determine the relative responsibility of the patrolman and the restaurateur, to discover 'who started it?', would be profitless. The provision of free or cheap meals to police officers on duty in the zones where they are known is widespread in America, though, in my limited experience, it is virtually restricted to officers of patrolman rank. Never once, when I went to restaurants in Carolina and Georgia Cities with officers of the rank of sergeant or above (or with Negro officers, for they seemed to be more 'correct' in these matters), did either I or my companion pay less than the proper price. Patrolmen explained to me that they would not accept the generosity of restaurateurs in this way if the latter expected any privileges in return. A case was quoted of a man who, because he had given the police free meals, thought he could ignore the parking regulations; he was promptly disabused of this idea, and officers stopped visiting his premises.[1]

While we were waiting at the restaurant, one of the officers mentioned to me that at places like this the waitresses often made a fuss of them. They said that the women seemed to be strongly attracted towards men in uniform. Often women telephoned headquarters to report a prowler in the vicinity of the house, as an excuse for getting a policeman to call; some officers got into trouble both with their wives and with the police department as a result of the accessibility of many such women. The officer added: 'You see this one here' – referring to the waitress who had just taken the order – 'I'll bet she makes a pass at one of us before we're through'. Later on he went into the restaurant for something; she came out of the door behind him, put her arm round his waist, called him her 'baby', and tried hard to flirt with him.

After dinner, the second officer took over as driver. The car received a call to a Negro household where someone said a child was being beaten. The house was quiet on arrival and the householder had no small child there; nor did she know of any neighbour with a grudge who might have been responsible for a false call. Then the

[1] The implications of 'mooching' are discussed on pp. 221–3 below.

officers went to serve a *capias instanter* on a youth who had failed to continue attendance at a driver improvement school which he had been directed to attend by the traffic court. He was not at home. His parents – who appeared very respectable folk – had an explanation of the incident, but the police, who had simply to serve the court order requiring that the person in question be held, could do nothing in the matter. They arranged for the youth to report at police head-quarters and went off to deliver two subpoenas for the court.

The next call was about a theft reported by a motorist – a youth who had left a car parked outside a cinema, and found when he came out that the valve cover and trachometer had been stolen from the engine. Nothing could be found in the vicinity to explain where they might have been taken. The officer later observed that he had once known the entire transmission to be stolen from a parked car!

Shortly after the car resumed patrol, a radio message came that it should report to headquarters, where the youth wanted by the court had called with his parents. On arrival, the officers explained to them that the order required them to take the youth into custody before bringing him before the court in the morning. The parents protested against their boy being put in gaol when they considered that there had been a mistake over the whole order. They were referred to the captain, who explained that he had no more power than the officers. Finally, on the advice of the police, though on their own reponsibility, the parents succeeded in communicating with the judge who had issued the order. He decided to cancel it and have the young man summonsed to court instead, so he was able to sleep in his own bed that night. There were no other calls for car 12 before 11 p.m.

One Friday, shortly afterwards, I rode with car 4 for the afternoon shift. During the first two and a half hours there was little activity. A call was received from a Negro lawyer to the effect that an old woman had been in his office in a drunken state, shouting abuse. The officers called at the law office, found which way the woman had gone and soon located her. She was Negro and aged about 70 years; her dress was unfastened and she was obviously unlikely to sober up for a while. They put her in the car and took her to gaol, where they tried to arrange that she would be released on bail as soon as possible. The officers – who were themselves Negro – felt it a terrible thing that a woman of this age, who ought to be worthy of respect from younger people, should behave in this fashion. Later on another drunk, Negro again, was taken to gaol, where – as so often happens – the gaoler recognized him as an old acquaintance. We ate a meal in a Negro café in the middle of the zone, just near to an intersection which is referred to as 'bloody corner' and 'murder corner'. During one of the years of the second world war, thirty-one murders had been committed either on this corner or within three blocks of it, and it had been reputed to be the worst 'corner' in the whole of the country. Before the slum clearance programme had been started, this had been a violent neighbourhood. When there had been trouble, the police had gone to the incident only in strength. This was the neighbourhood in which the first Negro officers had been obliged to prove themselves; it had demanded a strong arm and much courage.

Shortly after dinner, the officers received a call to headquarters. There they were presented with a Negro who alleged he had been robbed of his wage packet on his way home from work, but thought he might recognize his assailant. The officers questioned him closely and decided that the description fitted a man they knew, so they took the complainant in the car to see if they could find the suspect. Leaving the complainant in the car when they stopped, they looked through several establishments, particularly a certain pool-room. While they were still touring the area, a voice came over the radio: '1036' (a request to be given the air to make an emergency call); then '55 at Seventh and Church – send me some help here quick'. The driver of the car waited to hear no more, but raced away, siren sounding and roof-light flashing. The location of the call was an ominous one: two years previously a police officer had been shot near there, and only recently another had received a beating. After two or three minutes of hectic driving the car arrived at the spot. Seven other police cars were already there, their roof-lights flashing, and a small knot of people were gathered on the sidewalk. The officers went over and a Negro prisoner, handcuffed and with a bleeding head, was delivered into their custody. He was a young man of light build and ordinary appearance – he protested that he had done nothing. One officer asked: 'Then why did he put cuffs on you? You wouldn't have been arrested if you'd done nothing'. They put him in the back of the car and unlocked the handcuffs, then drove him to the gaol, allowing the earlier complainant to get out en route; he had found the recent drive so alarming that for a little while he had even forgotten his missing ninety dollars.

The incident had arisen when a traffic officer, accompanied by a reservist, had stopped a car containing two men and a woman, which was being driven in a reckless fashion. The officer was questioning the driver when another car drew up, and its driver (who was the husband of the woman in the first car) assaulted the first driver frantically. As his words had no effect, the officer then hit the new-comer over the head, put handcuffs on him, and placed all the parties under arrest. But then a threatening crowd had gathered, and since several of the men had offensive weapons and seemed inclined to use them, the officer called for help (the men I was with observed that reservists were not such reliable partners on occasions like this). By the time our car reached the scene, the uglier elements in the crowd had dispersed. The prisoner was handed over to the gaoler, but he speedily arranged bail through a professional bondsman who guaranteed the necessary $500; he could at the same time have arranged bail for his wife, but apparently preferred to leave her under lock and key.

Shortly after this incident, the car received a call to go to a woman who had reported seeing, in the vicinity of her house, a man she suspected of having earlier broken in and stolen a radio. Following her directions, the officers succeeded in picking up two men (like the other parties in the case, they were Negroes) who answered the description she had given. They were driven back, where the woman made a positive and convincing identification. The second suspect was released, the first man was detained in custody. (It was interesting to note how easily one of the officers apprehended people: he was a big man, 6 ft. 2 in. tall and about 230 lbs. in weight, and he had only to say to someone, 'Come on, get into the back of the car', to be obeyed quietly – it scarcely took half a minute.) The officers then checked the records at headquarters for the original report on the theft of the radio, and found none. Apparently, when other officers had gone to investigate the woman's original call, they had found no one at home; she had not telephoned again, so no report had been completed. The officers therefore made out the proper report, observing that now that the man had been found, the detectives would probably solve this and several other crimes, but that the

61

detectives would get the credit for it, and not the patrol officers who had caught the criminal. They went on to claim that the detectives at times made inquiries in the Negro section without consulting the patrol officers; the detectives might go to an address and ask someone the whereabouts of John Doe, unaware that they were speaking to the very man; he, of course, would give a misleading answer and then go into hiding.

Shortly afterwards, the car again received a call to the station, where the man who had been robbed of his wage packet was waiting. In the meantime, I had discussed his case with the officers. They were somewhat sceptical of his story because he seemed to have been duped remarkably easily; he bore no signs of any struggle, and there was not even a tear at the side of the breast pocket of his shirt from which his wallet had allegedly been snatched. In the interim the complainant in question had gone back to the places where the officers had looked, and had seen in the pool-room the man who had robbed him. The complainant may have shown himself, for by the time we got there the suspect had disappeared. The aggrieved party then went home, but the officers kept looking out for the suspect and visited a club he was known to frequent. At one point, the driver suddenly put the car into reverse and drove quickly back down the street; stopping, they went into a pool-room where men were playing cards; there was no money to be seen, but the officers were so sure that the men had been playing for cash stakes that they confiscated some of the cards and tore them up.

On other occasions when I was with officers on the afternoon shift, their activities included the following: three drivers who were on the road in vehicles with defective tail lights were cautioned. A driver who made an illegal turn against a red light was 'given a ticket' (i.e. a citation was issued against him); he could either plead guilty and pay a fine of $13, or attend court to answer the charge. Another driver was given a ticket for reckless driving because he 'spun his wheels' turning a corner (i.e. accelerated so fast that his rear wheels did not grip the road surface). The driver of a car suspected stolen was stopped, and his papers were examined. The driver of a car bearing licence plates for both this state and the adjoining one (where the driver worked) was told to remove the second. Two pedestrians under the influence of liquor were stopped, but allowed to continue since they did not seem to present any danger. A car was seen to wait through two green lights at an intersection; the driver was found to be drunk and was arrested. Another driver who was arrested by the traffic patrol because he did not have his registration certificate (and so might be driving without the insurance required by the laws), and who refused to recognize any liability to produce this document, was conveyed to the gaol. Five subpoenas were served upon witnesses, and one *capias instanter*. Four private complaints were investigated (one of nuisance, one of threat, and two of abuse) and the complainants advised. Someone apparently suffering an epileptic fit was noticed, tended, and sent to hospital by ambulance. An inquiry was made on behalf of a detective. A prisoner was visited in gaol to see if he was, by this time, prepared to state what he had done with a radio he was charged with stealing (the same man was convicted later that week, and received a sentence of not less than four years for breaking and entering and not less than fifteen months for larceny of goods less than $200 in value – which was considered an unusually severe sentence by the police).

Further cases which occurred while I was with the same shift may also be mentioned. A man reported that at work he had drunk from a lemonade bottle bought from a vending machine, and found it contained glass fragments some of which he might have swallowed. A prowler was reported by a woman late one evening (apparently a genuine case). There was a case of vandalism – some men in a car had driven into a man's front garden, torn up one of his flowering shrubs, and driven off with it (the car was later reported speeding but the police were unable to catch the driver). A number of juveniles had cast stones in slings, hitting a woman in a car, and breaking the window of an ice-cream van – the driver saw where one of them, a seven-year-old, ran to and took the police there; a small boy promptly burst into tears, giving himself away. The group was rounded up and taken into the juvenile bureau where the case was taken over.[1] On one occasion a patrol car made a rendezvous with the men in a neighbouring zone, at whose suggestion a road block was set up for

[1] *Table 3* shows that the incidence of crime among teenagers is heavy. It necessitates the operation of a separate juvenile bureau; 6 of the offenders charged with robbery, 17 with assault, 128 with burglary, 446 with larceny, and 30 with auto theft were persons under 15 years of age.

twenty minutes and drivers were asked for their driving licences and car registrations. The officers said that in this way they often picked up drivers who were drunk or without insurance coverage (if uninsured drivers are involved in accidents, this can be serious for the other party). A housebreaking was investigated. At another time the patrol car was called to a 'cutting': there had been a fracas at a disorderly house in a Negro quarter, and a woman had stabbed a man in the hand – the woman was taken to gaol in the wagon which had also covered the call.[1]

The morning shift resembles the afternoon shift in most respects, except that there is usually less activity; but the work is rather different on the night shift when there are fewer contacts with the public and the chances of tangling with an armed criminal are higher. Much of the patrol officer's time is spent – as in Scotland – on checking property. Each patrol car has spotlights mounted on either side, which can be operated from within the car. The driver of a one-man car checks premises with this light; if he sees anything suspicious he takes no further action until he has summoned a supporting car. The motor scooters which are employed on night-shift work have been criticized as ineffective because criminals hear them coming, but it is also argued that they have a deterrent value. Patrolmen can cover a larger area with a scooter, and such crimes as theft from automobiles have been considerably reduced by the scooter patrol.

Every Carolina City patrol officer, before he goes off duty, completes a daily activity report form, on which he records the cases on which he has worked, and the numbers of accidents investigated, searches made, buildings found open, street lights out of action, automobiles recovered, etc. He notes details concerning persons arrested, calls answered, and contacts made with members of the public (chiefly persons who are questioned but not charged). This gives supervisors a rough measure – though not necessarily a very reliable one – of how hard their subordinates work. In view of the greater difficulty in supervising men patrolling by car, some such check is probably useful in keeping people up to the mark. The idea (whether justified or not) that they may be evaluated in this way

[1] *Table 3* also shows that while the crime rate is higher among Negroes than Whites for most offences, the disproportion is greater for crimes of violence: rape, robbery, and assault.

PERSONS ARRESTED

TABLE 3 CAROLINA CITY – CRIME BY SEX, RACE, AND AGE

Crime	Males	Females	Whites	Negroes	Age in years				
					Under 20	20–9	30–9	40–9	50 & over
Murder and manslaughter	37	9	13	33	4	13	18	7	4
Forcible rape	31	0	5	26	12	9	6	3	1
Robbery	84	3	17	70	30	38	15	4	0
Aggravated assault	705	234	193	746	137	271	256	179	96
Burglary (breaking or entering)	458	19	170	307	262	127	61	23	4
Larceny, theft (except auto theft)	1,051	209	425	835	784	209	139	83	45
Auto theft	179	14	82	111	102	61	24	5	1
Embezzlement and fraud	219	50	227	42	9	100	85	55	20
Weapons (carrying, possessing, etc.)	91	5	22	74	24	36	23	8	5
Drunkenness	5,467	584	3,392	2,659	139	925	1,785	1,749	1,453
Driving while intoxicated	327	27	248	106	6	77	119	91	61
Gambling	124	26	46	104	1	34	50	32	33

underlies the complaint already quoted of a patrol officer that a detective would get the 'credit' for an arrest he had just made, and the observations of a Negro officer that 'They (i.e. white supervisors) say we don't work hard enough, but they've only to look at our records to see that it isn't true'. From another angle it is noteworthy that the Carolina City department uses standardized report forms for other purposes also; there are forms for general offences, alcoholic influence cases, and auto accidents, which reduce the labour of reporting (particularly important when the officers are better at shooting than spelling, and when they may have far more reports to complete per shift than the Scottish officer) and eliminate the possibility of any difference of opinion arising between patrolman and supervisor as to the correct manner in which to report an event.

GEORGIA CITY

Georgia City has a population of 500,000, 35 per cent of whom are Negroes. It forms the nucleus of a five-county metropolitan area of over 1,000,000 inhabitants. Its police department comprises 702 police officers and 103 civilians, excluding traffic policewomen (school). The present chief of police has been in office since the beginning of 1947; he is responsible to the Police Committee of the Board of Aldermen, a group consisting of the mayor and four elected officials, who meet at frequent intervals in police headquarters and who are responsible for the running of the department. For example, when a disciplinary charge is made against an officer, the chief suspends him and the charge is heard at the next meeting of the police committee, which decides both the verdict and the sentence.

The department is divided into five divisions, each in the charge of a superintendent. The divisional commanders are changed around at frequent intervals. The service division is responsible for gaol and building maintenance, communications, records, and special details. The other personnel in the division are two captains, six lieutenants, five sergeants, one policewoman, and sixty-one civilians. The detective division includes seven special squads (each commanded by a lieutenant) for dealing with auto theft, burglary, homicide, larceny, robbery, vice, and juveniles. Then there are sections for identification, special security, general investigations, and criminal investigations. In addition to the superintendent, there are two captains, nine lieutenants, seven sergeants, eighty-four detectives, two policewomen, and thirty-six civilians. The traffic division has men on three watches plus an extra day watch, and sections for safety education, control, schools, and accident investigation. There are three captains, four lieutenants, eleven sergeants, 134 patrolmen, 106 school policewomen, and four civilians. The uniform division mans three ordinary watches and two cover watches (to be described later), together with a plain-clothes section for night patrol. This division includes eight captains, eight lieutenants, eleven sergeants, 338 patrolmen, and two police-women. The training division is responsible for police training, civil defence, and personnel investigation; it comprises, apart from the superintendent, one lieutenant, one sergeant, and two patrolmen.

By way of explanation it should be added that in Georgia City – as in the other American police departments visited – the position of detective is also a rank, senior to and better paid than that of patrol-man. Also, that the chain of command is shorter than in British forces. An order from the chief passes through fewer intermediaries before reaching the patrolman; this means that lieutenants and ser-geants are often employed for much the same kind of work, and that there is less difference in their numbers – twenty-eight lieutenants and thirty-five sergeants – than in Britain, where there are three or four sergeants to every inspector.

The three ordinary watches change over at 12 midnight, 8 a.m., and 4 p.m. All the cars come into the headquarters, but since the traffic division watches change at different hours, its men are on the street while the uniform division is changing over. There are in addition some pointsmen who work a 10 a.m. to 6 p.m. duty. The likely alloca-tion of men, allowing for leave, sickness, etc., will be fifty to morning watch (12 midnight to 8 a.m.), fifty to day watch (8 a.m. to 4 p.m.), and seventy-five to evening watch (4 p.m. to 12 midnight). There will also be about thirty Negro officers working the 6 p.m. watch, which operates until 2 a.m. and provides additional cars and beat men for the coloured sections; and another thirty men on the night watch (8 p.m. to 6 a.m., two hours' overtime pay); working with the night watch is the Canine Corps (thirteen men all told) who patrol with dogs.

The day watch is likely to include one captain, two lieutenants, and two sergeants; each lieutenant and sergeant supervises a district in

F

which there will be five or six patrol cars and one or two wagons. Ten men will be on foot beats – at railroad stations, charity hospital, bus stations, parks – mostly older men, though one of the smartest officers is assigned to duty at the principal traffic intersection in the middle of the town. One man from each shift works also as dispatcher in the radio tower. During the day watch, practically all the patrol cars are manned by a single officer unless some 'roustabouts' (spare men) are available. This means that there are forty-five patrolmen reporting to four supervisors who report to one captain. The captain in charge of the watch is the 'field captain', and can requisition help from other divisions if necessary.

The evening watch uses its extra personnel to put up to twenty men on foot beats and to have an additional man in most of the cars. Work is allocated in accordance with the distribution of people – e.g. streets where people gather, theatres, sporting events. The morning watch is similar to the day watch except that men are allocated to police areas rather than people. The night-watch personnel are instructed to check all property in their zone after coming on duty; then, after they have had their meal, to check again; and finally, before going off duty, to make a third check; the remainder of the time they are to keep under cover and watch for burglars. When this watch was instituted a few years ago, I was told, officers patrolled on foot in places where they had never been seen before and this had a powerful deterrent effect. In British police terminology, the 6 p.m. watch and the night watch are 'cover shifts', because they provide additional police cover at critical times and places, supplementing the ordinary shift.

Georgia City police officers are required to report at headquarters already in uniform. They parade for roll call in the drill hall, where they are called to attention and inspected; however, the bearing of the men is much more relaxed than would be found in a military parade or at an inspection in a British station. The uniform is similar to that in the Carolina City force, except that the caps have no white top for the summer and have a round brim; the patrolmen remove the stiffeners from the caps, bending the front up and the sides down, and wear them at a variety of different angles.

The 6 p.m. watch (consisting entirely of Negro officers) is much smarter than the other watches at roll call. It consists of one lieutenant, one sergeant, and twenty-four patrolmen; and, at the time of my visit, an additional fifteen men were to be recruited. There are Negro officers also in other sections: seven detectives, five night-watch patrolmen, and three turnkeys (service division). Georgia City was, in 1947, the first large Southern city to employ Negro policemen. Initially they were under orders from the chief of police not to arrest white offenders, but in 1962 he issued a new order to the effect that all restrictions on the arrest power of Negro officers were removed. Though the Negro officers are organized in a separate shift, they appear to feel themselves members of the department to a greater extent than their counterparts in Carolina City, and their morale appears to be high despite the restrictions that lasted for fifteen years; this is largely due to their confidence in the chief of police.

Georgia City makes more use than Carolina City of one-man patrol cars. Their use is a subject of lively discussion in police circles. Georgia City started making regular use of one-man cars only when the policeman's working hours were reduced and the manpower problem became acute. But, though circumstantial factors precipitated the change in policy, there were good arguments for it from the standpoint of police practice. It was represented to me very strongly by one of the captains that, when the police had trouble with prisoners, it was often because the officers were over-confident or aggressive, and that this happened more frequently with two-men cars. If an officer was by himself, he had to use tact and persuasion. When I suggested that such a policy would be effective only if the courts punished men convicted of assaulting officers more severely than the policemen I had talked with believed them to do, the captain cited a case. A short while before, an officer had stopped a driver for a faulty muffler (exhaust silencer) and had given him a ticket. Later on, the accused drove up to the officer's car, bumping it slightly, and came over to say that he resented the officer's manner, that he was a no-good son of a bitch, and that his wife was probably a prostitute. The officer arrested him for insulting behaviour. The accused was found guilty and fined $300. Had there been two officers together, the captain said, it might well have been only a $25 fine because 'the police officer here is supposed to be able to take care of himself'. He thought that a similar view would be taken in the case of assaults. Other people argued similarly, that the older system invited the use

69

TABLE 4 GEORGIA CITY – CHARGES MADE DURING 1 WEEK BY THE ORDINARY WATCHES IN 3 DISTRICTS

	Morning Watch District 3			Day Watch District 2			Evening Watch District 4		
	4 Cars	2 Wagons	3 Footmen	5 Cars	1 Wagon	1 Footman	5 Cars	1 Wagon	2 Footmen
Drunk	30	1	24	17	3	5	41	3	19
Drunk and disorderly	0	0	0	5	0	0	49	0	0
Drunken driving	2	0	0	0	0	0	4	0	0
Disorderly conduct	15	0	0	3	1	0	59	0	1
Violating knife ordinance	0	0	0	0	0	0	2	0	0
Speeding	5	0	0	12	1	1	11	0	0
Stop sign	3	0	0	8	0	0	16	0	0
Red light	6	0	0	12	0	0	8	0	3
Illegal parking	1	0	0	3	0	0	3	0	0
Traffic offences	23	0	0	21	0	0	56	0	0
Total cases made	85	1	24	81	5	6	249	3	23
Total calls	190	78	0	99	0	0	379	85	0

Note: Georgia City is divided into four districts: No. 4 is the busiest and No. 2 the quietest from the police point of view – so the figures for the evening watch represent the busiest district at the busiest time, though they underestimate the number of cases by perhaps 20 per cent because men allocated to the district for only part of the week will have made cases that are not included in these totals. The figures for the day watch represent the quietest district at the quietest time. Some officers – as in most departments – go from week to week without making any cases at all. It should also be remembered that officers of the traffic division and of the two cover shifts will have made cases in these districts which are not reported here. The wagons will patrol when they are not conveying to gaol prisoners arrested by beat men or patrol cars; they do not normally answer calls, neither do the foot patrolmen who are not in radio communication.

of unnecessary force; and that the courts, being aware that the police were themselves inclined to punish the more bellicose offenders, gave lighter sentences. The chief of police himself observed that it would be possible (though not necessarily desirable) not only to go over to one-man cars but to let patrol officers go unarmed. After one or two unarmed officers had been shot, he said, there would be such an outcry that even the defendant's lawyers would be on trial. This is not to say that officers in the city ought to leave their guns at headquarters; but it does help to explain why increases in police power do not necessarily have the desired effect. It also provides part of the answer to the question asked by many American officers as to how the British constable can do his job without a gun.

The figures in *Table 2* show that patrol officers in Georgia City spend more of their time in active enforcement work than those in Carolina City or the Scottish city.[1] Most warrants are served by the detective bureau, and patrol officers call the wagon to take in arrested persons so that they will not be absent from their zone. The paper work involved in arresting and gaoling a person has been cut down to a few minutes only in the case of a routine offence like drunkenness. This does not mean, however, that officers take a nonchalant view of their powers of arrest. In the United States a high value is placed on individual liberty, and because people are aware of cultural differences within the nation they show tolerance of many deviations. The Georgia City officer in a busy district has little time to listen to trivialities, but this does not seem to make him any less considerate of people or less inclined to help them when he can.

To demonstrate how busy he can be, I cite a Saturday evening watch spent with a car in district 4. This is the busiest time and district, but the activity was apparently not unusual for a Saturday night. It was a two-man car, the one being an experienced officer and the other a relative newcomer. The area patrolled was in the poorest part of the city, with a mixed white and Negro population. During the eight hours we received eighteen calls, four of which were false. In three of these cases the address was non-existent, and in the fourth the householder knew nothing of the call. The officers thought that false calls were usually a blind: someone wished to take in untaxed

---

[1] *Table 4* sets out the charges made during one week in Georgia City by the ordinary watches in three districts.

liquor from a car to a house and telephoned about an alleged disturbance on the other side of the district to minimize the chances of a patrol car's passing at the wrong moment. Certainly a lot of untaxed liquor is brewed in or brought into Georgia City. In addition, there was a bogus fire alarm attended by three engines.

A call was received about a drunk in an automobile. It transpired that he was a man moving to lodgings in the city with all his possessions. He had been unable to have the room he had reckoned on, and, having nowhere else to go, went drinking and then went to sleep in his car. He was booked for drunkenness rather than for being drunk in charge of a vehicle. A wreck truck was summoned to tow his car in. His suitcases and belongings were checked and handed over to the gaoler, the car being impounded.

A man telephoned to report the theft of his car; he turned out to be intoxicated and to have been drinking with a companion who had since gone off with his car. Concluding that the other driver was probably intoxicated also, the officers first searched streets in the direction he was said to have taken but without success. On returning, it was clear that the man who had lost the car was too much 'under the influence' to take possession of it again should the other driver return, so he was told to step into the car and come to the police station where the theft could be recorded. On arrival he was led off into the gaol, still unaware of what was happening. He ought to have been told at the beginning that he was under arrest, but the police officers preferred to get things done as quietly as possible. Often, one of them said, when you arrest someone you have to argue with him all the way to the station. (That comment itself is interesting as an indication of how much the officer in practice tries to get the co-operation of the prisoner, however bizarre this idea may sound!) Later on they had another look around for the car. While they were doing so a report came over the radio of a man who seemed to be having an epileptic seizure in a street elsewhere in their patrol area; when the officers arrived at the spot, he was nowhere to be seen. Later they interviewed another man who alleged that his automobile had been taken.

A report came in of a domestic dispute. On the officers' arrival at the address, one of the two apartments was completely quiet and did not answer. The people in the other apartment denied knowledge of the call. Trying the first apartment again, the officers discovered that there were a couple there who did, after an initial disavowal, admit that they had been having a row, but said that they had now reached agreement. The police took no action. They were sure that it had been the people in the neighbouring apartment who had reported the disturbance, but that, for the sake of their own relations with the neighbours, they did not wish to acknowledge this. There was also a call to a white householder who had complained that some Negroes on the property at the rear of his house were creating a disturbance; they had since dispersed and no action had to be taken.

Two parties had called police headquarters, making allegations against one another. By chance, the police met first the white man who said that a Negro mechanic working on a car in a backyard garage had threatened him; the Negro had a different version. The officers told them both to be quiet and to keep clear of one another; should there be any further trouble, they were to call the police and not to try taking matters into their own hands.

A woman had called to complain of her husband's behaviour. He was on parole after being convicted of abandoning the family and of drunken driving, and his wife was responsible for the parole. The man had been drinking and had been abusive. He professed ignorance that drinking was a violation of his parole and might cause the court to revoke it. The wife, who had earlier declared she would tolerate him no longer, agreed to give him a last chance; no police action was required.

Another domestic dispute was attended, in which a woman complained that her husband was drunk and had injured her property by pulling out the ignition wires in her car. The police stood at the car and asked the husband, who was standing on the porch, what had happened. He came down to the pavement (this gave the officers the opportunity to arrest him for being drunk, should they wish; they could not do so if he remained in his house). The man denied mishandling the woman and disputed her ownership of the car. He said he had immobilized it to prevent her taking their niece who lived with them to stay in his mother's house; his mother ran a brothel and he did not want his niece to go there. The officers did not consider him really intoxicated. They reasoned that any man who spoke in this way of his mother was probably telling the truth and sympathized with his attitude. The man, who appeared resigned to arrest at one

73

point, offered to go and spend the night elsewhere, an idea which the officers tried to encourage. They told him he had been childish in damaging the car and warned both him and his wife to stop quarrelling. If there was another call to headquarters they (the officers) would be criticized for not having taken adequate action the first time, so they would come back and arrest them both.

There was another case of a wife complaining that her husband was drunk and insulting. It was a better house than the other one visited and had a Cadillac standing in the driveway. The wife, who seemed a quiet and respectable woman, was in an extremely nervous condition, weeping and slightly hysterical. The husband had accused her, among other things, of going with his brother, a man young enough to be her son. We went into the bedroom where one of the officers asked the husband – who was lying in his underclothes – what was going on. The husband was extremely argumentative. He refused to promise that he would quiet down and insisted that he could not be arrested for drunkenness in his own house. It became apparent that if nothing were done, matters would get worse. The officers told him to put his clothes on and to come out to the car, which he did, protesting. He asked why he was being taken in and was told he had to sober up. The man wanted to telephone the superintendent of detectives; he spoke of senior officers he claimed to know; he asked the officers if they knew how much he had in the bank. Then he said he was under arrest, wasn't he? The officers agreed (they were going to charge him with creating a disturbance, or a breach of the peace, or some such offence which obviated the difficulty inherent in an arrest for a misdemeanour in a man's own house). He wanted to buy himself off. After he had been taken into headquarters, charged, and gaoled, one of the officers expressed his indignation over people of this kind, who boast of connections and money, and then, when they see it is no use, try to beg or bribe their way out. He probably felt that morally he was the man's superior, though by no means his financial superior.

After this came a very curious story. A little and not particularly attractive woman of about 40 years was complaining that two evenings earlier, while intoxicated, she had twice been raped. She had been drinking and was lying on her bed when the landlady's married daughter brought two young men to her room and went away. The men raped her, though she had protested that she was too old. She had not shouted because she did not want to be knocked about, and anyway she had drunk too much to react as she might otherwise have done. One of the men came back shortly afterwards to ask if she would like some coca-cola but he had left when he saw that she was 'mad'. The next day she found a billfold on the floor, which must have dropped from the pockets of one of them and which identified a man of 22 years. Only today, nearly forty-eight hours afterwards, had she thought to telephone the police. The police officers told her that it was no use her charging rape after such an interval, because the courts would not listen to her story. A woman charging rape was supposed to have resisted and shouted, or at least to have reported the offence as soon as she had an opportunity to do so. Her only course was to go to the police station and swear a warrant for assault and battery against the identifiable man. Both officers privately expressed suspicions of her story, which, taken all together, seemed so improbable.

The final case came towards the end of the watch and took a long time to deal with. The parties were white, as they were in all the previous cases except where otherwise noted. The area patrolled was racially mixed, but cases involving coloured people were probably being given to a car with Negro officers. Someone had telephoned to report a disturbance, but the problem was more complicated. It centred on a household which had given the police trouble before. The father was a ne'er-do-well; the mother, who was no better, was a midget. Father, mother, and a visiting cousin had locked themselves in the house, and had got drunk on untaxed liquor obtained from the house opposite. The children, who appeared not to have washed for weeks, were badly in need of care and protection; they were regularly locked out and accustomed to scrounging food from the neighbours. There was a girl of 15, and boys of 13, 11, 8 and 6 years. The woman who had made the call did not live in the neighbourhood, but she frequently visited relatives in the street and had befriended the girl in the past. In the last few days, the father had twice tried to have incestuous relations with the girl and she was in a near hysterical condition. The mother – to judge by one of the stories – seemed to think that the sooner the girl was 'broken in' sexually, the better. The girl was induced to tell one of the officers how her father had tried to molest her, so the officers entered the house, arrested the three adults, and

75

had them carried away in the wagon. They had to collect the names of witnesses, and finally got an additional woman from a nearby street who knew the situation, and a young preacher who lived next door, to agree to testify. When one of the officers asked the woman who had made the call if the relations whom she visited could not be approached for this purpose, she said that they could not, as they were even sorrier than this family. To get witnesses in a street of this sort is not easy. The officers then had to collect the children, some of whom had run off in fear when the police came. The thirteen-year-old could not be found but the others were taken to the juvenile home. The elder of the two officers, who was accustomed to conditions in this district and who might be presumed to have become hardened to them, was much perturbed over the case. He would clearly have liked to punish the father himself. From the way he spoke, it was evident that he was indignant over the man's behaviour; indeed, it has generally been my impression that no matter how formal the policeman's behaviour in all except routine cases, he does feel a personal involvement in cases embodying important moral issues.

I also spent a Friday night in the district, riding with a supervisor. He took no calls himself, but whenever one of his patrol cars got a call that might be of a serious character, he went to see how it was handled. The supervisor dealt with two reports from pedestrians of a disturbance and a theft; he also had a drunk picked up by the wagon. The calls he covered included:

(i) A 'man down' call – a man had been 'phoning the hospital when he blacked out. He lived alone and it took a long time to contact a relative.

(ii) and (iii) Vehicular accidents.

(iv) A call that a man was beating his wife; on investigation it turned out that the woman was the more drunk and obstreperous of the two. Her husband told a fairly circumstantiated story of her entanglements with another man, who he now said had drugged her to try and get her to cash a cheque written in the husband's name. The patrol officer decided that the wife was the more worthy of arrest and had her taken away.

(v) A report of a man armed – this is an emergency call, but it was false in origin.

(vi) A 'drunk in auto' call answered by the supervisor; after a domestic brawl an intoxicated man had driven off but he could not be located.

(vii) A disturbance on a major street.

(viii) An assault on the same street, in which three Negro youths had attacked a white youth.

When patrol cars are getting frequent calls and have often to report their whereabouts over the radio, it is relatively easy for a supervisor to find out what his men are doing. One instance of supervisory methods occurred this same evening, when the supervisor I was riding with received a call to telephone headquarters. Over the telephone he was told that a civilian wished one of the patrolmen to telephone a particular number, saying that it was an emergency. The supervisor's permission had to be obtained before the message was passed on to the patrolman. In this case the supervisor had his suspicions. He believed that the patrolman was in difficulty: he had been told that he had separated from his wife but that she was still writing 'hot' cheques in his name. So he gave the message to the patrolman himself, stood by while he 'phoned, and inquired, tactfully, what the call had been about. As he suspected, it was not a proper emergency. He did not need to reprimand the patrolman. The knowledge that his supervisor knew that it had been unjustified was a sufficient warning.

These two samples of police activity are not, of course, representative of police work in Georgia City. There are large areas in the city inhabited by wealthy people with imposing houses and grounds. The police officer there has relatively little to do; indeed, one officer, telling a companion that he had once manned a patrol car in one of these patrol districts with a third officer, commented: 'We had a fine time with the women when we were over there.' These samples also underrate the amount of police attention that has to be given to traffic problems in Georgia City, when so many vehicles stream in and out daily. The police department now joins with the radio station and a private company in financing helicopter flights to report on the traffic flow. The helicopter is flown by an independent pilot, and a traffic sergeant accompanies him. One sergeant once caught an auto thief he saw from the air, by pursuing him until he ran into a school. The

77

helicopter landed in the playground and the sergeant went in and arrested the thief. Even speeding motorists are now apt to slow down if they notice a helicopter overhead.

FELSMERE CITY

Felsmere City, Massachusetts, is a small city (60,000 population) within the Boston metropolitan area. It has a police force of 120 men. The department is in the charge of the commissioner, who is a political appointee named by the city. The commissioner is a business-man who gives only part-time attention to the administration of the department. The day-to-day operations are the responsibility of the chief of police. Under him there are four captains, seven lieutenants, fifteen sergeants, and ninety-three patrolmen. One captain is in charge of records and administration, another of the juvenile bureau, and two are prosecuting officers at the courts.

Patrol shifts, each in the charge of a lieutenant, are: late shift (12 midnight to 7.45 a.m.); day shift (7.45 a.m. to 5 p.m.); and the early shift (5 p.m. to midnight). Eleven foot routes are patrolled in each shift. At night there will be five patrol cars on the street: one to each of four zones, and the sergeant's car. During the day there are two zone cars, the sergeant's car, a car used by the squad watching for liquor violations and vice, and another by plain-clothes investigators; a patrol wagon is also available. The lieutenant – at least during the daytime – spends much of his time in the station to deal with in-coming calls; at night he will go out to attend to important cases or to inspect his men. Patrolmen are allocated to shifts by seniority, the newcomers working the early or the late shift until there is a vacancy on days. When a day-shift man is promoted, he goes back to nights again.

In all the urban British police forces of which I have knowledge, men are allocated to a particular shift, and at intervals the whole personnel of a shift changes to a different shift, so that everyone works equal periods on the night, afternoon, and morning shifts. Under the system used in Felsmere City, while a man is young and active he works continually on the night shift; towards the end of his service he is entirely on days. This arrangement has its good points, for the older men are at less of a physical disadvantage on day work and are better at dealing with the people who come with personal troubles.[1] It does mean that a man may not wish to accept promotion and start again on the night shift; it makes the organization less flexible and introduces extra distinctions within the department, but it should be remembered that, unlike Scottish officers who (except for the most senior ranks) have to retire after thirty years' service, the Massachusetts officer has the same job tenure as other civil servants and may continue to the age of 65. Moreover, this system of allocating shifts according to seniority introduces a set principle and reduces certain injustices such as had occurred in the past when Felsmere City politicians had used their influence to have their friends put on the best shifts and the best beats, and to have anyone who angered them treated in the reverse fashion. The police departments of Carolina City and Georgia City adopt different procedures. There, a man is allocated to a particular shift (a recruit invariably starts on nights – apart from anything else there is less chance of a beginner embarrassing his department then because he is less in the public eye) and is moved to another duty as his supervisors think fit, though he may well be transferred if he asks for a change. A radically different method of arranging shifts, by allocating men to 'platoons' which change over every week, is gaining favour in some quarters, and may replace the current practice in some cities before long.

One of the most striking features of the Felsmere City police organization at present is its relative familiarity. This is in part due to the small size of the department compared with those previously discussed, but it is also in part a matter of policy. The present chief has reacted against the view of his predecessor who asserted that 'familiarity breeds contempt' and tried to enforce a more military discipline. Members of the department say that the previous chief obtained outward obedience but that people did not work any harder because of his attitude; indeed, they found ways of getting around the chief's demands. The present chief observed to me: 'At present we're like one big family – we'll have to see if it will work this way. If it won't, things will have to be changed.'

Some indication of the different character of police work in what, despite its being surrounded by the metropolitan area, remains a small city, may be gained from *Table 2*, which shows the incidence of

[1] The advantages of such a system are referred to at p. 253 of *Municipal Police Administration* (Institute for Training in Municipal Administration, 1961).

79

crime to be appreciably lower than in the cities previously examined. It should be borne in mind, however, that a comparison with the South may be misleading. The crime level in Felsmere City needs to be seen against the background of a relatively homogeneous population, together with the absence of poor white and lower-class Negro elements. For these and other reasons police patrol work resembles that in Britain, rather than in the Southern cities, in being oriented to a more benign supervision of the population. My impression is that the proportion of cases in which the policeman helps some citizen in distress, compared with the cases in which he takes action against a violator, is higher in Felsmere City than in Southern cities. Also, that when a patrol officer does see a violation he can more frequently assume that the violator is a citizen who tries to observe the laws, but through accident or negligence has failed to do so on this particular occasion. Something of this contrast may emerge from a sample of two periods of patrolling.

I spent from 9.15 a.m. to 5.30 p.m. one Monday in spring with a Felsmere City patrol car manned by two officers. The first call we had was from a woman who had telephoned to say that a pack of dogs from the street were running about in her neighbour's house. It transpired that the neighbour owned a bitch that was in heat, and she had gone out leaving a door ajar; about a dozen dogs had been running about inside. The next call was to a house where a woman had suffered some accident. She was a small woman of 61 years who had fallen downstairs; her arm was badly swollen and her shoulder acutely painful. The policemen – both men around 40 years – took charge of her in a friendly fashion, calling her by her first name. They drove her off to the hospital for examination, passing a message to her husband at his workplace about what had happened, and being careful not to let the cat out as they left.

The next task was to investigate a complaint from a woman that a flock of pigeons – for which a neighbour was responsible – were resting in the eaves of her newly painted house. They were a nuisance and their droppings were spoiling her paint. The officers located the house and the pigeons; they saw at the back an old barn that seemed previously to have had a pigeon-loft, and inquired for the owner. He turned out to be a man they knew. He explained that he had kept pigeons for many years but recently the Health Department had required him to 'cease and desist' from doing so; on their instructions he had boarded up the barn. Neither the Health Department nor the Society for the Prevention of Cruelty to Animals had been able to advise him what to do with the birds, which were now nesting on nearby houses. The officers concluded that the man had complied with the orders given him and was no longer liable for the birds.

After that we went for lunch. One officer took me into a restaurant; they contacted the other car and got the driver to give the second officer a lift to his own home; he rejoined us some twenty minutes later. We then went to report to the woman who had complained about the pigeons. She was a businesswoman who had opened a beauty parlour in her house and wanted it to appear smart. Understandably, she was most annoyed about the pigeons and rather reluctant to accept the officers' view that she had no remedy in law. An aggressive middle- or upper-class woman who knows how to press her viewpoint (and most businesswomen have to be mildly aggressive) is the sort of citizen the police officers least like dealing with, and such incidents require all their tact.

Shortly after this the patrol car had to perform its regular task of going to a particular spot on a main road to await the arrival of a school bus and see the children safely across. The chief of police has hitherto been able to resist proposals that women crossing-guards be engaged for this duty. He puts several of his older officers onto school duty, telling them to be friendly with the children, not just to see them over the street, but to get to know them; to find out how they get on at school and at home; to win their confidence. If children grow up to see policemen as friends and symbols of law observance, he believes, there will be less juvenile delinquency. The figures for offences by juveniles in Felsmere City, compared with those in neighbouring cities, tend to support this view and to substantiate his claim that, in the long run, it is cheaper to employ police officers for this task. Certainly, the children I saw always seemed greatly to enjoy greeting and joking with the officer.

Driving back from this duty the officers received a message to investigate a report that a telegraph pole was in a dangerous condition. A supporting stay had broken. This was reported so that the company responsible could send a repair crew. Then the officers went to the hospital, picked up the woman who had dislocated her shoulder – all was now well – and took her home.

Immediately afterwards, we were told that a woman had collapsed on a nearby pavement. She turned out to be intoxicated, and to be someone nearer 70 than 60 years of age. When the officers started to lift her into the car, she screamed wildly. Standing with her was a mentally deficient woman who was unable to give any account of herself, but seemed to belong with the other. She was taken into the car, too, then a few moments afterwards the first woman stopped screaming; the other was her daughter and it was she about whom she had been so anxious. Gradually the officers pieced together (from the daughter) an idea of where they lived; they were wondering whether it would be better to arrest the woman (in which case what would they do with the daughter?) or simply to take them home. Suddenly, the elder woman went cold. She was unconscious and seemed hardly to be breathing. That settled it. The driver switched on the siren and roof-light, and drove rapidly towards the hospital. Just before arriving, the woman recovered. The first problem was to have her examined by a doctor; but if he decided she had to be hospitalized, what were they going to do with the daughter? The hospital social worker could not help them. From 3.30 to 5.15 p.m. we waited for a doctor, and during that time the woman sobered up rapildy. By the time he came she was relatively sober, and he advised the officers that no treatment was necessary, so they drove the pair home. The officers discovered that the daughter was on ten days' leave from a mental hospital and had overstayed her leave by one day. They concluded that her presence had depressed the mother who had started drinking heavily, and after going out into the fresh air she had collapsed. They also remembered who she was; one of the officers had lived as a youngster in the same neighbourhood and she joked about what he had been like as a boy. This incident and some others brought out the remarkable personal knowledge both officers had of the residents of the city; this knowledge of the people they were dealing with seemed often to enable them to treat violators more leniently than would have been likely in Carolina or Georgia Cities.

It may be noted that on this particular day the officers could have gone off duty at 4 p.m., handing the case over to someone else, but they preferred to see it through. They got no overtime pay for this, but would probably be able to claim equivalent time off on some other occasion.

At one time the officers noticed some labourers digging up part of the road in order to make a connection with some pipe. They stopped and inquired why there was no police officer on duty and warned the foreman about this. In this locality any contractors who have to take up the road surface and in this way disrupt traffic are required by law to have a proper guard – who should be a policeman – standing by. The contractor notifies the police department, which in turn invites an off-duty man to perform this service; he is paid by the contractor. There is usually no difficulty in getting police officers for this job.

A little while later, I accompanied the early shift (5 p.m. to midnight) one Thursday evening, on foot patrol in one of the poorer parts of the city. The locality was described to me as a place 'where all hell can break loose' – referring, however, to violent matrimonial disputes and shootings rather than to mob action. The beat officer reports to the station and either walks out to his beat or, more usually, is driven out in a patrol car. There is no formal take-over from the previous patrolman on the beat. The beat officer has to 'ring in' to head-quarters every hour from automatic boxes mounted on standards at the kerbside. When he turns a key, this is recorded automatically, together with the time, at headquarters. If the beat officer is wanted, the dispatcher at headquarters will telephone to him at the box the moment he rings in. On this particular beat the officer is required to remain in the vicinity of the 'square' (a road intersection) until 8.30 p.m., because there is often trouble thereabouts.

On this evening the officer had received a complaint that some youths were congregating and creating a disturbance in a particular street. Shortly after arriving there he saw a group outside a drug store at the bottom of the street and warned them about the complaint. He patrolled several of the streets in the vicinity, twice calling at the address of the complainant for further details, but no one was at home on either occasion. Once more he cleared youngsters from the corner. As I recollect, the first time he addressed them in some such terms as: 'Now look, I don't want you gathering around here and disturbing the residents, so you'd better break it up.' On the second occasion: 'I told you to get away from here. If you don't go, I shall have to make you. Now, get . . .!' Then, when he saw a group sitting

G

outside a house: 'There's been a complaint about young people congregating around here and disturbing residents. I don't know if it's you who are responsible, but I think you'd better break it up and go home. All right?' Such remarks would certainly not be unrepresentative of the ordinary officer's approach to young people in this region. The Scottish officer on the other hand, would usually be more impersonal, less likely to talk about *his* wishes or to threaten what *he* individually might do. Where the Scottish officer can rely on his uniform to induce compliance on the part of many people, the American officer has to show a more active disposition. It is not easy to provide satisfactory evidence of any such difference between the two countries, but my observations of these relatively insignificant modes of speech and conduct make me feel that there is a difference of this kind.

Later in the evening, the officer saw a motorist driving the wrong way out of a one-way street, and stopped him. The driver had no licence or registration document with him. The officer pointed out that he could be arrested for not having them, and took a note of his name and address, resting his notebook on the car roof as he wrote them down. He allowed the motorist to go to his home – which was nearby – to fetch his papers, which he did in a few moments. After checking them, the officer asked where the man had been born and found that he had lived in a part of Felsmere where he himself had lived as a child. They exchanged reminiscences about a few people and places before the man drove off. The officer made three patrols away from the square and back again, checking property by trying the door handles of warehouses, shining his lamp over the windows, etc. On one occasion the lieutenant in charge of the shift passed, driving a car; he was wearing civilian clothes. At another time we went into a café for a cup of coffee. I left the beat officer a little before twelve, and shortly afterwards the patrol car came to collect him and drive him into the station. On the way back to headquarters, the officers in the car saw two boys behaving suspiciously in the vicinity of a gasoline station. The beat man pursued one of them, caught him, and got the name of his associate. Both of them were before the juvenile court at the end of the week, when they explained that they had taken the money because they wanted to run away from home. Being 14 and 15 years of age, they were sent to a special school for a certain time and put on probation for a longer period.

It should perhaps be added that the officer I accompanied on this shift was a Negro. I noticed nothing different in people's behaviour towards him except that he seemed to know quite a few Negroes who lived thereabouts and exchanged greetings with them as well as with a number of Whites. He himself did not consider that he had any extra difficulties as a policeman because he was a Negro, but he did resent delays on the part of the Civil Service Board over his appointment; although several Negroes had been appointed before him he sensed a wish to keep Negroes out.

On my first visit to the Felsmere police, I was struck by what appeared to the European as the loose discipline, and by the way the freedom permitted to the patrolman could so easily be abused. The chief of police told me that if a sergeant put a patrolman on a disciplinary charge for going into a restaurant to drink a cup of coffee, he would not accept the charge unless he was convinced that the man had been overdoing it. He was concerned that the men should take a responsible attitude to their work and not work simply out of fear of their supervisor. When I commented that on the early shift mentioned above I had seen no supervisor other than the lieutenant driving past in a car, the chief said that it was not surprising because the patrolman was a conscientious officer who required little supervision. But, he added, if a 'break in' was reported one morning and the man on night patrol had not seen and reported it, he would almost certainly be punished or reprimanded.

IN CONCLUSION

These three short studies have been intended to give a picture both of certain general features of police work in industrial countries and of particular features characterizing United States forces and in some ways differentiating them from those in Britain. It should be stressed that these studies draw on only a portion of the data collected about each of these departments. The account given here emphasizes some of the more demanding and puzzling tasks, but underrates the routine, the waiting, the boredom, the paper work: these things apart, it is, I hope, a fair picture. In the next chapter I shall offer some general comparisons between British and American practice, and try to explain the differences that are found.

CHAPTER 4

Aspects of Police Organization in Britain and the United States

In the first chapter it was argued that law enforcement was not an outside ideal that had to be 'sold' to people but that it was one aspect of social control. Communities cannot survive unless they can resolve internal disputes and discipline members who act antisocially. The law is only one agent of social control and its functions may be misunderstood if it is not related to other agents like morality, conventions, economic interest, neighbourly repute, etc. It was further maintained that the level of social control is related to the integration of the society. A small and homogeneous society is likely to be highly integrated: the incidence of crime and delinquency generally will be low, but the society will probably be conservative and resistant to most kinds of change.

By comparison with Great Britain, the United States is a country of low social integration. Millions of immigrants of different national background, language, religion, and race have combined to make a new nation, but, starting from such different points, they have not always found it easy to establish common understandings. This much is well known, and it will be readily appreciated that in such circumstances high crime rates are only to be expected. A second point of major importance is that Americans have had the opportunity to develop a virgin continent. To press ahead with economic growth has meant that great rewards had to be offered for commercial or industrial success. Both material resources and people have had to be mobile, capable of movement to wherever the economy needed them. Such mobility lowers the level of integration further.

An indication of the volume of such movements can be seen in the fact that Los Angeles, with a population of nearly seven million, is said currently to be growing by 1,000 persons per day and is expected to reach twenty million by the end of the century. Geographical mobility is important but, from the point of view of integration, social mobility up and down the status scale may be equally disruptive of accepted values, though it is more difficult to obtain statistical evidence of this aspect. In a rapidly developing country the businessmen are rewarded with high status as well as high salaries: they are the producers, the men who are taking the country forward. They draw upon the work of people in service industries – policemen, civil servants, teachers – but because these latter have no material product to point to, they suffer by comparison. This 'production ideology' tends, in the United States, to hold down the level of monetary reward in the service occupations.

It was also held in the first chapter that the policeman has to be seen as one of society's agents for social control. He does not serve an abstract ideal of justice. He can but put into effect his society's own norms of rightful or wrongful conduct. It would be foolish to expect policemen living and working in a corrupt society to be above temptation. Some sectors of American life are undoubtedly corrupt, and this needs to be taken into account when considering police practice. For example, on-the-job stealing by employees from their employers is said to cost American industry over a billion dollars a year, and the estimates of stock 'shrinkage' by theft in department stores are even higher. Then, in many of the cities which received the European immigrant groups, organized crime was the principal avenue open to them for obtaining political influence and ultimately social acceptance. The men of Italian descent who featured in Senator Kefauver's investigations had taken over the roles that twenty years previously had been played by children of East European Jews and before that by the Irish. Occupations that the wider society labelled 'criminal' could appear quite respectable to members of a recently settled minority. Steady and prestigeful jobs were scarce, and one of the objects of a politician's struggles was to obtain for his people a share of the work created by state and local government contracts. In some cities, different minorities have competed for employment as policemen, and the job has been seen as 'belonging' to a minority. This view of police work as a desirable job available to people with the right political and ethnic connections has naturally tended to tone down other possible interpretations of the role; for example, there is less motivation to idealism, but, contrariwise, probably less likelihood of its attracting sadists.

The involvement of police administration in local politics has been the subject of unfavourable comment by the chief of the Los Angeles Police who states:

'To be perfectly blunt about it, I think the political climate in the United States is not conducive to efficient, impartial, professional law enforcement. The police administrator finds it extremely difficult to hew to the line of professionalism and idealism and at the same time keep a group of political office-holders reasonably satisfied and happy . . . the very method of selecting and electing political candidates helps to create a climate in which it is difficult to administer the police service objectively and professionally. Political candidates must build up support in a campaign. They must have campaign contributions. And when they are elected they are followed by an army of people who have helped them and to whom they owe something' (Center for the Study of Democratic Institutions, 1962, pp. 4–5).

Another feature of the place of crime in American society which affects police work is that the stakes are high. A great deal of money can be won or lost on particular operations, so that the temptation to use violence is much greater. Certain kinds of violence were already legitimized by the tradition that the American hero is a frontiersman, cowboy, hunter, or soldier, with his gun ready to hand. The greater tolerance of violence and the gains to be won by it have meant that the policeman in the United States is much more exposed to the risk of violence than his British counterpart, and it would be strange if this did not affect his conception of his occupational role and the way in which he performed it.

LOCAL GOVERNMENT AND THE POLICE SERVICES

Both in Britain and the United States the organization of police services has been a responsibility of local government. In Britain, administrative efficiency has required a steady reduction in the number of police forces; they have been amalgamated into better administrative units. It may be doubted, for example, whether any police force of less than 500 men can provide adequate resources for training, promotion, etc., or maintain sufficient social distance between officers of different rank to ensure that private associations will not affect work efficiency. The British Royal Commission discussed this question in some detail and concluded similarly that the optimum size for a force was 'probably 500 or upwards'. In Britain there were at the end of 1962 158 police forces for a population of 53 million. Thirteen of them (twelve in Scotland) had establishments of less than 100; forty-nine had establishments between 100 and 199; thirty-five had establishments between 200 and 349; seventeen numbered between 350 and 499; twenty-nine, between 500 and 999; and fifteen, over 1,000. In the United States, by contrast, there are over 40,000 police departments for 175 million people; a very considerable proportion are departments of a few dozen men or less, and there is no significant movement at present for amalgamation of these smaller units.

In Britain the central government can exert a certain control over local forces through Her Majesty's Inspectors of Constabulary. These officers inspect forces regularly and report whether they are efficient. If they are considered efficient, the government pays half the cost of their maintenance. So if, say, a parsimonious local council is unwilling to buy the new police equipment that the Inspector of Constabulary considers necessary, he can threaten that next time the force will not receive a certificate of efficiency. There is no equivalent to this form of control in the United States, where the provision of police services is a responsibility of local government bodies over which – in this respect – state and federal institutions have little authority. The principal American institutions which make for uniformity in practice and for the raising of standards are the Federal Bureau of Investigation Academy, the International Association of Chiefs of Police, and the Police Institutes sponsored by several universities.[1]

[1] Lt.-Col David A. McCandless of the Southern Police Institute, Kentucky, comments: 'I suspect that the most important new developments in police training in this country are the mandatory municipal training acts. Since July 1960, for example, no police officer in the entire State of New York can assume his duties until he has received certification of successful passing of minimum basic training. The State of California's act is not mandatory but has provisions which are so attractive that most municipalities are taking advantage of the training offered. Several other states are following the lead of New York and California.'

The small size of many American forces means that they cannot offer any very attractive prospect of promotion to the ambitious recruit. In Scotland the recruit knows that he can in theory go up to the post of chief constable of Glasgow, and as commander of a force of over 2,800 men he would have a salary comparable to that of a cabinet minister. To be appointed a chief constable in Scotland a man must have served as an ordinary constable. In the United States, however, the best jobs in police administration are mostly political appointments, and the salary differentials between patrolmen and supervisory ranks are relatively small. Similarly, salary increases for length of service are smaller than in Britain. Only in recent years in the United States have local government bodies come to appreciate the advantages of having at the head of their police departments a professional administrator, who can run the department so as to achieve the ends of law enforcement without drawing too heavily upon the treasury.

British police officers at times complain about the difficulty of transferring from one force to another, but this can be done and is done. In the United States the difficulties are far greater, because the ideal of law enforcement is less separate from the other ends of the political machinery. In Britain, a local council selects its own police chief but the person selected cannot take up office unless his appointment is approved by the central government. In recent years the government has made it clear that it will not approve the appointment of chief constables who have not had experience of police work in other forces; this policy stops in-breeding and prevents a force getting too set in its ways. Again, there can be no American equivalent.

The selection of men for promotion to higher ranks poses a problem for police departments that is greater than for most comparable organizations because ability as a policeman cannot easily be gauged by written tests or other objective procedures. The policy laid down in Felsmere City, in accordance with civil service regulations, is that candidates take a written examination and that one of the top three is then chosen for promotion. This practice is defended as reducing the possibilities of political interference, but it is generally conceded that many excellent police officers cannot write a satisfactory examination paper and have no chance whatever of achieving promotion. The British system, whereby a chief constable chooses the appointee from among all those who have passed a qualifying examination, allows greater scope to subjective assessments of ability.

Police standards generally seem to be higher in Britain than in the United States. Physical standards vary from department to department in the United States, but there are more old patrolmen (because of the different retirement policy), more officers who have to wear spectacles, and more men who are over-weight or in poor physical condition. It is not easy to compare educational standards because of differences in the school systems, but my impression was that they were definitely higher in Scotland in respect of both knowledge of the law and command of the English language. More attention is given to training in Britain. For example, in the Scottish city a recruit is sent to the Scottish Police College which trains all probationary police constables and policewomen for the whole of the country. The recruit undergoes four weeks' intensive training there. He returns to his force for three weeks' local instruction, and is then allocated to a division where he is put on patrol with a more experienced officer. In the larger forces he will attend training classes every week and will receive on-the-spot instruction from his sergeant. After a while he may be allowed to patrol alone. After nine months with his force he returns to the Scottish Police College for a more thorough course lasting twelve weeks. At the end of a further period – some twenty-three months after joining – he takes a written examination with his own force. If he passes this and the reports from his supervisors are satisfactory, his two-year period of probation is finished and he is confirmed in the rank of constable. Should the reports received from the college after either of the courses, or the reports from his supervisors, be unfavourable, his chief constable may at any time during the two years declare that the probationer 'is unlikely to become a suitable police officer', and discharge him without appeal. This practice may seem harsh and open to abuse, but the American practice usually loads the dice on the other side. Training in the United States is conducted by local forces with some outside assistance. In the larger departments it usually stretches to about three months, supplemented by roll-call training and refresher courses later. Probation usually lasts for six or twelve months. Unsuitable recruits may not always be detected in this period and it may be difficult to force their resignation later.

The British police officer may not join a trade union, but he is represented by the Police Federation which is able to serve many of the functions of a union. The officers of each rank below superintendent elect one or more of their fellows to the local branch of the Federation, and branches are supplemented by national boards and organizations. Federation branches can raise with the chief constable a wide range of matters, including anything that can be shown to affect morale. The American policeman is much more vulnerable. Police benefit organizations have at times attempted to represent the views of the rank and file, but the leaders have been victimized. In some places Police Wives' Associations have been formed as 'front' organizations instead. In some departments there may be less tension between 'the men' and 'the bosses', and the civil service negotiating machinery may be adequate, but the American officer does suffer from the lack of a national representative body by comparison with his British colleague.

It is hazardous to generalize freely about American police practices because different departments vary so much. Dr James Q. Wilson of Harvard University has suggested that it may be easier to examine these variations by considering them in the light of two opposed principles (Wilson, 1963).[1] He refers on the one hand to departments run according to 'the system', in which the police department is subject to close political control; it reveals what in the eyes of the world is considered corruption, but administers rough and familiar justice understood by the community. On the other hand there is the 'professional' department, which is impersonal, free from corruption, and stresses technical competence, but is able to establish itself only under somewhat different political and social conditions. Wilson does not suggest that either type exists in a pure form, but that every department partakes in varying degree of the two principles; nor does he consider that either type can be judged as being necessarily better than the other.

The authoritative handbook *Municipal Police Administration* states:

> 'Control of the police force is a tremendous asset to a spoils-minded political machine, for the services which such police can render to the machine are legion. Fixing traffic citations has won many a vote and helped many a local campaign fund. Prosecution

[1] Dr Wilson is pessimistic about the chances of improving police standards in the big city forces; his assessment of the problems is essential reading for the student of contemporary American police work.

of minor and serious crimes can sometimes be arranged to suit the convenience of the person charged. By arrangement, an officer may fail to appear against a defendant or may prove a poor witness. Evidence may disappear or an investigation be incompetently performed. These are only a few of the possibilities which politicians have exploited in corrupt police departments.

When the police department is controlled by the machine, political influence begins with the appointment of the recruit, rallies to save him from discipline or discharge, helps him to secure unearned wages or disability benefits, grants him unusual leaves of absence, secures an unwarranted promotion for him, or gives him a soft job. . . . Politics in the force will gradually undermine the character of rank and file policemen. Most of them have families dependent on them for their daily bread' (Institute for Training in Municipal Administration, 1961, p. 10).[1]

Stories about police practice in departments corrupted by political influence can easily be assembled and there is little point in illustrating an obvious point over and over again, but to give British readers an impression of how what Dr Wilson calls 'the system' can work, reference may be made to a Massachusetts force that showed many of its traits. It should be added that, at the time of my visit, Massachusetts had the popular reputation of having one of the most corrupt systems of local government in the United States. A man who had at one time been a member of the department in question spoke of finding a house on his beat where liquor was being illegally manufactured in the cellar, prostitution was practised on the first floor, and abortions were carried out on the second. When he reported this to his lieutenant he was instructed not to go there again. The same man spoke of the disconcerting effect of having someone come up to him when he was on patrol and give him an envelope containing $100 without his knowing why. At one stage he took a promotion examination and was placed twentieth. A month or two later he went to headquarters to find out how many promotions had been made and how near he now was to the top of the list. He found that his name had dropped to forty-sixth, and when he inquired why, was told that it was none of his business. Then the sergeant spoke to him: 'You live

---

[1] Quoted by kind permission of the Institute.

in such-and-such a street don't you? Have you got a mortgage on your house? Well, if you want to be a sergeant, I'd advise you to take one out. It will cost you six thousand dollars.' Such stories may be true, and yet misleading unless kept in context. Police departments run according to 'the system' still catch criminals, display bravery, and show kindliness; this form of administration has developed chiefly in areas of immigrant settlement, and in the circumstances some degree of corruption was to be expected.

The Felsmere City police department had been subject to considerable political interference in the past and was moving towards more professional standards. Carolina City and Georgia City were further along on this path; officers there commented on occasions in former times when policemen on holiday from the North had introduced themselves and started a conversation on the sidewalk. They had been taken aback by such remarks as: 'This looks like a good beat, how much do you have to give the captain for it?' With different patterns of government many cities in the South and the West have avoided such influences. Many of the State police forces again are very different. The men wear big hats like the Canadian mounties and concentrate upon highway patrol. Many of them are quartered in police posts during their turn of duty, and can sleep at home only three nights a week. Qualifications for entry and standards of conduct are high. Some municipal departments are also much more demanding in these respects. In California, for example, the Berkeley department has for many years required two years of college study for acceptance as a recruit. In some departments a high proportion of men have taken university degrees; thus, in Georgia City, thirty-six members of the police department hold a bachelor's degree in law, and twelve a master's degree. The best American departments have a record in this respect unmatched by any British police force.

Sociological study can indicate how differences in police practice are related to the local context in which the police department has to operate. To show the interrelations sometimes appears as a way of excusing what goes on, whereas social science research seeks rather to assemble evidence so that administrators and politicians can make the policy decisions. In this case, lest it be thought that police corruption should never be left without condemnation, it may be well to quote the view of an American police chief, sometime President of the International Association of Chiefs of Police. Writing in the *Municipal Police Administration* handbook, Stanley R. Schrotel states:

'In the preservation of the constitutional guarantees of civil liberty, the police service has most certainly failed. False imprisonment, illegal search, "the third degree", special privilege, and denial of the due process of law are not the exception but are commonplace in many police organizations. Although these malpractices are rarely openly defended, they are condoned by far too many police administrators, and it is often these same administrators who clamour for elevation of standards of public service. When public indignation is aroused by reason of violations of civil liberties by policemen, the responsible administrators usually are quick to place the blame upon political interference, inadequate wages, weaknesses of the law, or lack of public support, instead of accepting the fact that they have failed to discharge their basic responsibility to the public' (op. cit. p. 463).

It is extremely difficult to compare police pay in the two countries because of differences in purchasing power and the problem of establishing any common denominator. Pay scales in the United States vary considerably, being much higher in the Northern and South-western cities than in the South.[1] However, it may be noted that in the United States departments visited, patrolmen stated that their pay was a little better than that of elementary-school teachers. The same held true at this time in Britain. Whereas in Britain pay scales are fixed nationally, in the United States they are decided by local councils, and this fact makes policemen more dependent on both local politicians and the electorate. In Massachusetts shortly before I arrived a referendum had been held in the eastern part of this state on a motion to increase police salaries. The police canvassed their own localities in uniform, explaining to citizens their case for higher pay. I had the impression, however, that while policemen in both

[1] Top patrolman's pay in Los Angeles and San Francisco approaches $7,700 per annum; in New York $7,630; whereas in Atlanta and Montgomery, the capital cities of Georgia and Alabama, top patrolman's pay is $4,936 and $4,140 respectively. The cost of living varies considerably, even if not to the same extent. These are 1962 figures taken from Samuel G. Chapman (Ed.), *The Police Heritage in England and America* (1963), a booklet which contains a useful brief comparison of police services in the two countries.

countries want more pay for its material value, in the United States higher pay seems to have greater symbolic value than in Britain. Many American officers seemed to think that their occupations would be more esteemed if pay scales were higher. British officers are less anxious about prestige: they appreciate that members of other occupations, e.g. ministers of religion, are highly esteemed without being well-paid. However, part of American officers' concern with pay as an index of public respect may be attributable to the relative ease with which they can earn additional income by taking on extra jobs in their leisure time. The American officer who is willing to undertake extra work usually need not feel that he is at the limit of his budget.

There is a major difference between British and American practice in respect of additional employment, which will be considered from another aspect in Chapters 7 and 8 below. In Britain, managers of football clubs, greyhound tracks, dance halls, etc., may arrange with the police for uniformed officers to supervise crowds, and will pay for this service. The policemen receive extra money but the arrangement is made through the chief constable and there is no direct relation between the employer and the policeman. Police officers may not take on any 'office for hire or gain' without the permission of their chief constable, and the interpretation placed upon this clause has usually been restrictive.[1] Though this restriction can be evaded to some extent by the constable, it does minimize police participation in any other kind of paid employment. In the United States, however, policemen are permitted to engage in a variety of extra work. In Carolina City a police officer may undertake off-duty employment in 'activities pertaining to law enforcement, such as: traffic control, crime prevention, and security duty . . . activities not allowed and not consistent with Departmental policy are such duties that would normally be performed by civilian personnel as: initiating checks, collecting worthless checks, checking customers out at cash registers, delivering merchandize to cars. . . .' Such employment has to be within city limits, and the officer in question has to notify the clerk how long he is working on each particular day and how he may be contacted. Men on security or traffic duty may wear police uniform. This policy enables the hardworking policeman to have a better built and furnished house than he could ever have on his police pay, and

[1] Cf. pp. 191 and 193–4 below.

to live on an appreciably higher standard than his British colleague. It is consistent with the local employment pattern by which, for example, a schoolteacher may work as an ambulance driver for the three-month summer school recess, or in the evenings. By making policemen available for duties connected with private establishments it reduces the pressure that might otherwise be put on the department to have some of these duties performed officially. In Georgia City a similar policy is followed. An officer wishing to take on an outside job submits a request that has to be countersigned by his superiors before reaching the chief; he has to specify the location, hours, and character of the work, and whether he will be wearing uniform. While performing such duty he has to carry a special authorization. Outside employment is limited to eighteen hours per week as a maximum. Stores which want extra detectives at Christmas time, sports promoters who want extra policemen, businesses which want officials to control traffic at their parking lot when a large number of drivers start for home, these and other people may approach police headquarters with requests for men. They can usually be found, as most of the men seem keen to earn an extra dollar, and they are paid by the outside employer directly. In Felsmere City very many officers have additional employment and it does not seem to pose any serious administrative problems.

The idea that an employer can hire a policeman seems strange to the Briton accustomed to thinking of the policeman as an officer of the Crown, and the same difference comes out in other respects. It is not uncommon in some parts of the United States to see a notice prohibiting the entry of unauthorized persons into an establishment, which concludes 'Police take notice'. This sounds, to the Briton, like giving orders to the police and strikes a jarring note. Another parallel feature is the large number of private police forces maintained by universities, industrial plants, etc.; these men are dressed like local police officers and are easily identified with them. A man accustomed to having police officers working at a low level of pay in his own institution – i.e. as his inferiors – is less likely to see a police officer who stops him in the street as exercising an impersonal authority.

Many of the comparisons between British and United States police standards appear to be much more favourable to the British, but it should be appreciated, first, that the British forces have, since the middle of the last century, had a more tractable population to deal with, and second, that they have been able to operate in a political context far more conducive to impartial police work. If these factors are considered it is difficult to maintain that the police forces of either country are more worthy of respect than those of the other. It could also be argued on the other side that top American police administrators have shown themselves more flexible than their British opposites in their readiness to modify established practices to bring them into line with current conditions and to introduce modern techniques.

An indication of the point from which police reform in the United States had to start is given in the reference of an American police author to:

'. . . the widely held beliefs that policemen are uneducated and of low mentality; that they are selected for physical strength and courage alone; that they are of doubtful honesty and integrity; that they are engaged in a continuous offensive against society; that they are often rude and domineering; that they get angry easily; that they resort to the illegal "third degree"; and that the only way to be safe from this tyranny is to have either wealth or "pull". . . .

Not all of these indictments can be fairly charged to any one police department; but, unfortunately, at various times and places each has been successfully proved' (Gourley, 1954, p. 136).

Many officers with whom I spoke referred bitterly to the old conception of the police officer as the meanest man in town. They recognized that it had not been without justification. The older men in the Georgia City department remembered officers who could barely sign their names and who were quite unsuited to the job, but who had been appointed by political influence. They could recollect occasions when men paraded for duty so drunk that they had to be held up at roll call. A policeman was expected to be a good-for-nothing, and was considered a real oddity if he attended church. The better officers had suffered for the worse, but in the last twenty years there had been a tremendous improvement. The calibre of the men was higher and they were acceptable socially; many policemen held office in church organizations and other bodies. Yet the old ideas could not easily be uprooted and it was still not unusual for someone to ask a police officer's children: 'Does your father work – or is he a policeman?'

Aspects of Police Organization in Britain and the U.S.A.

Municipal and state governments in the United States are coming increasingly to appreciate that to run a large police department (Chicago has 12,000 personnel; New York, 26,000) requires considerable administrative skill. Even in much smaller departments the chief has to be an administrator, not a policeman, and the realization of this is reflected in training programmes at police institutes, which are emphasizing the administrative and human relations side more strongly. What happens when this course is not followed is shown in the case of a New England town that suffered from a series of safe blowings at night. After a while the police chief got so worried that he put on uniform and started patrolling at night himself. He was reacting like a policeman, not like an administrator. In Carolina City and Georgia City a great deal of attention has been given to working out a form of organization in which no supervisor has more than eight men reporting to him and yet there is only a minimum of organizational steps between the patrolman and the chief; job responsibilities are made explicit so that there can be no overlapping; a check is kept on every man's activities to make sure that available manpower is distributed as economically as possible; civilian assistants are employed whereever possible; and mechanical equipment (like tape recorders) and standardized reporting forms are used wherever the police officer's time can be saved thereby. There is also an effort to teach principles of leadership and human relations by means of new techniques, and this, though not always necessarily successful, is an advance on the old view that leaders are born, not made, and that these topics cannot be taught.

Another feature of the American police departments visited which could not but impress the newcomer was the total absence of self-satisfaction or complacency. Officers from the chief downwards displayed a sense of pride in what had been achieved, together with a recognition that there was room for improvement. They asked for criticisms of what they were doing. At conferences they obtain speakers from organizations that they might be expected to dismiss as impractical, but they give them a tolerant hearing. Very many officers take the view that civilians may be able to tell them something about their job, and they listen to see if they can benefit from their contributions. In this respect the occupation does not seem like a closed guild in the way that the European visitor, noting the low prestige of the American police, might expect.

SUPPORT FOR THE LAWS

One of the most important features of British society, and one which causes the sociologist to regard it as more integrated than American society, is the general acceptance of the laws as being just and moral. The Royal Commission observed:

> 'No law can be considered satisfactory unless it commands wide popular support and its purpose is understood and accepted. We do not think that the present provisions of the law with regard to the parking of motor vehicles satisfy either test' (*Royal Commission on the Police 1962, Final Report*, p. 115).

That the parking laws require special mention in this connection serves to underscore the assent that is accorded the others. Many laws in America differ from one state to another, and there appear to be more instances than in Britain of people who do not regard particular laws as morally binding.

Many police officers in the United States believe that they are less protected and supported by the courts than is the case in Britain. An American police chief who had visited London commented to me that when he was there he saw a newspaper report that a man had hit a police officer while being arrested. The man was fined $25 for the offence for which he was arrested, and sentenced to a year's penal servitude for assaulting the officer. One of the patrolmen in Massachusetts said that he had talked with a constable on duty in the Liverpool docks and asked him if he had any trouble with roughnecks. The constable said yes, there had been one man, but he was now serving a seven-year sentence for assaulting an officer.[1] The patrolmen compared this unfavourably with a case in their locality, in which a man who punched a police lieutenant in the face was only fined $40. In Massachusetts, they alleged, a man got a milder fine for assaulting a police officer than for assaulting a civilian. They complained of the way some people disregarded police requests: one

[1] It is not easy to establish what are normal penalties for specific offences in either Britain or the United States, but as I write I see a report in the *Police Review* of 12 October 1962 that in a magistrates' court a youth had been fined £5 for assaulting an officer and £2 for using obscene language. The defendant appealed to Middlesex sessions, but the chairman there dismissed the appeal: 'Describing it as "impertinent", and, after commenting on the unsuitability of a fine as a penalty for assaults on the police, he substituted a sentence of three months at a detention centre.'

100

said he had gone up to a woman who had just 'double-banked' her car and asked her to park it elsewhere; she simply replied 'nothing doing' and walked off. (It is not easy to understand why a police officer should tolerate such behaviour, but this one apparently felt that had he taken official action it would have been difficult to get the support of the courts in view of the triviality of the incident.) In another Massachusetts force, patrolmen cited cases when the courts had – in their view – failed to support police officers. One said that when he was testifying in a case against a juvenile the lad shouted at him: 'My mother's an attorney – she'll get you for that!' The youth was not reprimanded by the court. The officers seemed to think that even if this eventuality was improbable, it was not impossible.

In Carolina City I was told that two and a half years previously a police officer had been shot by a Negro burglar who was convicted of murder and sentenced to death. The convicted man was still in prison awaiting the result of one of several appeals. The law's delays – which, as the infamous case of Caryl Chessman demonstrates, may be unusually drawn out in the United States – can be very discouraging to the police officer who is apt to see the work he does on behalf of society being countered by legal manoeuvring and by institutional inefficiency.

American officers complain about a series of recent Supreme Court decisions which make the task of the investigating officer more difficult.[1] They say that the stress in recent years on civil rights has been unaccompanied by any corresponding emphasis on civil responsibilities. In some respects American courts seem to be more severe than British ones. In the state in which Carolina City is located, for example, 'first degree burglary' is a capital offence for which men have been sent to the electric chair: a man who breaks into property at night where someone may be expected to be sleeping can be charged with this crime. Three young men who had broken into some unoccupied weekend cottages not far away and had been prosecuted for first degree burglary shortly before my visit had been given thirty-year gaol sentences. Offenders may be eligible for parole after serving a quarter of their sentence, but not all are paroled, and sentences for such offences seem generally to be heavier than in Britain. The

---

[1] Particularly the Mapp decision on 'search and seizure'. For a brief statement of one point of view, see Fred E. Inbau (1962), 'Public Safety *v.* Individual Civil Liberties: the Prosecutors' Stand'.

American criminal may have more justification if he feels that he might as well be hung for a sheep as a lamb.

Patrolmen in one of the Southern departments visited thought that certain laws were almost unenforceable because of the reluctance of the courts to convict. If a motorist was prosecuted for reckless driving but there had been no accident, for example, it was difficult to make the charge stick. If a motorist was convicted of drunken driving in the lower court, he would probably hire a lawyer and appeal the case to a jury in a higher court. Juries were extremely reluctant to find a man guilty of an offence which would cause him to lose his driving licence. It was also difficult nowadays to have men convicted on charges of loitering or vagrancy. One officer, saying how a light sentence often makes a policeman feel discouraged, recalled a case when he arrested a troublesome Negro who was pestering a waitress at the bus station. Although the man had a short while previously been convicted of this offence and sentenced to thirty days' imprisonment, he was given the same sentence again. The police officer felt very much inclined to resign in protest after this, because he thought that the man was potentially dangerous and that such treatment would give him the idea that he could get away with his bullying; next time he might kill a policeman.

In considering the problems of the American police officer· as compared with the British, it should be borne in mind that they cannot simply be listed and the responsibility for each one be placed upon some institution. The United States as a rapidly developing country with a heterogeneous population cannot help but make the role of the police officer (and the roles of many other officials too) more difficult than would be the case in a region of greater social stability. In the Scottish city during 1961 convictions were obtained for such offences, for example, as recklessly driving a pedal cycle, riding two on a pedal cycle, keeping a dog without a collar, allowing a horse to stray on a public road, leaving the engine running in an unattended car, etc.[1] The idea of charging people with such offences seemed only to cause amusement to American officers to whom I mentioned them: none

[1] Compare Durkheim's thesis that every society has to stigmatize some form of conduct to express its integrity and that even a society of saints would have its deviations – though they might be such as other societies would consider trivial (Durkheim, 1938, pp. 68–9).

of them attempted to enforce laws regulating pedal-cycle traffic (in fact there appeared to be none), smoking under age, etc. Only in a stable society can the minutiae of convention become invested with such moral quality that people feel they ought to be legally enforced. Something of the same difference is to be observed when Felsmere City is compared with the two cities in the South. The high crime rate in the Southern cities and the lower ratio of policemen to population mean that police officers have less time to worry about minor offences, but I doubt if that is the whole answer. A Felsmere City officer of considerable experience, and obviously able to deal with the roughest characters, shook his head over some of the 'bad boys' and 'bad girls' he had come into contact with through the school patrol. He was disturbed about them because he saw them as members of the same community as himself and he probably had children of much the same age. In the Southern cities differences of race and class seemed to divide officers from offenders much more sharply; maybe this was because the Southern cities were both growing rapidly as a result of industrial development whereas Felsmere City has had a relatively stable population for a fairly long time. Another incident which gave me the same feeling was when I spoke to a Felsmere City officer just after attending a juvenile court. At the court, the police had prosecuted three teenage girls for assaulting a fourth in an affair over a boy. The judge had thought it all a very silly affair and had simply 'continued' the case for twelve months so that, provided the defendants were of good behaviour, they would probably be discharged at the end of this period. The police officer was furious. He said that one of the youths had perjured himself and that the fourth girl had been so badly handled that she was afraid to attend school. The whole school had been waiting to see what would be happening and now they would think they could get away with all sorts of things. Juvenile delinquency by girls was a relatively new and disturbing phenomenon and now it would almost certainly increase. These were the sort of sentiments one might hear in Scotland, but I caught no echo of them in the South in police forces which were much more 'professional'.

Partly because of the relation of the police to elected local councils, partly because of the other factors mentioned, the American officer is subject to a variety of improper pressures, though it must once again be emphasized that the situation differs from one department to another. I have mentioned how in the past, at least, local politicians have in some places been able to interfere with the day-to-day operation of the department. Men in a Massachusetts force expressed a real fear of civil suits against them for actions taken while on duty, and of the fact that plaintiffs could demand – and be awarded – penal damages. The threat, 'I'll have your home', on the part of the powerful citizen is not an empty one. The same men also pointed out how their attempts to do their job could be frustrated by the system within which they had to work. As one said: 'A young fellow wants to get on, he wants to do his job – and before you know it, five or six other guys are looking at him and saying, "Well, what are you? Crazy? What are you going to get? You're not going to make sergeant. You're not going to make anything by doing this. It's going to be fixed." So the fellow has a tendency to run kind of lax. He does his job, such as protection of life and property, and the other parts that he could enforce kinda slip away from him.' An officer in another Massachusetts department said: 'You can either do your job, or you can take money to be short-sighted, or you can do nothing, which is what most of us do.' He went on to explain that one of the last things a night patrolman wants to come across is a drunken driver, for all too often such a case means only inconvenience and further grounds for cynicism. The policeman has to attend court the next morning (for which, until recently, he has not been paid) and the driver – who has previously got out on bail and engaged a lawyer, is likely to ask for a continuation of the case so that his defence can be prepared. A week later the case comes up for trial. The man is found guilty and he appeals to the superior court. When a hearing is fixed the lawyer asks for another date, saying he has to appear in a different court on the day in question. In this way he manoeuvres for a judge that he thinks may be more lenient. By the time the appeal is heard, however, the police officer is too dispirited to care: he has to attend court several times unnecessarily (at a time when, after working night shift, he wants to be in bed), for the defence lawyer wants to wear him down. Or the police officer can be the victim of a 'bag job', in which the prosecutor is in collusion with the defendant. The prosecutor tells the court he has examined the evidence and considers it insufficient, so he recommends the case be dropped. This sort of thing has a deplorable effect on morale. I remember talking outside a court with an officer who, I should think, was of well above average ability. 'There's not a man in the force who won't fix a ticket', he said with venom. What impressed me was not the statement but the bitterness in his voice: he took his standards from the exacting ideal of police service and hated the pressures which caused him to fall so far short of what he was capable. He went on: 'You mustn't stand with your jacket unbuttoned, like me, or leaning on the wall, like me. You mustn't go into a coffee shop except on police business. You mustn't fraternize with the people when you're on patrol. But a cop who tried to obey all the regulations would have a hell of a time. All the others (i.e. other cops) would be after him.' Police efficiency cannot be considered apart from the efficiency of the local government machinery and from an economic system which offers much greater rewards in private industry than in local government, so that the most able people do not go into such work.

The question of improper pressures was best illuminated for me by a very simple incident when visiting a municipal police department. An officer in the traffic department was showing me the various forms they used, when he held up one and said, with what I thought to be just a faint tinge of pride in his voice: 'Now this is the "no-fix" ticket'. It was a form for reporting a driving offence, which had a carbon copy that had to be sent forthwith to the courts, so that the charge could not simply be dropped by the police officer. That such a form should be called 'the no-fix ticket' speaks volumes.

THE POLICE AS AN ORGANIZATION

In the case of certain occupations it is fairly easy to agree on criteria of organizational efficiency. Armies are efficient in so far as they can defend national interests by military action; the fishing industry is organized to catch large quantities of fish at an economic cost; motor manufacturers are efficient if they produce reliable and inexpensive vehicles, and so on. But the police have to meet many criteria and it is difficult to compare the value of success in one direction at the expense of shortcomings in another. For example, a police force which solved more crimes but which treated suspects with undue severity would be in one sense more efficient, but its practices would excite public protest. The police are given a variety of objectives but they are simultaneously subjected to a host of restrictions concerning the ways in which they may attain them, and the interplay between ends and means is much more complex than in most organizations. The efficiency of the police may therefore be less important than their reponsiveness to the community they are required to serve.

How best to organize a police force or forces in a democratic state is in fact a complex political problem. Britain and the United States have approached it by relying on the constabulary concept – the idea of a policeman as a civilian, armed with few legal powers other than the citizen's. This solution was evolved in relatively small well-integrated communities and its application in modern industrial cities has created special difficulties – though whether any other solution could have avoided them is open to question. In former times it was possible to have a police system in which constable was the only rank and the local policeman was directly responsible to the community. Nowadays this is impossible. As the density of population increases and police work becomes more complex, so an organizational superstructure has to be developed; this point was well appreciated by a Georgia City supervising officer who remarked to me: 'The only justification for us people in higher ranks is to see that the men out on the street do their job properly.' Bureaucratic organization is needed to coordinate activities, to provide specialist services, and to supervise performance of the various tasks. Though the creation of a superstructure may solve certain problems, it usually creates new ones as well. The nature of the organizational problems which face the police may perhaps be illuminated by comparisons on the one hand with the professions and on the other with bureaucratic structures of the administrative type.

Professional organization has many distinctive characteristics, but one of the most striking is the relatively shallow hierarchy of ranks. Some churches have created a ladder of differentiated offices but other religious movements have recoiled from the idea that one leader should possess spiritual authority over others. Law, medicine, architecture, and the other established professions are founded on a common role in which all the members practise, and which decides the character of the occupational group. All medicals, for instance, are 'doctors'; it is their shared experience and interests in this role which give the profession its unity. At the same time, nothing hinders the proliferation of the medical hierarchy more than the need to preserve the individual doctor's role as an independent adviser to his patients. One of the reasons for this relative egalitarianism is that there is no very great variation in skills: the gap between a general practitioner and a medical professor is much smaller than that between a railway porter and his general manager. Another reason is that in most cases the activities of a professional man are directed towards serving the needs of an individual client, so that in his client's interest he has to be independent; the occupation has to face outward towards its public and not inward towards its own values.

Other kinds of occupation tend to develop a highly formal organization in which everyone is ranked and given a carefully delimited set of tasks. Sociologists term this kind of organization 'bureaucratic', though without intending any of the disparagement which is often implicit in popular use of the adjective. Work organizations tend to be bureaucratic when they have to coordinate the activities of large numbers of persons of varying rank and skill, when the ends served by the organization are relatively stable so that the same principles can be applied over and over again, and when the organization as a whole possesses a certain independence from its public. Examples of bureaucratic organizations include the armed forces, the civil service, the nationalized industries, and many large industrial concerns. Though such organizations can never be entirely inward-looking, employees in them sometimes direct their energies to internal values (preserving solidarity with colleagues, interdepartmental faction-fighting, etc.) instead of concentrating upon their official task of serving the public. The greater the differences in rank, the more they tend to inhibit communication between people on different rungs of the ladder, to provoke antagonisms, and to divert people from their real tasks to jockeying for promotion or to exercising their privileges for the pleasure of showing their own importance. In many organizations hierarchies are essential, but they do not work so well in practice as on paper.

The organization of the police resembles that of a profession in several ways. It, too, is based upon the common role of constable. Inspectors and the more senior police officers do have a few legal powers the constable lacks, but they are relatively unimportant. Basically, all police officers, from the top to the bottom, exercise the obligations and enjoy the privileges of the constable's office. The distinction between a police sergeant and an inspector is not like that between a sergeant and a lieutenant in the army. All policemen are called 'officers'; there are no 'other ranks' or 'enlisted men'. Except for a few chief constables in England, all the policemen in Britain have begun as police constables, and, if they have since advanced, have been promoted up the same ladder. Moreover, though there is a diversity of ranks, the difference in skills is relatively small. A Scottish policeman may wait twenty years or more before he is promoted sergeant and then, if he is lucky enough to catch the eye of his chief or to have his various superiors retire at the right moments, he may climb well up the ladder past inspector and chief inspector to superintendent, chief superintendent, assistant chief, or perhaps even beyond, in half the time it has taken him to become a sergeant. The formal qualifications of senior officers are often no greater than those of senior constables; their promotion being due to qualities of intelligence, discretion, industry, etc., which are notoriously hard to measure. Like professional people again, policemen often provide a personal service while remaining independent of the person for whom they act; it is not stretching the use of the words to say that they, too, are called to a case and treat it as their judgement directs. They are motivated more by a personal assessment of what ought to be done in the circumstances than by any desire for personal gain, and the ideal of public service is an important element in the motivation of many police officers.

Similarities between the police and bureaucratic organizations are also apparent. Many police forces are large and complex, requiring a considerable headquarters staff. Procedural rules and disciplinary procedures are needed. There is a precise and hierarchical arrangement of ranks and offices, of deputies and relief personnel. As might be expected, police forces are also apt to display some of the endemic sicknesses of formal organizations: internal disputes over jurisdiction; abuse of rank; concentration upon reporting procedures to ensure that one is 'in the clear' instead of upon the job to be done, and so forth. However, there is a difference between the police department and many bureaucracies in the way in which most activities are originated. In an industrial concern, for example, the key man is usually the managing director. Responding to a change in market conditions, he may order that production of a certain line shall be stopped, or, approving suggestions put forward by the research and development division, he may have a new production line set up. The pattern of activity is in most cases started from the top, and where subordinate sections make representations they need approval from above. Similarly, in a civil service department it is directives from the upper reaches which lay down the basis for dealing with people from outside. But most police activities are originated by members of the public: motorists, drunks, lost children, people leaving their houses empty, football crowds, housebreakers. Information about these events reaches the organization through the men at the bottom. Every case is unique and any one of them might spell trouble for the whole organization if the policeman who is first on the scene makes an error of judgement. His supervisors are in a very real sense dependent upon him, but they cannot always be looking over his shoulder to see what he is doing. Thus the cases with which a police force deals are mostly fed into the organization from the bottom; but the men at the top, if they are to maintain their position, must control their subordinates. They must establish uniform procedures and see that they are implemented. Therefore supervisory activities are originated in a downwards direction. However, as will be shown later, supervision is not straightforward in an organization like the police. Subordinates have to be allowed, even encouraged, to use their discretion, and this means that it is not easy to force a lazy policeman to take the measures his supervisors consider appropriate. In this mixture, therefore, of independence and subordination, police organization seems again to lie between the types of the profession and the bureaucracy: it looks outward towards members of the public, but, because policemen do not receive their remuneration directly from clients, their organization has to employ a disciplinary stimulus to supplement the service motivation that characterizes the dutiful officer.

The question of whether the police are or can become a profession has often been raised. The International Association of Chiefs of Police examined the implications of the term in the 1930s; and on the British side Sir John Moylan maintained in 1948 that the police had become a profession (Roddenbury, 1953, pp. 111–15; Moylan, 1948). Disputes on this issue can only be barren, for while the police possess some elements of the professional role as it is understood in Britain, they cannot but lack others. Moreover, the character of professionalism is changing and it is no longer possible to establish clear criteria as to the occupations which can claim such a title. Commissioned rank in the navy and army used once to qualify, but today the ways in which it differs from the recognized professions are more striking than any similarities. Many lawyers are employed full-time by corporations; doctors work for insurance companies and industrial concerns; many engineers, architects, and clergymen have little independence. 'Professional status', it would seem, no longer relates to a distinctive set of social relationships but instead denotes a rough rank on a scale of social status.

EXPOSURE TO VIOLENCE

Policemen feel that they are more involved in their jobs than most people are, and that this is inadequately recognized. They may be assaulted or insulted just because of their occupation, and run a greater risk of being assaulted or murdered in the execution of their duty than do the great majority. Consequently, policemen look with sympathy upon any of their number who get into trouble because of an error of judgement. Such an error in a situation where he has to act quickly may, after all, cost a police officer his life. For example, I was told of an American detective who shot an innocent youngster in an alley, believing him to be a dangerous escapee, and who had to serve a two-and-a-half-year gaol sentence. Police opinion towards him had been sympathetic, whatever the public thought. Public indignation and police sympathy are both understandable reactions to such events. In theory, the police officer in Britain and the United States is personally liable for any wrongful action of his while on duty, so that a citizen can, in theory, sue for wrongful arrest and claim punitive damages. In practice, this sort of thing is very restricted, and the British Royal Commission has recommended that police authorities should now be made liable for such actions. The same issue comes up in a different form over damage to police vehicles. The police officer often feels that he may be called on to pursue another driver at the risk of his own life; if, in these or other circumstances, he should damage the vehicle he is driving, it seems (to him) harsh that the damage should be investigated and that he should be liable to punishment although he was doing his best.

Aspects of Police Organization in Britain and the U.S.A.

This last issue introduces a major difference between police-public relations in the United States and in Britain, a difference that some police officers would consider the most critical of all. The British policeman knows that the chances are infinitesimal that any seemingly ordinary person will be carrying a gun and will shoot at an officer. Few burglars carry guns. Indeed, it has been alleged that criminals in Britain disapprove of those of their number who carry guns because they consider it likely to result in severer counter-measures. While the British police officer may have to deal with an armed man, the odds are that he will have some forewarning that the situation is dangerous. (One exception should be noted: the recent increase in wage snatches and bank robberies by armed men who are prepared to shoot represents a relatively new tendency which may have far-reaching consequences.) In the United States, however, many policemen have to be continually on the alert for shooting. As I write I see in the current issue of the monthly police journal *Law and Order* that thirteen deaths of police officers on duty are reported – eight by shooting and five in motor accidents – all except one of which occurred within a four-week period. During 1962 a total of seventy-eight law-enforcement employees were killed in the line of duty. Forty-eight officers were victims of direct attacks by criminals, most of them dying from gunfire. Over a three-year period, 26 per cent of police officers killed by felons were responding to 'disturbance' calls (family quarrels, man with gun, etc.); 12 per cent were investigating burglaries in progress; 22 per cent were dealing with robberies or pursuing robbers; 25 per cent were attempting other arrests or transporting prisoners; 11 per cent were investigating suspicious persons and circumstances; and 4 per cent were killed without warning by deranged persons. Of every 100 United States police officers, ten were assaulted at some time during 1962; the highest incidence of assault was in the biggest cities, but a greater variation occurred on a regional pattern – the rate in the South Atlantic and East North Central regions being 16·1 and 14·7 per hundred police officers, compared with 4·7 in New England (*Crime in the United States*, 1961, pp. 21–3 and p. 110). Comparable British figures are not to hand, but they must be a small fraction of these.

The possibility of violence affects the American police officer in many ways. I was told in Carolina City that most police officers there had at one time or another been threatened by people who wanted to settle a score. Most officers in the city carried a gun, even off duty, either because of such threats or out of habit. Officers there regarded even the motorist who had been stopped for a routine check as someone who might open fire. When asking patrolmen how they responded to various kinds of people, I inquired whether, if a motorist whom they had stopped were to get out of his car, they would not regard this as more cooperative and respectful behaviour than if he simply stayed at the wheel? No, they said. They preferred a driver to remain in the car so that they could come up to the driving window from behind and he would have to turn his head to speak to them.[1] In this way they could watch him best and it would be more difficult for him to point a gun at them. They added that the previous year a criminal on the run had driven through the state and had twice been stopped by patrolmen: on each occasion, as they had approached the car, he had shot them dead. Judging from the fact that the two slain officers were apparently unprepared for gunfire and the effect that such incidents would have on police officers in the neighbouring communities, it would seem that the caution the men expressed to me was partly a result of the trouble the previous year. However, the greater likelihood that someone stopped for a minor offence may be a dangerous man who thinks he has been tracked down, and the more general availability of weapons in the United States, must make the policeman more suspicious of people he does not know. In Georgia City, the few officers to whom I put this question about the motorist did not respond in the same way, but when the two officers referred to in Chapter 3 were taking into their car the drunken driver who had been making a disturbance, he asked if he might get some cigarettes out of the glove compartment in his own car; they refused, observing to me that he might well have a gun there. Except in New York State, it is not difficult for the ordinary citizen to obtain a permit to carry a gun; this is quite legal, provided he does not conceal the weapon. The Constitution is widely interpreted as giving a man the right to a gun to defend himself and his property. It would certainly seem that in

[1] American practice is for a police car to stop a motorist by driving behind him with roof-light flashing and siren sounding; if he does not pull to the side but attempts to speed away, the police pursue and possibly shoot. The usual British practice is for the police car to come alongside or in front and wave the driver down; American police would consider this suicidal.

112

the South, at least, most white men and many Negroes like to have a gun available. To the visiting European it appears as if the revolver is the prime symbol of virility: a man without a gun or a man who cannot shoot is a poor creature. When people possess guns there is a standing temptation to use them even when circumstances do not justify their use, and this increases the policeman's burdens considerably.

The possibility of violence affects not only the American policeman's conduct towards members of the public but also his relations with fellow policemen. In situations of danger, patrolmen make very heavy demands of solidarity upon their brother officers. If two men have to go into a house containing a man who is suffering from some mental disorder and threatening people with a gun, it is essential for each one to know that the other is backing him up. In such situations some men cannot withstand their fears – let us say they find an excuse for covering a window instead of going up a staircase – and they let their partner down. The feeling of obligation to a brother officer helps a policeman to do his duty in such circumstances; it has to be one of the principal values in the culture of the patrolman. Some men – who are considered to be in other respects excellent policemen – just cannot master themselves in these situations, so they are given desk jobs or other less exposed positions.

The British policeman is much more favourably placed in these matters than his American colleagues. While in the United States I was told a story about a London bobby which highlights the difference. The policeman was pursuing a burglar over a warehouse roof when he trod on a skylight, fell through, and remained there hanging by his hands. Hearing his shouts, the burglar returned, helped him up, and was arrested. In court shortly afterwards he received a lighter sentence in recognition of his action. I do not know whether this story is true, but I do not find it difficult to believe; yet in America such an event would be altogether extraordinary: the criminal would never help a policeman if he had to injure his own interests by so doing. In the struggle between police and criminals in Britain, both sides abstain from certain methods. It is not an all-out war, and the policemen are happier without guns strapped to their belts. They can count on more support from members of the public and they are less dependent upon their own colleagues. But quite apart from situations requiring direct action, both British and American policemen are subject to a general pressure from the public, consisting of minor incidents which add up over the years. Complaints may be made against officers which are without foundation, but nevertheless the men may feel that the investigation of the incidents by the chief has harmed their careers; cases of injustice may be infrequent but still loom large in the patrolman's view of the matter. Members of the public complain that they pay for police services and insist that they therefore have a right to particular benefits. Policemen are subject time and again to cheek and abuse from people, which are so calculated that they are not quite serious enough to merit prosecution; they often feel that the mass media are unfair to them, and they may suffer in their private life on account of their occupation.

SOLIDARITY AND DISCIPLINE

The need for support in situations of danger and the feeling of common identity arising from public pressure have important consequences for police organization. The demand for solidarity is extended to cover matters which have nothing to do with danger from criminals. One American officer, explaining this, remarked: 'Sometimes during the night shift everything is quite dead. If you met some girls and they were willing, you might go off into the bushes with them. Now if you can't trust your partner over something like that, you know you won't be able to trust him in an emergency.' Thus it would seem that patrolmen may support their fellows over what they regard as minor infractions in order to demonstrate to them that they will be loyal in situations that make the greatest demands upon their fidelity. Though they accord more latitude to their colleagues in such matters than their supervisors would wish, patrolmen will not tolerate behaviour which they regard as liable to bring policemen generally into disrepute. If an officer is dismissed the force on good grounds, the men may be very severe on their former colleague who has fallen from grace. They know that if he gets into trouble it may well be headlined in the local newspaper as 'Ex-policeman sentenced', etc.[1]

[1] 'A recent issue of a weekly St Louis Negro newspaper captioned a story with a headline "Ex-policeman is charged with stealing supplies from school". After investigation the story was found to be true. The man was suspended from the Police Department on October 18, 1935 – twenty-seven years ago. One wonders how many other occupations are expected to make contemporary atonement for acts of past employees' (*The Police Chief*, January 1963, p. 9).

He is still identified with them despite his dismissal, and he can do them much harm. I remember a senior officer observing to me: 'Not long ago we had to dismiss a man for drunkenness and unbecoming behaviour. Last Friday a report was passed out that he had been seen drunk in the square and had been threatening his wife. There wasn't a car that wasn't trying to get him.' To have him behave like this in public was a cause for more shame than any publicity following an arrest.

In the American departments I visited it seemed as if the supervisors shared many of the patrolmen's sentiments about solidarity. They too wanted their colleagues to back them up in an emergency, and they shared similar frustrations with the public. Having themselves been patrolmen they could sympathize with their view of some of the regulations and may have been inclined not to look for possible misdemeanours as long as there were no complaints. In the American forces the supervisor could not use his rank to the same extent as he can in Scotland, and he usually had less power to spoil a man's career. The practices in American cities whereby the men work from headquarters (instead of proceeding individually to their beats), gather in the locker rooms, and frequently patrol in pairs by automobile also make it easier for the patrolmen to preserve a common front, so that the supervisor is obliged to go carefully. It should be added that of the three departments with which I was best acquainted, supervision seemed to be strictest and most impersonal in the largest, and of a much more familiar kind in the smallest. The size of the unit inevitably influences the social distance between supervisors and their men.

As an example of how a supervisor is inclined to exercise his powers more discreetly in the circumstances that prevail in the United States, I would cite what happened at a motor accident. A bus and an automobile had been in collision and when I reached the scene with the sergeant, one of his patrolmen had taken charge. Two injured men from the car were propped against the fence and an ambulance was on the way. Both vehicles remained in place – the bus half across the road. The sergeant saw that cars were having difficulty in getting past the bus. He could have ordered the patrolman to have the bus moved, or have suggested to him that this would be a good idea, but the patrolman was in charge and the sergeant did not want to interfere if he could help it. So he stood and directed traffic near the bus.

After a few moments the patrolman saw how the traffic was building up and got the driver to move his bus.[1] This is only a minor incident and many supervisqrs would have been less concerned not to interfere with the patrolman, but it does contrast with the position in Britain where the sergeant would almost certainly have taken charge immediately.[2]

Where men are allocated to patrol duties in pairs, the question of whom a man has to partner becomes very important. In Georgia City there were no permanent partners in the patrol cars, but in Carolina City two men might be teamed up together for a long period. I was told that if you could not get on with your partner this made your tour of duty very miserable. One patrolman, after emphasizing that an officer saw more of his partner than he did of his wife and family, and that on night shift things could be very dull, went on to recollect that once he had been paired with a man who used to spend all night looking for stolen cars – 'He was really keen on this'. The officer added: 'That's quite all right with me; as long as you've got something to do it doesn't matter so much what it is.' If you really could not stand your partner, he said, you could ask the captain to put you with someone else, and if he said he could not, then you could ask to go on foot patrol. In this department it was said that two particular patrolmen had been together for five years without speaking to each other; their commander found this impossible to believe. The supervisors try to put men together who are compatible and do not tend to 'goof off' together; some supervisors like to make frequent changes, others say that a good pair should be kept together. In the United States this question of partnering is clearly of some importance to the way the patrolman sees his job, and is often of particular importance when Negro officers are employed.[3] It might repay closer attention in a subsequent investigation.

[1] Compare also the action of the supervisor described on p. 77 above.

[2] Americans are notoriously unwilling to accept positions of subordination, and this contrast may be found in other organizations too. One Carolina City officer had served in a United States army unit which was stationed alongside the Black Watch (a Scottish regiment) and he commented: 'Why, a man with one stripe in that outfit had more rank than a master-sergeant in ours.' Certainly a sergeant in a Scottish force has 'more rank' than a sergeant in most American police departments, and the American patrolman has more opportunity to remonstrate against instructions he dislikes.

[3] Cf. Kephart (1957, pp. 71, 78–81) and Banton (1963, pp. 18–20).

The size of the organization is another important factor in supervision. In a large department the problem faced by a supervisor who wants his men to prosecute more cases of, say, illegal parking or improper automobile lights is similar to that of the works manager who wants the men on the factory floor to increase their production. The men have various reasons for resisting, and some of them may be quite defensible, but that does not affect the structure of the problem. If they are to resist, they must follow a common policy. If the manager is to increase output and cannot change the framework within which the problem is set, he will have to break their front and put pressure on individuals and small groups. It can be the same in police work. A former New York City police captain observed to me: 'The chief makes decisions and then the locker room makes decisions.' The locker room decides informally, and perhaps even without realizing that it is doing so, just how much work is to be done. If a man shows up his colleagues by working too hard, or if he is lazy and wants to spend most of his night shift sleeping in the car, or if he carries tales to supervisors, then the others will ostracize him. His partners will ask to be put with someone else, and if no one wants to work with him then there is little chance that his superiors will view him with favour either. In any organization, breach of informal understandings about output arouses the strongest feelings, and if the supervisors encourage tale-bearing – as the weak ones are tempted to – false information is fed to them and the morale of the organization suffers.

When, for these and other reasons, supervision is weak and the demands for solidarity are strong, the patrolman is bound to take his cue from his peer group. This can have deleterious effects. A former member of the Denver police department, in discussing what went wrong there, stressed that a new recruit was not accepted by his colleagues unless he conformed to their norms. When investigating a burglary in a store, police officers might put some additional articles into their pockets (indeed they were sometimes encouraged to do so by the owners who pointed out that they would recover from the insurance company anyway). The new recruit was aware that he was being watched to see if he, too, was going to help himself to a wrist watch or a new pipe (Stern, 1962). Similarly, in the old days in a large Massachusetts force, a recruit was promptly taken by an older officer into a speakeasy and given a drink. The pressure to conform must

117

have been overwhelming. When, in response to public pressure or in resentment at their low status, police band together, they may carry their solidarity too far. When policemen support one another in wrong as well as right, public hostility increases and the police become even more of an outcast group. The sort of situation that can result is reflected in an incident related by Judge Adlow: a prominent public figure who was appointed a special justice (in Massachusetts) said at a banquet to honour the appointment: 'I wouldn't believe a cop if he stood on a sack of Bibles' (Adlow, 1947, p. 17).[1] He was never appointed to a criminal sitting, but even so the incident was startling.

Like members of the better American forces, Scottish policemen feel rather ambivalent about occupational solidarity. They would like to stand by their colleagues unquestioningly but know that they cannot do so. In many situations they identify themselves with the public as well as with the policeman, for they are out of uniform themselves for many hours a week. As citizens they want the police to be 'theirs' and not the servants of some distant authority. This was the feeling that caused one keen and successful police officer to remark in discussion, 'The natural born policeman should be strangled at birth'. Though policemen in Britain sometimes refer to members of the public as 'civilians' this usage is misleading, for they do not draw a hard and fast line between themselves and the public. In a democratic country the police cannot organize themselves as a solitary group apart from society, because they have no 'product' that can be separated from their public relations. The nearest thing to a raw material that they can 'process' is the criminal, but criminals cannot be separated from the public. Many police scandals have centred on cases in which policemen treated someone roughly, believing him to be a criminal when there had been a mistaken identification. Had he been the man the police thought him the public might not have complained.

British policemen have much less cause than American ones to feel that they must keep together in face of the public. Their organization can therefore tolerate more internal strains than could be the case

[1] Compare the career of the Boston mayor James Michael Curley and the Newburyport mayor described in W. Lloyd Warner's *The Living and the Dead* (1959). In 1962 a Massachusetts man was re-elected to the state legislature from prison where he was serving a sentence for having earlier turned his office to his personal profit.

across the Atlantic. There is a longer hierarchy of ranks in Britain;[1] pay differentials are greater; the sense of opposition between 'the men' and 'the bosses' (and vice versa) seems stronger; discipline is stricter; constables show less solidarity with one another, and more competitiveness. Supervision generally is much closer and more demanding, both because in British conditions it is easier to insist on higher standards and because policemen have fewer crimes and incidents with which to deal. In so far as British policemen feel socially isolated it is less because the public rejects them than because both the public and the police themselves require such conduct of officers that they are bound to feel set apart.

This portion of my argument can easily be misunderstood, and it should be emphasized that I am not here concerned with the merits of either system. In the United States, public pressure on the police is stronger, which causes the police to band together more. This of necessity reduces the supervisor's power and makes it harder for a police chief to eliminate illegal behaviour within his department. In Britain opposed interests within the police can more easily find expression because the organization as a whole is under less pressure from outside. More attention can be directed to maintaining or improving standards, but the opportunity presented by better public relations is not necessarily used to the public benefit. The British supervisor can, at times, use his greater power to behave despotically and glory in his personal achievement.

There are many contrasts between American and British police practices in respect of discipline and deference between police officers. In most Scottish forces sergeants and constables salute officers of the rank of inspector and above. A constable calls a sergeant by his rank, and anyone senior he addresses as 'Sir'. Inspectors and sergeants may address constables by their first names but the reverse is rare. An older constable might address his sergeant by his first name but this is not common. Nor would constables and sergeants necessarily see a great deal of one another off duty, because men are transferred on promotion. If a group of men are constables together and one is promoted sergeant, visits and informal contact between the promoted man's family and the others' families will be reduced, not

---

[1] Many police departments in the United States have no office of assistant chief, unless – as in Carolina City – its holder also has charge of a division.

because the new sergeant is snobbish, nor because the others are envious. The friends he has left behind will be reluctant to do anything which might be construed by their colleagues as ingratiating themselves with the new supervisor: the pressures come from the peer group.

In the United States the constraints of rank are much weaker. In Felsmere City I never saw a police officer salute; nor did I ever see an officer above the rank of lieutenant wearing uniform. In Carolina City I was told that saluting had been abolished. In Georgia City – the largest and most impersonal department – saluting was said to be a convention unsupported by the regulations. Men saluted at roll call or outside headquarters but rarely on any other occasion. From the way people spoke of such matters it also seems unlikely that differences of rank in any of these departments would constrain off-duty contacts as much as they can in Scotland.

In Scotland constables are often referred to by number. I remember being told that I could accompany PC 99 on one shift and where to meet him. He was notified that I was coming. I met him, he introduced himself as PC 99, and we spent almost eight hours together; at no point did I learn his name or was it necessary to ask it. In Felsmere City, by contrast, I remember getting in a car: the two officers in the front seat promptly shook hands, introduced themselves by their first name and last name, ascertained my names, and addressed me on a first-name basis. At one point in the conversation one officer mentioned his age and turned round to ask 'How old are you?' This kind of familiarity is unusual in Britain. In the American South, officers are more inclined to address one another by their last names but the same contrast holds in many ways. In both the Southern forces, officers could be identified by a name-tag over the breast pocket; a British officer is identified by the number on his shoulder. In one American department nicknames were used freely: for example, when an officer in headquarters was asked the where-abouts of Lieutenant Hare, he could call over to the dispatcher: 'Joe, see if you can find where Rabbit is'. Somewhat contrary to this characterization of the American uniform and manner as the more individual, is the British practice whereby a policeman wears war-service ribbons, and ribbons denoting the award of police decorations, over his breast pocket; American policemen wear no ribbons or symbols of this kind.

Aspects of Police Organization in Britain and the U.S.A.

In a Scottish police headquarters there will rarely be anything in any of the officers' rooms – even the superintendent's – which identifies it as the room of a particular individual. In the United States, however, there may be a variety of personal decorations. A man who has attended a training course or obtained a law degree will have the certificate framed and hang it on the wall. In the room of a senior officer in one of the Southern cities it was noticeable that on the top of the desk lay a Bible, and a portrait of his wife stood in a frame. In the bookshelf behind him was a book, *Why I am a Methodist*, and several others about Sunday-school teaching, with a large picture of Jesus on the wall over them. These would never be found in the more impersonal setting of a Scottish police headquarters.

The same contrast appears in almost every sphere. Scottish officers rarely remove their caps when entering a private house; whether or not it is the intention, this practice serves to conceal the youth of some of them and to cover features by which they might be distinguished. One of the functions of uniform is to emphasize the role someone is playing and to minimize individual differences among the people who have to play it. It makes the people who have to play this role appear interchangeable. In the same way, a Scottish constable speaking to a civilian about another policeman is likely to refer to him as 'another officer' or 'the other officer'. It is not necessary to mention names. When I have been with American officers they have been more ready to remove their caps and to refer to their colleagues by their names. Their approach to members of the public also seems more familiar.

American views about police discipline are more free and easy than those obtaining in Britain. In Chapter 8 I shall try to explain why this is to be expected and why things that appear deplorable to a British policeman do not, in the United States, necessarily have the same consequences as they would in Britain. For example, one patrolman in Felsmere City, who had to watch conditions outside a school as the children came and left, used his own car to drive from his house to the school and then into headquarters to pick up the daily information sheet. He said that his chief did not object to the use of private cars in such circumstances; it is much more difficult to get from place to place by public transport in the United States, and to have had the officer conveyed by a police vehicle would have been more expensive.

The Policeman in the Community

In Britain, policemen are not allowed to smoke on duty, and a strict supervisor who catches the same man smoking twice – however discreetly – will probably put him on a disciplinary charge. In the American departments I visited police officers are not allowed to smoke in a public situation (e.g. directing traffic) but they may smoke in a patrol car if it does not interfere with the execution of their duty. A superior officer in one department said: 'I think most of the men have the sense to throw down a cigarette when speaking to members of the public.' However, from my observations, they readily spoke to people with a cigarette or even a cigar butt in their mouths. Probably to enforce a regulation about this while public attitudes were permissive would evoke such resistance that little would be gained. In any case, the smoking of tobacco seems a minor matter compared with chewing it. In some parts of the South a police officer will chew tobacco and spit it out all over the place.

In Carolina City (which may be fairly representative in this regard) I was told that the principal occasions for disciplinary action centred upon damage to vehicles, trouble with women, and drinking. The last two chiefs of the Georgia City force have struggled to put down drinking by police officers in any circumstances, and, according to their discipline regulations, police officers are not allowed to consume intoxicating liquor at any time whatsoever; in practice it is unlikely that any action would be taken against a man for drinking in his own home. The attraction of a police uniform for many women is, however, a more difficult matter to deal with. Police officers – especially in the South – have expressed surprise to me at the way a girl will come up and talk to a policeman when she would speak to no one else. It is not unusual for a police officer to be able to make an assignation in this way, and tales are common of respectable women who come into town for an adventure and make advances to policemen. Supervisors as well as men get involved in such affairs. In one of the Southern cities visited, officers on patrol were continually surveying the feminine scene; they joked that when approaching the principal intersection in the town centre it was police practice to slow down and time their arrival for the red light so that they could watch the girls crossing. Standards of female pulchritude are high in the South. Not only did the policemen watch the girls but it was evident that the girls were aware of the attention they got from the police, and the policemen's wives were also inclined to be suspicious. It could easily happen that a young police officer went astray; if his wife complained to his superiors but nobody else said anything, the man was warned unofficially. If the other woman brought the matter up, or if some member of the public complained, the matter had to be handled officially. Only recently a young policeman with a wife and three children got involved in this way: he was told that he would have to give up either his mistress or his job. He chose to resign and the department was sorry to lose him because he was a good officer. This occupational hazard seems to be quite characteristic of police work in the United States, but I have never heard it mentioned in Britain.

In connection with these questions it is also necessary to explain that in some American departments disciplinary standards cannot be maintained strictly because otherwise the level of turnover among the personnel would be too high and men are expensive to train. A police chief assured me that one West Coast police department has its own branch of Alcoholics Anonymous, and he justified it by saying that their recruitment problem was such that they could not afford to dismiss a trained and competent police officer because of a personal weakness, unless it was clear that it was going to affect his police work.

Just as American officers show less deference towards their superiors, so they are inclined to be more easy-going in their dealings with members of the public. An American police chief mentioned that he had been very impressed by the demeanour of British policemen. They bore themselves well, and were smartly and uniformly dressed; they handled the public courteously and they always appeared to be doing something, never merely waiting or hanging around. Even if only watching traffic at a road junction they stood in a way that showed they felt themselves to be on duty. The British policeman has an exemplary role – he is expected to show other drivers how to drive and other citizens how they should behave. Police drivers, for example, are given additional training and a higher standard test; they are by common consent the best drivers on the roads. The British policeman's uniform makes him highly 'visible': he stands out from the crowd. People are conscious of his presence and the policeman is unconsciously aware of this, and the pressure makes him the more inclined to act in an exemplary fashion. American policemen are less uniform in appearance: dress varies from department to department; variations in height are greater, and in some localities patrol officers may wear spectacles. American policemen are often conscious that they stand out among the citizenry but it sometimes seems as if they exaggerate the extent of this. In Carolina City two officers with whom I was patrolling were convinced that many citizens were only awaiting the opportunity to get their own back on the police: if they were to stop somewhere for pleasure, they said, someone would telephone and report them. They pointed out that people would see me riding in the car with them and would know that, because I was sitting alone in the back seat, I could not be under arrest. They would suspect that the policemen were giving one of their cronies a ride and would report them. When I later asked the afternoon shift captain about this he said that no one ever had telephoned about me; he thought that detectives, liquor control, and other plain-clothes law-enforcement personnel rode so often in the patrol cars that no one took any notice. On the other hand, it should be added that when police officers misbehave in public, people do telephone headquarters. Another example of the same sense of 'visibility' occurred when sitting at lunch in a restaurant. Two police officers were present in uniform. They drank water while the rest of the party had beer. One officer noticed that his neighbour's glass had been placed in such a way that people at other tables might think it his; he was embarrassed and pushed it aside, at the same time glancing at the other officer (his superior) to see if he had noticed. Had he taken a glass of beer, I was assured, it was quite probable someone would have telephoned to the chief. Yet by contrast I cannot recall ever having seen a uniformed policeman sitting in a restaurant in Britain.

To a visitor the difference between the British idea of the policeman as exemplary and the more familiar American conception was evident in driving habits. In my experience, American police officers drive no better than ordinary members of the public: they slow down instead of stopping at stop signs, start forward before the green light appears, do not always signal their intentions, exceed the speed limit without good cause, and so on. In most forces they receive no training in driving additional to that which they have had as civilians. Some of them are allocated to cars with insufficient experience and cannot drive in traffic for a full eight-hour shift. British notions of decorum do not obtain. For example, the driver of one patrol car saw a woman who was a hospital receptionist and whom the officers had often met and joked with. She was driving in the outside lane. He drove in on her nearside, put the gear-box into neutral, and accelerated to make the fan belt race loudly and give her a fright. This sort of joking would have been deprecated in most American departments, but it is almost inconceivable in Britain.

Some American police officers would wish their men to be more dignified and impersonal like their British colleagues. A change in this direction might be welcomed by the American public but I am inclined to think that it would be restricted by other factors. If British constables were to patrol an American town the public would probably think them stuffy and unfriendly; they might resent their detachment, preferring the American-style policeman who seems 'human' and approachable. There would also be resistance from the patrolmen who would see this as a policy unrelated to the nature of the job to be done, and unnecessarily military.

In America the police are less removed from civilian social life than in Britain. People feel that policemen are employees of the community, hired to perform the task assigned them. They are not an outside agency serving the government or an ideal. This is revealed in many ways. For example, in Carolina City and many other places, the police crime files containing the report of the officer who first went to the crime, and other information, are open to journalists who have the right to come in and consult them. Naturally the detectives withhold information they do not want the press to have, but the very idea of journalists having a right of access to any police files is a strange one to the visitor. Again, the Los Angeles chief of police remarks: 'It is important to note that every member of the department has the right to talk to the press about what he is doing. We make no attempt to muzzle our officers.' Compare this with British practice. In the Scottish city any letter from the police – until recently, even from a superintendent commanding a division with headquarters at an address different from that of the City headquarters – contained the superscription, 'All communications should be addressed to the chief constable', and had his address on it. Some of these differences

125

are explored further and more systematically in Chapter 8, but for the present it is necessary to emphasize again that the conception of the tasks of police forces vary from society to society. In Britain, the police have been given more freedom to organize in accordance with their view of how the job is best done, and have built up a self-sustaining tradition. This, along with the other circumstantial factors discussed earlier, gives the British police officer a considerable advantage over his American colleague.

CHAPTER 5

Police Duty

It was argued in Chapter 1 that the policeman on patrol is primarily a 'peace officer' rather than a 'law officer'. Relatively little of his time is spent enforcing the law in the sense of arresting offenders; far more is spent 'keeping the peace' by supervising the beat and responding to requests for assistance. Chapters 2 and 3 documented this thesis. It may be that under modern conditions, with the spread of the telephone, the dissolution of small communities, and the increased sense of participation in the wider society, the public are now more disposed to notify the police when offences are committed, and that to this extent the need for routine patrol is reduced. More officers can then be allocated to specialist work in criminal investigation, examining vehicles, investigating accidents, plain-clothes duty, etc. This is indeed the tendency, but patrol work remains the principal activity of most British and American forces; it is the problems of this kind of work and the attitudes to which it gives rise that most characterize the culture of police work as an occupation.

My argument that the patrolman is primarily a peace officer is, however, based less upon any calculation of how he spends his time than upon a consideration of how he responds when he has to deal with offences. In my experience the most striking thing about patrol work is the high proportion of cases in which policemen do *not* enforce the law. Usually they have good reasons for not invoking it, and they act within the limits of their discretionary power as this is recognized by custom if not by statute. Yet the exercise of discretion poses very serious moral, social, and administrative problems. Who, after all, is the policeman, to decide what the legislature intended? Thus a British police writer observes:

'It is an open secret that many police forces, in order to provide a suitably impressive margin, do not prosecute motorists for exceeding the speed limit in towns unless they are travelling at 40 m.p.h. or over. The police have over-ridden Parliament and made law for themselves. . . . Despite the advantages of police discretion, in principle it is bad . . .' (Elmes, 1963, pp. 13–14).

And a chief constable states:

'to demand that (the policeman) should exercise some sort of discretion, and refrain from enforcing certain laws . . . demands of him a judgement and a sense of responsibility which is scarcely reflected in our treatment of him when we fix his salary in relation to that of other public officers' (Williams, 1954, p. 271).

In the training of police officers, both in Britain and in the United States, the recruit is told that he must never play judge and jury. His job is to bring the offender to court, and what the court decides to do with him is no concern of the policeman's. As might be expected, it is not easy to maintain such a distinction in practice, and the officer who makes the charge takes a lively interest, as an individual if not always as a policeman, in the court's decision.

The decision to invoke the criminal law and put a man on a charge must be in the first place that of the police officer who sees the offence or makes the initial investigation. But there is bound to be variation in the way many thousand different policemen respond in similar circumstances. Quite apart from any variation in their understanding of the law's requirements, some will be temperamentally lenient and others strict. If the initiation of criminal proceedings depended only on the judgement of individual constables there would be serious discrepancies. To guard against this, senior officers lay down rules for the guidance of their subordinates. In Scotland, two further provisions make for uniformity. First, a constable's charge has to be approved by a superior officer before it is taken further. Second, prosecutions are not conducted by the police but by the Procurator Fiscal, an independent official, who decides whether or not to prosecute, and indeed has statutory power to direct the police in the investigation of crime. However, whereas there are safeguards to prevent the invocation of the law in unsuitable circumstances, it is more difficult to guard against the injustice which may occur when a patrolman improperly neglects to initiate proceedings.[1] This is something that is almost impossible to control. As a Carolina City police captain explained to me:

'You drive into this town with a defective muffler (i.e. exhaust silencer). When a police officer stops you, you tell him that it broke on your way in and you're going to a garage to get it fixed. He lets you go. On the next corner you get stopped again and the officer there lets you go. But on the third corner there may be a third officer who gives you a ticket. There's nobody that can say he's wrong. The fact that the other two let you go is irrelevant: each police officer makes his own decision on his own responsibility.'

If it be assumed, for the moment, that variations like this are bound to occur, the administrative problem is this: if the third officer is ill-advised to prefer a charge, proceedings can be stopped before they reach court; but if the first two officers were wrong – in good faith or not – it is almost impossible for the supervisor to revoke their decisions. Actions of this sort have been called 'low-visibility' decisions because it is so difficult to keep them under review. When someone is let off who ought not to be, let us say because of class discrimination or bribery, as serious an injustice is perpetrated as when a wrongful charge is preferred or an illegal method is used to obtain evidence. The withholding of punishment demonstrates the use of arbitrary power and a contempt of law just as much as illegal punishment. The case against giving the police any discretionary power cannot therefore be completely answered by any conceivable tightening up of police procedures.

This question of the non-enforcement of the law by the police has been examined in detail by Wayne R. LaFave of the University of Wisconsin Law School (LaFave, 1962, pp. 104–37 and 179–239). He holds that there are three chief objections to the view that the police should exercise no discretion in law enforcement. First, it has not yet been proved feasible to draft a criminal code which unambiguously encompasses all conduct intended to be made criminal; equally,

---

[1] In some circumstances (e.g. minor offences against public decency) the police may feel obliged to report a case for prosecution if a complaint is laid, even though they believe that the incident would be best ignored.

it seems impossible for the reform of the law to be able to keep pace with changing conditions and opinions. Second, those charged with enforcing the law do not have the resources to enforce all the laws effectively: if all major road junctions were to be kept under continuous observation and all offenders charged, there would be no police for other duties. Third, individual circumstances vary in such a way that justice cannot be achieved merely by the enforcement of rules. What for one man is a novel experience may for another be a punishment. As Justice Breitel observed: 'Mere arrest may destroy reputation, or cause the loss of a job, or visit grave injury upon a family. Hailing the arrestee promptly before a magistrate, though serving due process, may be no boon, indeed, to the innocent or technical violator.'

In support of LaFave's contentions, it may be added that if full enforcement is desired, then the police, as presently organized, are not the right body to try and effect it. Many features of police administration in fact militate against full enforcement. In both Britain and America the police are to an appreciable extent subject to local government control; they may not be able to raise from local taxation as much money as they believe they need if they are at odds with the community. In many situations the police are heavily dependent upon the public for information concerning crimes and criminals; people will not collaborate in such inquiries if they feel that they are not getting a fair deal from the police. Consequently, police forces everywhere trade pardons in return for better public relations: first offenders and others are regularly let off in the belief that they will feel they have been given a fair chance. Then it has to be remembered that policemen, as individuals, participate in the same society as the people whose conduct they are supervising. The offender may be an old friend, a relative, a brother policeman, or just someone with whom they sympathize. Police officers usually see the offence from the point of view of the offender, and they often feel that he should also see it from their's. LaFave states:

'In Wichita the point has been reached where the police often avoid arresting for traffic offences because of the loss of respect engendered by such action. Assigning even to traffic work has become a personnel problem because the officers are subjected to considerable abuse and vituperation by the citizenry. When a traffic offender is written up, the officer really has to "sell" the ticket, sometimes talking to the offender for up to fifteen minutes' (ibid. p. 222n.).

I was not aware of traffic offenders presenting this sort of problem in any of the American departments I visited, but the point is very relevant. Policemen do not like taking aggressive action unless they believe they have public support, and they often refuse to enforce the law upon their fellow citizens if they believe it would be unfair to do so. Full enforcement would require policemen to be far more detached from society than is possible under the present system.

LAW ENFORCEMENT AND POLICE DISCRETION

Quite separate from the question of whether the police should have any discretion in law enforcement is the question of how they in fact exercise the discretion they are acknowledged to possess.

At some times and in some districts, the police enforce legislation more strictly than the letter of the law allows. In the rougher neighbourhoods they will disperse groups from the street corners to prevent the conditions arising in which fights and disturbances most easily start. A larger group on the pavements at the end of a church service or in a middle-class neighbourhood will be left undisturbed. Offences such as obstructing the highway, loitering, and vagrancy are difficult to define objectively, and the laws governing them are used by the police to frustrate activities that seem likely to cause trouble. The police will also utilize the law more rigorously in dealing with known criminals, for it may be dangerous to allow them the same latitude as the law-abiding citizens. However, as my research has focused on patrol rather than detective work, I have not attempted to collect information systematically on such matters. The only example of what seemed over-enforcement to come my way was a case mentioned in Chapter 3, (p. 74 above) when a drunken man was arrested in his own house on grounds which seemed legally dubious but humanly justifiable. His wife was on the verge of nervous collapse, and from his demeanour it seemed as if he would go on harrying her; though there might technically be no assault, there was a possibility of the situation's becoming much worse.

LaFave describes seven cases in which the police arrested or charged a particular offender though they would not normally have invoked the law for the offence in question. These cases were ones that came to attention in the American Bar Foundation survey of the administration of criminal justice, and they illustrate not over-enforcement in particular cases so much as under-enforcement in the majority of instances. They fall into five categories: arrest to avoid a strain on police resources (arrests made at a domestic dispute because brawls in the household had necessitated police calls in the past); charges to maintain respect for the police (abusive motoring offender); arrest to maintain public image (social gamblers who made no attempt to conceal their activity); arrest because of an opportunity to punish a criminal who had been able to avoid convictions on more serious charges; arrest to aid in investigation of another offence (murder suspect arrested on vagrancy charge). In the same survey, cases were also recorded of non-enforcement: because of ambiguity in legislation or doubt as to the legislature's intentions; because a warning was considered sufficient; because the conduct in question was common among the offender's section of the population; because the victim did not desire prosecution or the offender's own conduct invalidated his claims; because the prosecution would achieve nothing, would lose the police public respect and support, or would entail disproportionate punishment for someone guilty of only a minor offence.

It seems clear from LaFave's discussion and from my own experience that in both Britain and the United States, where minor offences are concerned, under-enforcement is a general rule. It is advisable, however, to distinguish between cases in which the policeman does not invoke the law because of the nature of the offence and those in which he fails to do so because of the character of the offender. Regarding the first category, policemen feel that it is fruitless to proceed against offenders if the courts are unwilling or reluctant to convict people for the offence in question. Thus in both countries, officers complain that it is difficult to get a conviction for dangerous driving unless such driving contributed to an accident. Carolina City officers had many tales to tell of how persons convicted of a motoring offence would fight to retain their driving licence, and of how juries were sympathetic towards them; the prospect of a long tussle in the courts may make the police reduce the charge in the belief that this improves their chance of getting a conviction that will not be reversed on appeal. They also said that it was no longer much use bringing charges for loitering or vagrancy. A different illustration of the same principle is found when a man charges larceny against a woman to whom he has given money, expecting her services as a prostitute in return, and he has been tricked. In such cases it is considered that the complainant does not come to court with 'clean hands' and either the court may be unwilling to treat it as a case of larceny or the police may be unwilling to prosecute.

Social control cannot be maintained by enforcement of the criminal law alone. There are many instances of wrongful behaviour which can only be punished by civil actions. Frequently members of the public are unwilling to take such action either because the matter at issue is too trivial or because they do not have the public good at heart. Certain it is, though, that they often expect the police to act for them. LaFave writes:

> 'When a woman called precinct headquarters and reported that in the course of paying for her meal in a restaurant she had been bilked out of some money, the lieutenant answering the call suggested she report to the station so that a complaint could be made out against the person who had cheated her. When the woman indicated she only wanted her money back, the lieutenant said, "Then, madam, you have the wrong department. Please call the lonely hearts club". He then hung up the phone' (op. cit. p. 212n.).

Similarly, in Georgia City a man came up to a police lieutenant and reported that he was unable to collect his property from an apartment where he had been living because of threats from his former landlord. The officer suspected that the complainant had been living in a homosexual relationship with the other man and thought that it was not the job of the police to do private citizens' dirty work, so he declined to take any action.[1] How far enforcement of the law in some of these borderline cases is a responsibility of the police rather than of private citizens is open to argument.

At times, strict enforcement of the law would be contrary to public policy or to the ideas that once were termed 'natural justice'. Thus

---

[1] Compare the recent objection of an English judge to hire-purchase companies' using the county courts as debt-collecting agencies.

policemen everywhere have discovered that if a woman complains on a Saturday night that her husband has come home drunk and has assaulted her, it is often futile to arrest the husband. Many policemen who have done this have found the man difficult to subdue and before they have got him out of the house they have received a hearty crack over the head from the now doubly aggrieved wife who has changed sides and come to the aid of her ill-used spouse. Whatever happens on the Saturday night she may well appear at the gaol next morning with his breakfast and the announcement that she is unwilling to give evidence against him—for she, after all, has to live with the man and it may be long enough before he forgives her for having called in the police. Should the case go to trial, however, and the man be convicted, it is certain that the wife and children will have to bear most of the financial burden of the sentence imposed by the magistrate. Policemen naturally doubt whether the ends of justice are served by prosecution in cases like these. An officer in Felsmere City said jocularly that the law of assault and battery was suspended on Christmas Eve—not because assaults were frequent, but because no court sat on Christmas Day and the police had no authority to allow bail on this charge. Being unwilling to keep a man away from his family over Christmas they preferred, if his behaviour had not been particularly objectionable, to charge him with disorderly conduct or some minor offence that permitted bail. Not only the time and season but the place also may be relevant to a decision whether or not to enforce the law. The police will turn a blind eye upon drunks and revellers in some neighbourhoods, who, if they were to appear on the main streets of the town, or amid the traffic, would be arrested immediately.

An English example of how the police may use discretion in deciding upon the allocation of their resources between different kinds of law enforcement was provided in 1963 by an announcement by the chief constable of Southend. He stated that though cases of shoplifting brought to his notice would be thoroughly investigated, he did not intend to prosecute the offenders at the public's expense unless there were very good reasons for doing so.[1] Such a decision may be defended if it gives the police more time to investigate serious

[1] Doubts about the legality of this statement were expressed in questions in the House of Lords on 2 April 1963.

crimes. It is also clear that shopkeepers have benefited from high-pressure salesmanship and from the open display of goods which excites the customer's desire to possess them; if their methods lead to more shoplifting it is reasonable to expect that the cost of counter-measures should be borne by the shops rather than by the public purse. Moreover, a fair proportion of petty shoplifters are not the sort of offenders who are best dealt with by a routine prosecution.

Sometimes police treatment of an offender is influenced by his personal characteristics. Some citizens try to obey the law because they believe that they should, and not because they fear the police (though they may do that too). If they make a genuine mistake (a traffic offence, perhaps) and are treated in the same fashion as a persistent offender who simply took a chance on it, they feel offended and may in future concentrate upon dodging the police instead of upon observing the law. If the police enforce traffic laws rigidly they may reduce motorists' commitment to the prescribed norms and the level of observance will fall. Every society acknowledges the additional claims of the person with a good record, and the principle is acknowledged in court when a first offender with a notable war record is given a lighter sentence. People do not see the law as concerned only with shortcomings; they expect previous good behaviour to tell in their favour, but there is no good means whereby the police or the courts may calculate people's moral credit. The law-abiding citizen also gains psychological rewards from his good conduct, paid in the coin of self-esteem; if he is prosecuted, this is apt to destroy his image of himself as a good citizen. Whether or not the law has been fairly administered, if the offender feels unfairly treated he is no longer so strongly motivated to obey the law. An awareness of the feelings of their fellow citizens underlies the belief of many Scottish policemen that traffic offences are often best dealt with by a verbal warning. Sometimes they only draw the driver's attention to his mistake and say no more.

This view of the relation of law to morality is particularly relevant to traffic offences. It seems reasonable to suppose that there is a point in traffic regulation beyond which increased enforcement provides only diminishing returns. The uniform treatment of all offenders leads motorists to regard a traffic citation as a natural hazard, and to have a citation issued against oneself is merely bad luck and not a

135

criticism of one's performance as a citizen. This would appear to be the attitude of many drivers in the United States, and the contrast can be highlighted by comparing the figures of citations for Carolina City (200,000 population; 132,000 registered motor vehicles) and for the Scottish city (474,000 population; 70,000 registered motor vehicles). In 1961 the Carolina City police issued 21,000 citations, approximately 90 per cent being for hazardous moving violations, and the remainder for no driver's licence, defective muffler (silencer), etc. The captain in charge of the traffic bureau stated:

'The 21,000 citations issued last year are very definitely under what we consider to be a justifiable amount to cope with the accident severity. Should this Bureau have an additional 40 per cent personnel increase, the number of citations issued would probably double, which in our opinion would still not be sufficient to meet the standard set forth by the National Safety Council because of the population and the number of vehicles registered in this area. I do feel that there is a saturation point which could be reached in any given locality; however, due to the personnel shortage, this point is far beyond reach at the present time and will be for years to come.'

For the Scottish city during the same year the figures show 4,994 offences reported under the Road Traffic Acts regarding motor vehicles, and 3,080 persons apprehended or cited. The chief constable's annual report further states: 'The motor patrol officers reported 2,393 owners and drivers of motor vehicles for various contraventions of road traffic legislation. They also administered 11,023 cautions to motorists and other road users for minor infringements of the law, not serious enough to warrant Court proceedings.' The preponderance of cautions over citations in the Scottish city suggests that they are felt to be more effective in dealing with most offenders. Some American states have a system whereby minor offenders are given an official warning by the Registrar of Motor Vehicles: if they are reported and already have three warnings against them during that year their licence is suspended. But independently of warnings the Carolina City figures suggest that motorists there heed only punitive action on the part of the police. Other American cities show a similar state of affairs, and higher rates for the issue of citations. As the level of social integration falls, the efficacy of verbal cautions is apt to decline. Presumably, therefore, there will be a tendency for British cities to follow the American pattern. Certainly recent 'courtesy campaigns' by English forces, relying upon the issue of cautions, have had less effect in diminishing the incidence of fatalities than have campaigns embodying stricter enforcement.

The action policemen take after stopping a motoring offender is often influenced by the demeanour of the driver. If he adopts an abusive attitude he is more likely to be charged. In the United States policemen may justify their taking a stricter line in such cases by arguing that it is necessary to maintain respect for the police.[1] In Britain police officers do not have to be so concerned with this aspect of the matter and a different interpretation seems necessary. If a constable approaches an offender knowing that he can either administer a caution or put him on a charge, he needs, in order to make his decision, some additional information about the driver and the circumstances that caused the offence. If, say, he finds that the driver passed the 'Halt' sign because his daughter in the back seat had just been stung by a bee, he may well take no further action. But if there are no special circumstances he is inclined to ask whether, if he lets the man off, he will be more careful or less careful next time. If the driver is quiet and apologetic the odds are that a warning will be more effective, but if he is one of the loud-mouthed type this is less likely: such a driver may conclude that if only he is belligerent enough, he can shout himself off, and that therefore he need not be careful. The offender's demeanour supplies the policeman with information relevant to the decision he has to make, and the decision, though on a subordinate level, is of a judicial character.

Other factors also make for under-enforcement. The volume of legislation today is such that no one individual can possibly remember all the actions that have been declared criminal. In Britain the road traffic law is now so complex that an ordinary patrol officer will be able to recollect only its more important provisions, and it may well be that some officers take action on matters that others believe unexceptionable. As he is personally liable for his decisions and can be made to pay damages if a civil action charging false arrest is upheld against him, the policeman who is unsure of the law may

[1] Cf. LaFave (1962, p. 231).

prefer not to take action (LaFave, 1962, p. 190). Some citizens also receive preferential treatment because of their special relation to the police: local politicians, the police chief's wife, brother officers, and so on. In a good police department any one of these would be prosecuted if he or she committed a serious offence and they can never be certain of preferential treatment even in minor matters. The Scottish press recently reported that in a routine check two constables stopped a car and found that the driver had not signed her driving licence. As the driver was the wife of their inspector they did not report her, but told her to show her licence to her husband. The inspector summoned the constables and reprimanded them for failing to report an offence. (The reader may ask himself what he would have done in the constables' position.) Normally, however, there is a risk that if the police prosecute someone close to them for a minor misdemeanour like a parking offence or a smoking chimney, it may put too much strain on the human machinery by which more important laws are enforced. Around almost every occupation there seems to be a little cluster of privileged persons who get some benefits—like cheaper services—from the people who practise the occupation. With the police, as with other occupations, to try and cut this away completely would not only be extremely difficult but would reduce the effectiveness of the people on the job. The police officer who would prosecute his grandmother for jay-walking would be someone with a deviant set of values.

Another aspect of the problem which is more relevant to circumstances in some American towns arises from social differences within the community. In some lower-class neighbourhoods different standards are customary, and if the police try to enforce the norms of the wider society this only induces the local people to cover up for one another because they do not wish the police to intervene in such matters. LaFave discusses in this connection police tolerance of offences such as bigamy, the carrying of knives, and assaults with knives in Negro neighbourhoods, and he points out that if the police insisted in prosecuting whether the aggrieved parties wished it or not, this might only lead to a drop in the number of offences reported (ibid, p. 208n. and p. 231n.). The sociologist, William Foote Whyte, in his account of the social structure of racketeering in a Massachusetts Italian neighbourhood observes that there is a contradiction

138

between the policeman's formal obligations and the relationships he needs to build up in such a community if he is to keep the peace. The policeman who takes a strictly legalistic view of his duties cuts himself off from the personal relations necessary to enable him to serve as a mediator of disputes in his area. Yet the policeman who develops close ties with the local people is unable to act against them with the vigour prescribed by the law (Whyte, 1943, p. 136).

In order to determine the best course of action in any particular case, a policeman must be able to separate the sheep from the goats. For the village policeman this is relatively easy; he knows the people he sees on his rounds and he has a good idea of their character. The city officer, however, meets many people he has never seen before and it is harder for him to tell from their appearance and behaviour what manner of men they are. He has insufficient information about many of the people he has to deal with, so it is very important that he should have good judgment in handling them. The most common complaint of supervising officers in urban police departments seems to be about what they consider the stupidity of some of their younger officers, whose lack of judgement creates problems for their colleagues and supervisors. This question came up in a recorded group discussion with some Scottish probationary police officers, and I reproduce some extracts (slightly edited) from it which are relevant to the present chapter:

I[1] What sort of case had you in mind when you spoke of special constables (i.e. reservists) who wanted to go booking everyone?

E Well, there was a drunk. In my opinion he was fit enough to get himself home but the special wanted to lift him. I just told him that you don't lift any person that you see staggering.

I This question of lifting somebody who is drunk but not too drunk is an interesting case because it bears upon the exercise of your discretion, doesn't it?

E Yes. It's just something you pick up.

[1] I signifies the author.

139

ɪ Now this is something you've learned on the beat, is it not? How much were you told about the use of discretion in your training? (*Looks round the table.*)

ᴄ It's just common knowledge.

ᴀ It comes to you every time you're on, more or less.

ʙ It's something you pick up that you're no' told, it's just . . .

ᴇ What I mean, you just seem to be able to judge straight, you just look at the person, it just sort of comes to you, 'Oh, he'll make it O.K.'

ᴅ Most of police work anyway is common sense.

ᴄ Common sense, aye.

ᴅ I was out with a special one day, it was on one of the outlying beats, and there was this chap and he was drunk, lying on the ground. Well, I knew that the chap lived in that area. The special was all for taking him down to the box to get a van out to take him in. I spoke to the chap and after a while I managed to get his address and I took him home. The special was gey quiet after that. He would rather have seen the police take him in.

ᴇ What did you do after you'd taken him home, like?

ᴅ That was it finished.

ᴄ We do that quite often in our force, too.

ᴅ You would take him home?

ʙ (*Interrupting*) We never do that. We get a bloke drunk and incapable, and suppose he was lying outside his own doorstep, in the roadway, we take him home and go back the next day and book him for being drunk and incapable.

ᴇ I wouldn't agree to that.

ᴅ If you know a person is near his home I think it's unfair.

ʙ What do you lift a drunk for? Because he is a danger to himself is one of the reasons. I mean he could be run over lying outside his own gate as lying five or six hundred yards away

140

. . . and you find next Saturday night he's lying outside his door again.

D I don't mean to say that if it were a regular habit I'd let him off with it. . . .

I This may be a difference of opinion or it may be a difference in practice between two different forces. Where would you say (*to* D) that you picked up this idea that you should take this sort of customer home? Wouldn't you have picked it up from older men?

D I picked it up from a constable that got on very well with the public.

I (*to* B) But you, in your force, must have seen other police officers going round and charging the man the day after?

B Well, that was the habit. As far as I'm concerned, I mean.

D That's your procedure.

B This is my own opinion. I mean, I'm no' wanting to be number one popularity boy in the town. I've got to do the job. When I came into the force I swore I would discharge the duties of constable. The thing as far as I can see it is, it's all right to be lenient. I mean, if you catch a boy stealing apples, you're no' going to drag him to the office and charge him with theft. I don't know about the rest of you but back to when I was a boy, I ken I've stolen apples: it was part of the process of growing up. But a bloke lying in the middle of the road is a danger to himself plus a danger to other road users. (*To* Banton) You're a civilian, let's bring you into this. You drive along the road and you don't see the bloke on the dark side and you run over him. You'll remember that for the rest of your life. You've always got it on your conscience that you've killed this bloke. I think that you are duty bound to charge him.

D I don't say I'd blame you for that, but I've found that any person I've helped is a good source of information regarding any other inquiries I've got.

141

B Can you honestly sit there and tell me that some drunk that you've helped into a house has ever benefited you later on?

D Yes, that beat I was referring to is one of our roughest beats and there's a lot of. . . .

B (*Interrupting*) And how does this bloke come to give you information?

D Well, you see, if I meet the chap and I have an inquiry, I'll maybe ask him, 'Have you heard anything?'

B How did he ken it was you helped him that night?

D Because his wife pointed me out to him one day.

I (*A few minutes later*) If, let us say, you picked up a man drunk who occupied a fairly responsible position in the community and you thought, 'Now, if I put this man on a charge this is going to be a far more serious matter for him than it would be for someone who was a farm labourer. Everybody is going to hear about this; the man's reputation will sink and it will be a very severe blow to him.' Would you be inclined to exercise your discretion differently? (*Turns to* C, *from a country station.*)

C No. We find that it's entirely the same, no matter who they are. If you do that once you may as well pack up and go.

D Quite. Why do you think he should be favoured anyway?

I I'm not suggesting that he should be.

B Why should they be? Because one bloke's got £50 in his pocket and another one's got five shillings and the two of them's committing the same offence, you're no' going to say that the one's a decent bloke because he's got £50.

I No. The argument would be that it was a more severe punishment for the one man than for the other.

B Oh yes. I mean I'm agreeing with you there. I mean his status in life is probably far better, but that is outwith the police; we have nothing to do with that.

E We had a case when we were instructed to go round and book those who had no parking lights and the Provost was one of them. He was booked for it and the constable who booked him was up in front of the chief constable the following morning. I disagree with that. The Provost was committing an offence the same as any other person. . . .

In discussions of this kind, the failure of the parties to take up questions and the way they mould them are often as illuminating as what they actually say!

This extract, apart from illustrating one of my sources of research material, points up some of the possible differences in the way young constables define the social situations they encounter. It mentions something that many officers can corroborate: a minor kindness to an offender may dispose him to supply useful information on other occasions. The range of situations with which the new constable may be confronted is so varied that instructors cannot cover every contingency and they have to depend on the constable's common sense. How, the supervisor will ask, can you teach a man common sense? Either he has got it or he hasn't. The usual policy is to rely upon his picking up the general principles by accompanying more senior men. From the recruit's point of view, also, this delicate balance between contrary obligations may be a source of embarrassment. 'Everything about this job's so vague', one complained, 'no matter what you're doing you can always be told you should be doing something else.' The regulations all too often tell a policeman what he must not do, and fail to indicate what positive steps should be taken. Yet this quality of judgement which is so difficult to teach or to measure is nevertheless one of the things that are looked for when promotions are to be made. A Carolina City supervisor commented on a patrolman who had recently asked him whether, if he saw a man driving a vehicle late one evening, with a dealer's registration plates and two girls inside (i.e. presumably using a motor dealer's registration for pleasure and not for purposes of trade), he would give him a ticket. The supervisor said that his action would depend upon what the man said. Whereupon the patrolman remarked that he would certainly give him a ticket; the law was clear and his job was to enforce it. The supervisor replied that this attitude of his explained why he was still a patrolman after fifteen years' service.

It is important, therefore, to consider the sources from which policemen draw their ideas as to the way in which they should exercise their discretionary powers. Apart from their training, the example of their colleagues, and the advice or instruction of their supervisors, two sources are especially influential. In the first place there are the courts. In the long run a police officer can go only as far as the courts will let him; the man who lacks a sense of judgement will probably come to grief in court some day. The courts provide a good expression of the consensus of responsible opinion, and to a certain extent (more marked when the police view and public opinion differ) they tend to sit in judgement on the arresting officer. The policeman learns in court what cases the court will accept. For example, an American officer said that a judge had once thrown out a prosecution of a motorist who had turned out of the centre lane of traffic; there had been a violation, but since there had been no accident or hindrance to other drivers, the accused was discharged. The policeman soon discovers – if he did not know it already – that offenders who have the money to engage an attorney are treated with more consideration and have a better chance of acquittal. In this way he learns the values by which his society is really ruled (as opposed to the ones praised in ceremonial speeches) and how to operate within this context. Policemen generally agree that there is one law for the rich and another for the poor; many of them accept this as one of the facts of life without in any way approving it. The police officer is frequently a critic of society; through what he sees in the courts, as well as on the beat, he is in an unparalleled position to observe the machinery of society in operation. It also seems as if the procedure of the courts has an indirect effect upon the culture of the police occupation. Several times when I have been with a group of policemen I have been struck by the readiness of members of the group to argue against almost any proposition stated by one of their number or to point out other interpretations of his facts. The policeman knows that any of his decisions may later be judged in court and he gets used to anticipating arguments that could be advanced against them. In the same way he will readily play devil's advocate to one of his colleagues.

In the second place, a policeman derives much of his sense of judgement from his participation in the society he polices. Out of uniform he is subject to exactly the same controls as any other citizen. He mixes with other citizens on an equal footing and soon hears what they think about the police. British and American officers will readily comment upon the way the press and the public fail to appreciate their problems and rush in with criticisms; they are very conscious of this criticism and much of it impinges on their private lives. The resulting awareness of the public's point of view influences many of a policeman's decisions in the course of his daily work. Many times, when discussing his treatment of an offender, has an officer observed: 'I know that if I were in his place I should feel so-and-so'. In a colonial or military-style police where the officers live in barracks and do not mingle with the public this kind of understanding must be greatly reduced. The influence of a policeman's private roles upon how he performs his public role is of the utmost importance, and it is not limited to his off-duty experiences. While on patrol the policeman learns a great deal about human nature which may later stand him in good stead.

Like so many aspects of police work, the question of discretion in law enforcement is not something that can be considered apart from the topic of supervision or from the policeman's role in society. Later passages in this and subsequent chapters will also hark back to this matter, but sufficient has been written to show how problematic it is. Indeed Roscoe Pound, the great lawyer, once wrote: 'A balance between rules of law . . . and discretion, which will give effect both to the general security, and the individual life, with the least impairment of either, is perhaps the most difficult problem in the science of law' (Pound, 1930, pp. 40–1). LaFave concludes his survey of American practice:

> 'The first step is to elevate police discretion from the *sub rosa* position it now occupies; the role of the police as decision-makers must be expressly recognized. Then, as has been found possible with respect to other administrative agencies, the areas in which discretion properly may be exercised must be delimited, principles to govern its exercise must be discovered. Only then can it be said with certainty that police non-enforcement does not contravene some of our most cherished democratic values' (ibid. p. 239).

The British sociologist is bound to feel that even this is insufficient. Consider a recent English case in which Miss Pat Arrowsmith, the

advocate of nuclear disarmament, was prosecuted under the Highways Act for obstructing the highway. She addressed a crowd in a
place often used for open-air meetings. The police asked her to call
the crowd in closer so as to minimize the obstruction; she and the
crowd complied, leaving some of the road clear. The partial obstruction continued for twenty minutes, after which she was charged. On
appeal it was argued among other things that many meetings were
held in that place and that the police often helped by keeping a free
passage for traffic. The Lord Chief Justice said he could not concern
himself with 'what happened on other occasions'. The police, he
added, 'cannot prosecute every obstructor of the highway but must
exercise a wise discretion when to prosecute'.[1] Was Miss Arrowsmith given the same latitude as other offenders? No administrative
principles can ensure equity in circumstances so dependent on the
vagaries of human judgement. The only long-term solution to the
problem of police discretion is for the police and the public to
share the same norms of propriety. Some modern tendencies, as I
have indicated earlier, are making this ideal more and more difficult
to realize.

LAW AND MORALITY IN POLICE WORK

The observer who tried to predict, from a knowledge of the
criminal law alone, what actions an ordinary policeman would
take, would not be very successful. To explain what the policeman
actually does it is necessary to see his actions as being governed
much more by popular morality than by the letter of the law; most
often morality and the law coincide, but when they do not, it
is usually morality that wins. According to popular morality it
is wrong that a wife and children should pay twice over for the
husband's drunkenness; right that people should have a little
extra leeway on Christmas Eve;[2] right that roughnecks and criminals
should be treated more severely; right that a man who is bullying
his unoffending wife should receive some correction. In the same

[1] *Arrowsmith* v. *Jenkins*, Queen's Bench Division, 6 March 1963, as reported in
the *Police Review*, 23 August 1963.
[2] As Durkheim suggested, integration varies not only between village and city
but between workday and holiday; when the collective ceremonies are re-enacted,
such as at Christmas or a coronation, integration is increased, and with it the
individual's moral claims upon society.

way, I was told by a supervising officer in Scotland that if one of their men failed to help an old woman who obviously needed assistance to cross the road, and this was seen by one of his superiors, he would be reprimanded although there was no law or regulation which stated that he should help such people.

It is noticeable how policemen prefer to work within the popular morality, and to persuade rather than prosecute. They see their office as being vested with moral authority as well as legal power. Authority has been defined as 'rightful power'; power itself is not necessarily rightful. Legal power, like physical power, gives one man the ability to force another to do his will. But if this power is seen as rightful, as authority, the second man will probably comply with the former's wishes because he feels morally obliged to do so. In these terms policemen possess both authority and power. Many criminals will not consciously recognize policemen as having authority over them, and in these circumstances the police attempt simply to bring the men before the courts. They are not concerned to justify themselves to the people they have arrested because they are sure of the approval of the remainder of the community. But in most situations the police seem to expect those with whom they deal to regard policemen as being morally justified in dealing with them as they do. They try to get offenders to recognize explicitly the norm of proper conduct and to agree to observe it more carefully in future. If they do have to 'book' someone they prefer to have him believe that he deserved no better. I have seen more arrests in America than in Britain, but there I was struck by the familiar behaviour of the arresting officers towards the people they had arrested, and the extent to which they were willing to argue the rights and wrongs of the issue with them.

This preference of policemen for taking actions which even the people who suffer from them have to concede are morally right, seems to be a fundamental factor in explaining why the police are so often reluctant to enforce the law. The margin they allow the public is usually generous. For example, in Carolina City the police operate a speed check, a device actuated by two tubes which are placed across the road a set distance apart. The time I saw it in operation it was placed round a bend on a road restricted to 35 m.p.h. Drivers were not given a citation for speeding unless their speed exceeded

44 m.p.h. Even so, the police did not like this to be thought of as a trap, so they issued a notice on the preceding day stating that they would check speeds on a certain road. They indicated the road but not the exact place. This notice was broadcast along with other news on a local radio transmission. At higher speeds they allowed a margin of 5 m.p.h. but–and this was characteristic–if the driver had exceeded 55 m.p.h. they would reduce his reported speed to 54 m.p.h. unless he had been driving recklessly, because driving in excess of 55 m.p.h. on other than certain highways was a state offence for which a relatively severe penalty was prescribed. (It is also possible that by reducing the reported speed the officer increased the chance of having the accused plead guilty and of therefore saving himself the trouble of a court appearance.)

In the Scottish city I have seen policemen show what seemed remarkable tolerance for parking offences. A constable on patrol in a central street, which was particularly liable to traffic jams and in which parking was forbidden, twice found cars parked there–one considerably more than the regulation distance from the kerb. He went into a succession of shops to try to find the drivers and to ask them to remove their vehicles. He explained to me that although drivers were not allowed to wait for any time at all where 'No Waiting' signs were displayed, the police normally took no action unless they waited for more than twenty minutes.[1] As will be remembered from Chapter 2, there is a special parking patrol in this city. When I referred to it in conversation with the superintendent of the division, his immediate response was to explain that this patrol was not established to increase the number of prosecutions but to keep the major streets clear. The patrol's job was to help drivers and shopkeepers, not to harry them. This was a very defensive reaction compared with that characteristic of American police departments. By their standards the enforcement of parking regulations in the Scottish city would appear lax, for the patrol I accompanied normally allowed rather

[1] The officer could not have proceeded against the motorist without a supporting witness; in these circumstances he would not ask a passer-by to corroborate but would seek out a fellow policeman, and when he had found one, the two of them would have to keep the parked vehicle under observation for twenty minutes if they were to prefer a charge; in all probability it would have been driven away before then. The reluctance to prosecute should therefore in this instance be ascribed primarily to the law and to police organization.

more than the regulation time before re-checking the vehicles parked in restricted areas. Consider the following incident. We came up to a spot where a driving school had an office in a central street, and no cars were supposed to wait immediately outside the office. Two cars from the driving school were waiting there and two more came up. About ten minutes later two of them were still there when two instructors came out of the office, separately. The first, who had seen the policemen standing watching, said, 'It's all right for you chaps' (implying that he knew he was infringing the regulations but could see no easy alternative), so one of the policemen told him he should take his car to one of the side streets to do his paper work. The second instructor came out and the policemen asked him, 'How long are you going to leave your car there, Sir?' and went on to say that he would do better to leave it in a lane to the left. The instructor blushed and remarked, 'I've been on your job, too'. The policemen walked off; they said their superiors required evidence of fifteen minutes' waiting (two witnesses) even opposite a 'No Waiting' sign before they would approve a prosecution. The interesting feature from a sociologist's standpoint is not the correctness or otherwise of the policy adopted (the increasing pressure on parking space may well have long since caused the police to be less lenient than they were at the time of these observations), but the implicit opinion on the part of the police authorities that it was more effective for police-men to go to such lengths in relying on persuasion rather than prosecution.

In every police force I have visited, some policeman has at some time volunteered the remark that it is a serious thing to deprive a subject of his liberty. One man in Scotland explained this view, saying that one never knew all the circumstances of a case, such as what had happened at home to the man who went out and got drunk. In a discussion with probationers one man expressed considerable regret at having taken the legally correct procedure in a case against a juvenile, because he afterwards learned more about his circum-stances and felt that he could quite properly have been cautioned instead of having a blot on his career that could never be entirely removed. Policemen both in America and in Scotland have been known to resign after only a short spell of duty because they felt so guilty at having arrested people, and I have heard men with twenty years' service say that they still feel guilty whenever they have to charge someone. It would seem, therefore, that when dealing with the more ordinary offences the policeman frequently identifies to some degree with the person arrested and feels as if he has betrayed him. In the old days the executioner was supposed to ask for his victim's pardon before he beheaded him, and many policemen seem to know the same feeling. They tell stories of how people they have arrested have afterwards turned out to be really bad characters, or have later reformed and thanked the arresting officer. These stories are doubtless true, but their telling does tend to assuage any such guilt.[1]

The fact that a police officer is himself a member of the community whose norms he has to enforce accounts in large measure for the difference between the everyday actions of the peace officer on patrol and the more exciting deeds of his colleagues on the screen. Because the policeman is a member of the society, he perceives the behaviour of his fellow members in moral terms as good or bad, and not as constituting a market in the way a manufacturer or retailer might see it. He can get more satisfaction from his role when he feels it has moral support, and consequently he will relax the law's provisions in order to win the goodwill of the offender (who will feel he has been leniently treated and therefore ought to try harder to observe the law in the future) or to bolster his own feeling of being a human and goodhearted person rather than a sort of hanging judge. Thus a Scottish police officer once remarked in discussion: 'The essence of a good cop is the man who can book a man in the morning and be able to hold a friendly conversation with him in the evening.'

If police organization encourages the development of in-group solidarity among its officers, it is likely to remove them more from the informal control of community expectations and to reduce their

[1] A parallel can be drawn between the policeman's 'betrayal' of the person he arrests and the conduct of people responsible for someone's being committed to a mental hospital. Erving Goffman discusses the various stages by which persons are brought into this unattractive status and points to the way different agents deal with their guilt about depriving the patient of his freedom. He adds: 'His (i.e. the patient's) showing consideration for those who are moving him towards the hospital allows them to show consideration for him, with the joint result that these interactions can be sustained with some of the protective harmony characteristic of ordinary face-to-face dealings' (Goffman, 1961, p. 141). Cf. also Goffman (1956, pp. 473–502, especially p. 497).

moral authority. A former captain from a large American police department testified that when his department had attempted to reduce crime in certain neighbourhoods by employing a 'saturation' policy and flooding these districts with policemen, the results were three-fold: (i) the crime figures for the neighbourhood rose because the police observed more offences, and the public, seeing police officers nearby, reported more offences than they otherwise did; (ii) serious crime was displaced to other neighbourhoods; (iii) police brutality increased because, being in groups, the police tended to gang up and observe norms of police solidarity. The results of putting two officers together in a patrol car illustrate the same point. The Georgia City police had recently adopted a policy whereby only one man was allocated to a patrol car, though in the busier zones a temporary partner was usually given him. Many officers there and elsewhere disapprove of this practice, pointing to cases in which officers have gone to calls by themselves and been injured. In Georgia City I was told that, on the contrary, trouble with violent prisoners usually derived from over-confidence or aggressiveness on the part of the police officer.[1] In the event of a possibly dangerous call extra cars would be sent or the first officer would await reinforcements. Most cases of trouble with prisoners came from two-men cars. An officer who was by himself had to use tact and persuasion, to exert moral authority and not unadorned power. A similar view is expressed by an American police administrator writing in a leading handbook:

'An officer patrolling alone must give first attention to beat duties. There are no distractions other than those he is obligated to notice on his beat, and he is completely self-dependent for his own safety and welfare. It has been demonstrated that an officer patrolling by himself in a car is actually safer than when accompanied by a brother officer. The presence of a second officer appears to discourage reasonable caution, either because of pride that prevents the second officer from observing danger or because of failure to take suitable precautions lest the companion interpret caution as cowardice. When an officer is alone in a patrol car he knows that he has no one else to rely upon in the event of trouble. Consequent-

[1] See p. 69 above.

ly he is cautious in stepping into dangerous situations and is better prepared to take care of unexpected emergencies' (Institute for Training in Municipal Administration, 1961, p. 242).[1]

The offender who is approached by a single officer, it would seem, sometimes offers no resistance because the policeman is not abusive or threatening. If there are two officers and they exceed their moral authority, relying upon superior power, the prisoner may be more inclined to rebel.

Many anecdotes could be cited by policemen to support the thesis that even criminals recognize the moral authority of the police when it does not interfere with their own plans. A Scottish detective was searching a store in which some burglars were thought to be hiding. There was no sign of them. Then the detective thought he saw a bale of straw shift slightly. He brought his baton down hard on the top of the bale and there was a fearsome yell. A man was hiding inside it and he had caught the blow on his spine. He was hospitalized and later convicted. Sometime afterwards the detective was promoted sergeant in the patrol branch and he had occasion to call at this man's house. Seeing him on the doorstep, the wife called 'George, look who's come!' and ushered him in. George – who had reason to bear him a grudge – came and shook his hand vigorously, congratulating him on his promotion. George's son had got into trouble and he proposed to thrash him severely. He said: 'I don't want him to grow up like me. It's too late for me to change now, but he's got a chance to lead a better life.' George's responses to the policeman and to his son's delinquency were both situational responses attitudinally inconsistent with his response to other, apparently similar, situations. Likewise, if criminals trust a detective not to reveal the source of his information and not to use it against them, they will be more ready to help him in his inquiries; but if he ever adopts the deceitful attitude common in the criminal fraternity he loses their respect immediately. Thus, whatever they say about the police, criminals may behave as if they expected policemen to maintain the truth-telling standards of the wider community.[2] However, some

[1] Cf. 'One-man Patrol Cars', *The Police Chief*, May 1963, pp. 18–24.
[2] I am indebted to John Mack of Glasgow University for observations on this point.

writers insist that police morality operates on the same level as that of the professional criminal, and that both respond to expediency rather than to principle. They say that between detectives and criminals there is a working relationship which blunts the moral issues.[1] Maybe there is truth in both these viewpoints, though I know too little of the subject and of the variations in place and circumstance to guess how much truth there is in either. Yet I am inclined to think that the criminals' partial admission of the moral claims of the policeman may underlie the viciousness with which they have treated convicted former policemen in some American penitentiaries, as if the ordinary criminals argued: 'I never had much of a chance, but you did. You're lower than us; you never had any right to tell other people they were doing wrong.' However, American policemen with whom I discussed this, while reiterating that other convicts treated former policemen so roughly that such men sometimes had to be put in solitary confinement, insisted that it was because in the eyes of the other convicts they were still identified with the police. The relatively greater reluctance of the public in the United States to recognize their police as possessing moral authority also ties in with the very much more restricted use of women in the police service there.

In describing the moral element in the interaction between the policeman and a member of the public, it is relevant to observe that when an officer answers a call he usually meets the complainant and not the violator. Usually the complainant emphasizes the moral wrong that he or she has suffered and not the legal wrong, if any. The complainant says that someone else has done wrong and, in explaining what it was and why it was wrong, he or she inevitably reaffirms what in the circumstances would be right or moral conduct. Consider a trivial but representative case. Two American police officers went to interview a woman who complained of a neighbouring boy's behaviour. Several of this boy's brothers and sisters had been in trouble with the police, and their mother would not cooperate with them. The boy was emotionally disturbed but because he was friendly with her son the complainant had allowed him to come to the house and had been considerate towards him. But the boy had behaved badly and in the end she was obliged to forbid him the house and to tell her son to avoid him. The boy had responded by making anony-

[1] Cf. Parker (1963, pp. 7-8).

mous threats over the 'phone, by breaking the garage windows with shot from his 'BB gun' (airgun), and by insulting her in public. She could stand it no longer and wanted the boy to be checked. Notice the following features of the case: the woman sought to justify her own actions in the matter; she was complaining that the boy's conduct was morally inexcusable; she did not know whether it constituted a legal offence and never spoke about legal remedies; she wanted the police to put pressure on the boy and his parents so that he would behave better, not that they should take him to court. This is typical. By complaining of the boy's bad behaviour the woman implicity reaffirms the accepted view of how boys ought to behave. When the policeman answers a call, as often as not it is this reference to how someone ought to have behaved that he hears first. He is reminded of what morality expects at the same time as he is told of an offence.

Being members of the society themselves, policemen share the same values as the other members. If the society is corrupt the policemen will be to some degree corrupt. If the society sets store by differences of social class, this will affect the police both as an occupational group in the class hierarchy and in their dealings with people of varying class. This means that the police will use their discretion in ways which diverge from the ideal of perfect justice but which conform to the pattern of social control. A police force of Martians who did not share the imperfect norms of the population and who obeyed an extra-terrestrial philosopher would scarcely be as effective in the long run as a human, if imperfect, police department.

The personal involvement of the police officer in the popular morality and in the emotions of the people he has to deal with is at times striking. Locking up drunks soon becomes a routine, but personal distress rarely loses its power to move a man's heart. I remember going with two Scottish officers to deliver a message: they had to tell a woman that her husband had been drowned on holiday. When we got to the door one of the policemen said to me: 'You go in instead of me. I can't stand these things.' Then I have noticed how in the event of a bad case, like that of the father who interfered with his daughter (see pp. 75–6 above), even a hardened patrolman feels moral indignation over a man's conduct. Many an officer has at some time or other dipped into his own pocket to help the children of someone he has locked up. Such incidents are not surprising once attention has been called to them, but their significance for the character of police work can easily be overlooked nonetheless. The moral involvement of policemen extends into other areas too. When the court fails to pass what the officer would consider a sufficiently severe sentence on an offender he feels that a negative judgement has been passed on his own commitment to social order. Then just as a policeman may feel guilty about having arrested a person, about having deprived him of his personal dignity as well as his liberty, so may he feel guilty about having failed to arrest someone if this failure results in the degradation of the social self of the man or of some other member of the society.[1] For example, an American officer mentioned that one Christmas Eve he had seen a man staggering homewards with several parcels that looked like presents for his children. As it was Christmas Eve the officer decided not to lock him up. Next day he learned that a little further along the man had been hit by an automobile and injured. He still felt guilty about not having taken the man into the gaol for his own protection.

Popular morality, of course, changes. A generation ago a policeman could punish a troublesome juvenile by giving him a good cuff on the head, or he could clear up a case of wife-assault by giving the offender a taste of his own medicine. In some of the poorer districts in both Scottish and American cities public opinion used to support such sanctions because it considered them appropriate; now it no longer does so.[2] In the increasingly complicated circumstances of life in industrial societies, informal controls languish; the powers and responsibilities of many roles – teachers and doctors as well as policemen – have to be more closely defined because the public are no longer so willing to place the same trust in them. Formal controls displace shared understandings and the people who have to play these roles complain that they have lost status.

[1] The phrase 'some other member of the society' is not an unnecessary circumlocution. In the American South many Whites would not perceive Negroes as having a dignity that could be degraded by arrest in the same way as a white man's.

[2] An example of this is provided by a recent case in northern Scotland. A policeman hit a foul-mouthed and cheeky juvenile, giving him a bleeding nose and a bruised lip; because of the attention drawn to the incident the government appointed a tribunal of inquiry (cf. *The allegation of assault on John Waters*, Cmnd. 718, 1959).

155

WORK AND SUPERVISION

There is a sharp contrast between the dramatic public ideal of the policeman's role as it is sometimes pictured on television, and the reality that is known by the people who have to play it. 'Work' for the policeman means persistent observation at times when he is bored, answering stupid questions, satisfying niggling supervisors, studying his books, and doing all sorts of odd jobs. The recruit often thinks of his new office in more romantic terms, and when he first goes on patrol he is subject to what has been termed 'reality shock'.[1] An older officer in an American city said that he spent his second day as a policeman on the streets with a more experienced colleague. The latter took a telephone call from headquarters, turned round, and said, 'Come on, we've got a job'. 'What is it?' the recruit asked with suppressed excitement. 'We've got to go and bury a dead rat', the older man replied. This can scarcely be representative, but as the only public agency open twenty-four hours a day the police do sometimes get some strange tasks. A recollection of this contrast has prompted the practice of a senior officer in the Carolina City police, who keeps on his desk a plain brass door-knob, so that he will not forget the hours he had once to spend checking doors. But the moments of glamour and danger are also important to most police officers' conceptions of their role. Many join the police because they want 'action' and there is always the chance that the next sixty seconds may present the patrol officer with an incident requiring all the courage he has. Many of the younger American officers prefer to work on night shift when they can concentrate upon catching criminals, which they see as their real work. It is remarkable, too, how frequently I have been assured by officers I have been accompanying on patrol – in Scotland and in the United States – that it has been an unusually quiet night; either the laws of chance do not apply to patrol work or the busy shifts impress themselves on the patrolman's mind so strongly that all other ones seem to fall below standard.

Breaking in the recruit is often a painful experience for both parties. A favourite theme for stories in the *Police Review* is that of the older policeman's alarm when a probationer is detailed to patrol

[1] By Everett Cherrington Hughes. Compare the work in Edinburgh by Hewan Craig on the middle-class teacher who goes from the training college to a school in a rough working-class neighbourhood.

with him. So often the recruit is all too well-informed and energetic but has little appreciation of the complexity of the human material with which he has to deal. One American patrolman expressed a strong dislike for having to partner men who were new to the job, for many of them nevertheless thought they knew it all and would readily tell their partner what to do. Often, he complained, they were the type who loved to exercise authority, and would arrest a man without knowing on what charge they were arresting him. He recalled one newcomer who had given a citation to a driver because the bulb in his tail light had burned out. The senior man said to him, 'Maybe he didn't know it had burned out'. The recruit said, 'He's supposed to know'. 'Do you know', the first man asked, 'if any of your six bulbs have burned out?' and the other had to admit that he did not. Apart from the pressure of his colleagues other experiences induce the over-confident young officer to conform to the pattern established for his role: his apprehension about how he will react to danger; how he will respond when for the first time he has to deal with a sudden death; what he should do when he is subject to abuse from juveniles that is not quite sufficient to justify arrest.

It will be argued that an appreciation of the policeman's moral involvement in society is essential to an understanding of some of the current controversies and grievances among policemen in Britain. In the United States the moral elements do not seem to permeate police affairs to the same extent, which fits in with the general impression that American policemen are less committed to the social order (i.e. because of higher crime, their own lower prestige, and the way in which loyalties to an ethnic group often counter-balance loyalties to the total society). Two broad issues on the British scene which seem to bring out these fundamental assumptions are those of the scope of police work (particularly with reference to the delegation of minor duties to civilian auxiliaries) and the super-vision of patrolmen in the cities.

An American sociologist has maintained that members of any occupation attempt to find means of relegating unwanted duties to categories of workers beneath them, thereby keeping the clean work and getting rid of the dirty work (Hall, 1957). An example of this is provided by the introduction of ward maids to take over some of the less agreeable of a nurse's duties. But it would appear from British experience that a 'professional' work ideology tends to maintain the diffuseness of an occupational role and, in certain circumstances, to inhibit the creation of subordinate categories. Among nurses, the introduction of degree courses and the trend towards stratification by qualifications are subjects of heated controversy. Underlying much discontent of schoolteachers in the west of Scotland has been unease over a government policy which would 'dilute' the occupation and increase disparities between teachers of different qualifications. The police present a third instance. They have been criticized for not making more use of civilian employees, policewomen, and auxiliaries generally. Policemen may complain about having to do work they consider beneath the dignity of the law, such as impounding stray dogs or putting out 'No Parking' signs, but the only auxiliary occupation they have welcomed has been the school crossing-keeper's. The Police Federation roundly condemned the introduction of traffic wardens. The effectiveness of policewomen in dealing with juveniles is acknowledged but they are said to be no substitute for a man on the beat.

Two related factors responsible for some of the resistance on the part of the police are those of the utilization of scarce manpower and of organizational flexibility. Major football matches and other big events create pressing manpower demands; if clerical and other auxiliary jobs are being performed by policemen, these men can be called upon for patrol duties, giving senior officers a useful reserve of men. Similarly, if everyone is qualified to carry out the common role, men can be moved around fairly easily and directed to substitute for someone sick or on leave. The more specialized jobs become, the less flexibility there will be of this kind. On the other hand, certain jobs such as those of mechanics, car washers, cleaners in small county stations, etc., have been taken over by civilians, and policemen would not now wish to have them back. The number of civilians and policemen employed continues to rise steadily.

Yet it is doubtful if these considerations, even combined with any temperamental reluctance to adopt new methods on the part of senior police officers, constitute a sufficient explanation of police resistance to what they regard as dilution. British police officers seem to resent specialization and the employment of civilians, because such developments strike at the conception of the police officer as personally committed to the people he protects, and substitute a more technically conceived, limited-liability kind of role. It is the officer on foot patrol who is regarded as the representative policeman. The tasks he performs are so varied that he has to be an 'all-rounder'. The challenging variety of these tasks develops the capacities and understanding of the policeman in a way that few occupations at his socio-economic level could do, and police officers say that the variety of duties is one of the most satisfying features of the job. Like a nurse, a policeman performs many unskilled and unpleasant tasks because he sees himself as providing a service rather than fitting into a bureaucracy. The conditions under which police work is carried out underline the distinction between policemen and others, so that policemen emphasize their shared experience and common status. The work of divisional plain-clothes officers in the Scottish city illustrates this to some extent. The outsider might anticipate that they are in plain clothes so that they will not be recognized as policemen. In practice they do not work incognito. If they are not recognized personally (which frequently happens) they regularly stand out among the people with whom they are mixing. They assume that many bystanders will recognize them as policemen so they behave much as they would were they wearing uniform. Their tendency is to keep to the common role of constable, not to emphasize their special characteristics.

American police officers (especially in those cities most affected by the spoils system in local government) have been inclined, to a greater extent than British policemen, to see police work as a means of obtaining a steady job; they have resisted proposals to make over any of their work to civilians because they have seen this as robbing policemen of employment. American experience in connection with specialization may, however, provide the answer to a question which has been raised in Britain but which cannot easily be answered here because of the greater uniformity in police practice. The question is whether specialization, by improving police efficiency, improves police-public relations, or whether, by reducing contact and understanding between the parties, it affects relations adversely. Perhaps both may be true under different conditions. On the negative side it can be pointed out that, as previous chapters have shown, many of a policeman's contacts with the public are of a welfare nature. One

159

author states: 'It has been estimated that at least 90 per cent of all police business is not of a strictly criminal nature' (Gourley, 1954, p. 136). A research worker who studied the police department of a town near Felsmere City concluded: '26 per cent of all calls received at the station over a two-week period were requests for information; almost 50 per cent of all calls do not involve matters of a "police" nature' (Del Pesco, 1952). Good public relations may well depend on the marginal services provided by the police; if the citizen gets help when he needs it and meets officers in cooperative relations as well as in the occasional adversary relationship, he may view them more favourably. The police chief of Felsmere City was expressing the view of many policemen when he argued (p. 81) that it was good policy to have policemen supervise school crossings and meet schoolchildren in the role of someone who gives help rather than punishment. If the public perceive policemen only as authority figures, they will be less ready to come forward with information and assistance than if they have been able to build up more friendly ideas of them through less one-sided forms of interaction. On the other hand, it has been argued by Dr A. L. Goodhart, in his dissent to the majority report of the Royal Commission, that public approval depends mostly upon police efficiency; if householders know that the police are efficient in catching most of the burglars and hold-up men they will be less inclined to resent interference with their own liberty (*Royal Commission on the Police 1962, Final Report*, p. 164). The American police campaign for professionalization has aimed at raising standards and at having officers concentrate upon the tasks that require the specialist attention of a trained policeman. According to this conception the police administrator should be able to practise his profession any wherein the country, and local control must give way to proven principles defining the most economic utilization of financial and human resources. Loyalty to a national ideal of law enforcement must take precedence over considerations of local popularity. In the United States this movement – which is clearly in line with Dr Goodhart's conception of the police role – has been gaining strength, and seems to have had a salutary effect upon public relations and popular appreciation of the police. I believe that studies of American attitudes towards their police, and of the methods employed by top American police administrators, are of far greater relevance to British conditions than is usually believed. The visiting Briton is impressed by the differences, but underneath the surface lie common problems, and there are lessons to be learned from American experience.

A second issue which can be better understood in the light of the earlier analysis is that of supervision. How best to supervise people's work is always a problem, but it is more acute in the case of the police than in most occupations. This is because supervision is by its very nature a two-edged weapon. The more closely people are supervised, the more they bend their energies to satisfying the supervisor instead of to doing the job.[1] The two are not the same, and it is usually easier to separate them than the superior realizes. If the supervisor interferes too much, the worker does nothing unless he is sure he can justify himself. When superiors try to supervise too closely, their subordinates combine to frustrate them. The superiors retaliate by encouraging tale-bearing, and people no longer direct their energies to the goals for which they were recruited.

It might be expected that the problem of supervision will be relatively slight in country districts. The village constable working 'discretionary hours' probably sees the children into school and then goes off to dig his garden; he does not go out on patrol again until he thinks the circumstances require it. To a significant extent the village constable is his own master and is kept up to the mark by the expectations of the local people. If he is not doing his job properly his superiors will learn of it (and they will have their own checks upon him anyway) but when the nearest sergeant is ten miles or more away, the local man has to be allowed considerable independence. In the city force a much larger number of policemen have to be under close control. Men have to be moved between shifts, patrol areas, and other duties to allow for leave, sickness, and special events. More can go wrong, for the problems that arise are often more complex and cannot be sorted out on a personal basis; senior officers are often apprehensive about the trouble that can be caused if the first policeman at the scene of a crime makes a mistake. Therefore the urban policeman is much less his own master; he is subject to controls which are bound at times to seem frustrating and are apt to reduce his desire to get on with the job as he conceives it. Add to this the complication that different kinds of supervision are required: whereas the

[1] There is an excellent discussion of this point in Gouldner (1954, pp. 159–62).

youngster often needs guidance and restraint, the old hand may be inclined to take things easy and needs to be prodded into action.

This expectation was borne out by a series of discussions held at the Scottish Police College with probationers on second-stage training. They all had about nine months' experience of patrol work with their own forces. The men from the cities expressed considerable concern over relations with supervisors; the men from the county forces very little. The country constable had one superior immediately above him; he soon got to know this man and to understand what he wanted. The urban probationer might be moved around a lot to gain experience, coming under a series of different supervisors whom he never got to know in the same way. The constable has only to meet one autocratic supervisor to be ever on the watch for a repetition, and resentful that he should have to be so.

One practice was mentioned several times, and occasioned complaints from probationers echoing the far stronger criticisms I had sometimes heard from more experienced constables and sergeants. Periodically, senior officers decide that their men have got too lax in some respect and that far too many people are leaving cars parked without lights or are leaving dustbins (trash cans) at the kerb without lids for excessive periods, or that some other relatively minor offence is becoming too flagrant. They have warnings issued and then instruct their men that after a certain date all offenders are to be reported. These instructions arouse a resentment that at first surprised me. One patrol officer said he objected to the implication that he had not previously been doing his duty. In a discussion it was said:

B We had one case where the superintendent just issued a memorandum about good relations with the public and then proceeded to say that every motorist parking without lights was to be booked and that no exceptions were to be made. There was one case of a man who regularly put lights on his car. He dashed home one night to run into the toilet. By the time he came back to his car one of the inspectors and two constables were standing outside. The two constables had to book him. They knew him, they were friendly with him, but the inspector was there and it's a matter of 'If you don't book him I'm going to book you for neglect of duty'. Well, I'm not saying in that case it will make an awful lot of difference but someone who is on the borderline, who conscientiously puts his lights on every night, and then gets booked for that ten or fifteen minutes. . . .

I You say you don't suppose it will make a lot of difference?

B Well, he is friendly with the police and realizes it wasn't the policeman's fault, but some people think we just take a delight in booking them.

This opinion of B's may provoke some doubts. If the motorist was in the house so short a time, why had he not his lights on when he drove home? How can booking an offender be regarded as 'the policeman's fault'? However, the extract is not cited to support the constable's view but to illustrate an attitude that is not uncommon. The whole incident is, I submit, more readily comprehensible in terms of the analysis offered in this chapter. First, superior officers are faced with the general tendency of patrol officers to under-enforce the law. It is fairer to the public to tighten up all round, after a warning, than to have some constables exercising their discretion quite differently from others. Second, the resentment of the patrol officers stems from their implicit belief that discretion is essential to their role if they are to fulfil *all* its obligations, and they dislike orders which restrict their use of discretionary power.

Another of several examples which showed that feeling ran high on this issue came when one probationer described how he had been reprimanded by his sergeant for warning someone who had been shouting in the street. The sergeant said he should have charged him for a breach of the peace, and the probationer concluded, 'I'm not paid to warn'. Three others in the discussion group remonstrated with him. One urged that a warning is often more effective than a prosecution. Another advised, 'The last thing to use is your book'. But the first man responded, 'From now on I'm going to *book*'. Vehemently he asserted that he was not going to expose himself to this kind of talk from his sergeant. He was saying in effect: 'If the sergeant won't let me use my discretion, I won't, and we'll see where that gets him'. Other urban probationers thought their superiors did not regard them as capable of doing a proper job. One said he had been told, in as many words, not to try doing anything until he had a year's service. This must be totally unrepresentative, but some old-fashioned supervisors remain sceptical of the new methods of instruction. It will also be appreciated, in view of the discussion of 'reality shock' earlier on, that it is extremely difficult for any police supervisor to keep alight the slender flame of a recruit's enthusiasm.

A Swedish police officer once remarked to me: 'Some supervisors still don't realize that nowadays it's not sufficient to order a man to do something; he must be motivated to do it' (i.e. be stimulated to do it out of a sense that it needs doing). This observation summarizes aptly many of the lessons which social scientists' studies of work organizations have spelled out in detail. The changeover from more military-style ideas of discipline to notions of leadership is one that many industries and institutions have had to attempt in recent years, and in some quarters the process is by no means complete. The extent to which a particular activity raises questions of discipline may, however, depend upon the mode of organization. In Carolina City and Georgia City an officer used printed forms for reporting offences and incidents: these were various forms, each with spaces for the information relevant to the particular kind of incident. Police duty attracts the active man rather than the one who is good at expressing himself on paper, so such forms can be very helpful. From what little I saw of this side of their work, some American officers seemed to be no experts in spelling, but I never heard any complaints from the men or their supervisors about the manner of the reports. On the other hand, report writing is a recurrent topic of complaint among Scottish police officers – especially constables. Relatively few standardized forms are used, but the problem does not seem to be simply one of providing the requisite information. Stories are legion. One inspector deleted '. . . secured by chain and padlock', indicating that the report should be re-submitted with the phrasing '. . . secured by padlock and chain'. A sergeant directed that a report be written in a different way, but when it was re-submitted unwittingly ordered that it should be rewritten in the original fashion. Some constables who have had reports returned have been bold enough to rub out the pencil corrections and send them in again; they have been accepted. The writing, correction, and acceptance of written reports – whatever else they may connote – are to an important extent a question of rank. They

164

are bound to be a means of showing who is the subordinate and who the superior. The former must submit his report, the latter can accept or reject it; he can always find something 'wrong' with it if he wishes because there is no objective means for determining what is correct. One way of raising morale, or of strengthening officers' personal motivation, is to keep the number of controls to a minimum and, where controls are needed, to see that they relate impersonally to the substance of the matter and tone down any influences stemming from differences of rank.

Parallel to the problem of supervision is that of promotion, which is closely bound to it. This description will have shown that many qualities are demanded of the policeman and that they are not such as can easily be assessed in written examinations or in interviews. Selection for promotion is therefore bound to depend in some degree upon the favourable opinion of supervisors, and British policemen continually allege, 'It's not what you know but who you know' (this principle, of course, is honoured in other occupations too). If people believe that promotion does not necessarily reflect merit then it is no disgrace to fail: 'There's many good men still walking the beat', policemen say. If the day ever comes when the long-service constable is regarded as someone who has 'failed' then there will be serious personnel problems.

CHAPTER 6

The Control of Interpersonal Relations

At the beginning of this book it was held, in accordance with George C. Homans's argument, that social control is a property of states of social relations. The level of control, be it high or low, is determined by the kinds of social relationship between the people who make up the society, and by their effectiveness in getting people to follow prescribed patterns of behaviour. Control is maintained by the rewards and punishments which are built into these relationships and which are evident in the giving and withholding of esteem, in the sanctions of gossip, and in the institutional, economic, and moral pressures which underlie the behavioural patterns. It is present, therefore, in every relationship; what form does it take in police-public contacts?

In relations between people of similar status, when one party behaves in a fashion the other considers praiseworthy, the other is likely to reward him by expressing verbal approval or some mark of regard, whether it be a deferential tone of address or a more material acknowledgment. If a man fails to behave according to general expectation, the other person is likely to express disapproval; if the former continues in this deviant behaviour the latter may use what is normally the ultimate sanction of withdrawing completely from the relation. In relations between unequals, as between employee and employer, this sanction is normally available to both parties, though the personal cost of abandoning a job is usually greater to the worker than to the employer. But in relations between a policeman and a member of the public (let us, following American practice, call the latter a 'subject' for short) freedom to break off the relation is often absent. If a subject stops a policeman to ask him the way, he is free to withdraw when he wishes; but should his behaviour be suspicious the policeman might detain him and he would have to offer an acceptable explanation of his conduct to win release. This element of constraint distinguishes police-public interaction from nearly all other forms of social relation.

It should not be thought, however, that subjects cannot control police behaviour. As a rule, people do not approach the police for assistance or with a complaint unless they have some idea of what action the police are likely to take. They do not wish to involve themselves in a relation that is going to be more trouble to them than benefit. A Scottish sergeant testified that in country districts people will rarely give you information about their neighbours' misdemeanours because they have to live with them. They will talk in a roundabout manner and drop the advice, 'It might be worth your while walking up so-and-so glen one of these evenings'. In such a situation the man is trying to control the policeman's behaviour by having him discover an offence without the speaker's being identifiable as the informer. He can do this because he knows how the policeman is likely to respond. At other times countrymen will go to very considerable trouble to get into touch with a police officer with whom they are acquainted. Trust, in this connection, is frequently a matter of predictability. An American writer has concluded:

'Probably the one single element which is responsible above all others for the unparalleled cooperation prevailing today between the police and the public in England is the complete integrity of the police under the law. They enjoy popular confidence and esteem because the people know they will not overstep the safeguards to individual liberty provided under the law and rigorously protected by the courts' (Davies, 1954, p. 148).

This is a lawyer's view. The sociologist will emphasize that the public in Britain are able to trust the police because the actions of individual officers follow a common pattern so that the subject knows what to expect. Many studies of intergroup relations lay great stress upon this factor. For example, Negroes frequently assert that they would rather live in a society where racial discrimination is customary and open than in one where acts of discrimination are infrequent but unpredictable. In the former case, they say, they 'know where they stand'. In the latter, they may never meet discrimination but they are continually wondering whether it is not going to hit them next time, or whether what happened to an acquaintance last week is not going to happen to them before the day is out. So it is, too, with policemen. The man who has once suffered bad treatment at the hands of an individual officer never knows whether the same or worse is not going to occur again next time.

The establishment of uniform and predictable modes of action is not a matter for the police alone. They cannot respond in a standard fashion unless they know their behaviour will be correctly interpreted by subjects. The officer in the United States is less predictable than his British colleague partly because, in a heterogeneous population, common understandings are less inclusive. The American officer cannot rely upon the authority of his uniform, but in dealing with subjects must establish a personal authority by proving what a good guy he is, or what a dangerous one. For the relationships between the policeman and the non-criminal subject to serve both parties' ends, they must understand each other. They must both be members of a community, sharing values and modes of communication.

THE ALIEN COMMUNITY

The effectiveness of the policeman as a peace officer lies in his participation in the life of the society he polices. This proposition has been reiterated earlier and to some readers it may seem self-evident. I do not believe that this is the case. On the contrary, there is evidence to suggest that the policeman's sense of participation varies considerably and that his performance of duties is related to these variations. The evidence comes from places where the gap between police and public is large, in colonies, in Northern United States cities, and from Negro communities in the Deep South, but there is every reason to suspect that the same factor is at work, usually to a milder degree, in all societies. Different police duties bring officers into contact with different sections of the public and this is likely to influence both their attitudes and their behaviour on the job.

A writer with experience of colonial administration takes up the question of police-public relations to illustrate one of the causes of corruption. The African farmer, he says, is barefoot, but 'the policeman is wearing a pair of large, shiny boots, and this difference may stand as a symbol of their relative ability to protect themselves'. The policeman has knowledge of the law, contacts with government officials, and powers of arrest. The farmer does not understand the law very well and sooner or later he will infringe one of its provisions. If the policeman then demands a bribe, the farmer is relatively helpless. To complain to the constable's superior is likely to be ineffective. Even if he should spend a considerable sum to engage a strange lawyer from the city, and should win his case, he gets only temporary satisfaction, for he knows that all the police in the locality will be watching for his next mistake (McMullen, 1961).[1] Only through a political movement does the farmer have any real control over the policeman; instead of the two men seeing infractions from one another's standpoints and responding to the same moral ideas, they see each other as belonging to different communities. There are few internal controls built into the relationship, and the chief constraints upon the policeman are those deriving from the discipline of his own organization. Where the farmer is weak the policeman is tempted to use his power to obtain money; where the farmer is wealthy it is he who is tempted to use his money to buy some of the policeman's power to shield his own activities. Thus one of the practices which arises to bridge the gap between the policeman and the community is corruption.

Another is violence. In some of the cities in the Northern parts of the United States the police departments have been demoralized by political control, poor leadership, and low rates of pay. The life of many districts seems competitive and raw; individuals pursue their own ends with little regard for public morality, and the policeman sees the ugly underside of outwardly respectable households and businesses. Small wonder, then, that many American policemen are cynics.[2] 'After a while you don't believe that anyone tells you the truth', said one man. 'The favours that you do for people bounce back on you because the guy who came up with the sob story was

[1] The position of a colonial-style police, trying to enforce laws unsupported by the local system of social control and seeking to have witnesses testify truthfully when they are subject to contrary community pressures, is the theme of Philip Mason's novel *Call the next Witness* (1945). Introducing his story, Mason maintains that the problem of the police in India is not that of finding their man so much as of getting honest witnesses to court.

[2] 'I do not know how police officers can escape from being cynics' (Holcomb, 1950, p. 10).

lying.' Couple this experience of the public with the policeman's feeling that in his social life he is a pariah, scorned by citizens who are more respectable but no more honest, and it need surprise no one that the patrolman's loyalties to his department and his colleagues are often stronger than those to the wider society. The patrolman has little moral authority and he cannot identify himself with the entire community to the extent that his British colleague does. To make the public comply with their orders the policemen in such localities have to adopt a familiar manner, and when this is insufficient they feel obliged to employ violence in order to coerce an obstinate person into obedience or into evincing more respect for the police. William A. Westley, in a study made in a mid-Western city at a time when police morale and standards seem to have been very low, asked policemen in what circumstances they thought officers were justified in 'roughing a man up'. Twenty-seven out of seventy-three men (37 per cent) replied that violence might be justified when a man showed disrespect for the police – no other set of circumstances received such frequent mention (Westley, 1951, 1953).

If a policeman uses violence in order to make a truculent offender show more respect for the police, he is, according to Westley, requiring that the man show respect for him as an individual; his action is not intended to exact respect for law and order and for the policeman as its representative, but simply for him as an individual. It is a response to a situation in which he believes that other people regard him as a social failure and a person of little account: he cannot maintain his self-respect if people who flaunt such an attitude are allowed to get away with it, and he knows that the courts will give him little support. As one officer said:

'There was the incident of a fellow I picked up. I was on the beat and I was taking him down to the station. There were people following us. He kept saying that I wasn't in the army. Well, he kept going on like that, and I finally had to bust him one. I had to do it. The people would have thought I was afraid otherwise.'

Westley is careful to point out that many policemen in this force condemn violence and some even take desk jobs in order to be away from it, but that the circumstances are such that none of them will condemn its use by colleagues or will report them for it.

Westley describes the police officer in the town he studied in the following terms:

> 'He is regarded as corrupt and inefficient by, and meets with hostility and criticism from, the public. He regards the public as his enemy, feels his occupation to be in conflict with the community, and regards himself to be a pariah.'

Some support for this highly coloured picture can be drawn from the fact that 70 per cent of the men he interviewed were strongly opposed to the idea of any son of their's becoming a policeman (Westley, 1951, p. 213). Though some elements of the attitude Westley describes were undoubtedly present in a large Massachusetts city visited by the author (some twelve to fourteen years after the period when Westley did his research), he could not believe from his conversation with officers that they held so pessimistic a view of themselves or their job. They insisted that their role was important whether or not the public appreciated it, and criticized society from a moral standpoint instead of accepting its judgements. Nevertheless, an experienced member of the department held that Westley's analysis of the use of violence was equally applicable to his own force: it was imperative to exact respect, and it was respect for the individual, not for the uniform – 'a matter of personal pride', as he put it. 'You must do something, even if it's only a slap across the face.' Then he went on:

> 'When someone rings you to fix a ticket you always ask "Did you give the officer any back talk?" and if they admit they did, or if they start explaining a lot, you take no action. For example, my brother rang me once. I asked him this and my brother said "I only told him I was in the right and I didn't see what the hell he was doing hiding behind a tree". So I said "Well if that's the way it was you'd better find someone else to fix it for you".'

In Westley's study two other sets of circumstances that policemen consider may justify the use of violence are discussed: in order to obtain information which will enable them to apprehend or convict an important criminal, and in order to punish sexual offenders. It is often difficult for the police to get people who have been victims of

171

sexual attacks to testify in public and submit to cross-examination, so the police may well feel under a moral obligation to act in defence of society when the law cannot do so. It is important to note, however, that Westley does not consider the use of violence in such circumstances as a choice between moral obligations, nor does he convey any feeling that the police, too, are participants in society. In both cases he represents violence as a reaction to social pressure. A policeman, he says, is motivated to track down criminals in order to advance his own career and to still the criticism of a censorious public. Similarly, a policeman is impelled to brutalize a suspected sex offender because public hysteria generates pressure on the police and not because they share the public's view of such people. This element in his interpretation reads strangely to a European, but he is describing police work in conditions that are also foreign to European circumstances.

A gulf may arise between the police and the public where, as in the instance noted above, the police feel alienated from society. A comparable situation occurs where the police see a section of the population as not belonging to their own society. The results may be even more distressing. In words which quite clearly are chosen to describe cold facts rather than to express personal feelings, the President's Commission on Civil Rights concluded:

'A comprehensive review of available evidence indicates that police brutality is still a serious and continuing problem. When policemen take the law into their own hands, assuming the roles of judge, jury, and, sometimes, executioner, they do so for a variety of reasons. Some officers take it upon themselves to enforce segregation or the Negro's subordinate status. Brutality of this nature occurs most often in those places where racial segregation has the force of tradition behind it' (*Justice*, 1962, Book 5).

What struck me most forcibly when talking with ordinary white people in the American South was the way they would always refer to Negroes as 'they'; there seemed to be no situations in which White and Negroes belonged as 'we'. This observation is a commonplace in the sociological literature but its continuing validity can still impress the visiting European. Most Whites did not see Negroes and themselves as being members of the same community. At no time did I get the impression that white police officers felt the same involvement in the rights and wrongs of life in the Negro district as they did in the white districts. An officer who came across a Negro woman who had been badly beaten by her lover showed none of the feelings of indignation and sympathy he might have revealed had she been white. There were some exceptions, of course, as there usually are, but generally speaking the white policeman saw beatings and stabbings as customs of the Negro sections, like shooting craps. Many years earlier at the time of the first world war, a captain of detectives in a Southern town told a writer on police matters: 'In this town there are three classes of homicide. If a nigger kills a white man, that's murder. If a white man kills a nigger, that's justifiable homicide. If a nigger kills a nigger, that's one less nigger.' He was not saying that this was the way things should be, merely that it was the way things were. Something of this feeling that crimes between Negroes are no concern of the Whites and of white courts of justice remains in many parts of the South. The courts will give a Negro convicted of assaulting another Negro a sentence only a fraction of that which would have been imposed had the parties been white. If the courts take this view it is hard for the police officer not to follow suit.

In many American towns – even in the Deep South – Negroes have been engaged as police officers to patrol Negro districts. The principal reason for this has been political: by promising that suitable Negro applicants will be hired, white politicians have been able to win Negro votes. Where the Negroes are not allowed to vote, there are no Negro police. However, there are also good police reasons for the use of Negro patrolmen. A Negro officer in one Southern city argued convincingly that before the introduction of Negro police, Negro citizens were not getting proper protection. Negro bullies were allowed, by white officers, to get away with all sorts of offences against other Negroes, in return for the information they supplied. Often, too, Negro violators were able to satisfy white officers by telling them a tale no Negro would have believed. White officers in the past had arrested drunks, but they had never worried about drunken men who neglected their wives and children. Negro officers, on the other hand, were concerned with the moral issues; they had many times proceeded against people for this sort of offence and been instrumental in reforming them. A white officer would not try

173

to reform a Negro offender and probably could not do it anyway. Where a white officer might charge a Negro violator under the municipal ordinances with disorderly conduct or cursing in public, and have him fined $15, he (the Negro officer) would charge him for every offence he committed, possibly including, in such a case, the use of obscene language in the presence of females, which was punishable under state law and might entail a sentence of up to twelve months' imprisonment. He took as serious a view of offences against Negroes as of offences against Whites and thought the dignity of Negro women equally worthy of protection. Under-enforcement of the law by white policemen had been a means whereby the Negro community was kept subordinate.

When Negro police first went on patrol in this city, many Negro toughs boasted that no Negro police were going to arrest them. As a result the pioneers had to win respect in the Negro lower-class districts by the strength of their arms, and they had to make many charges for such offences as idling and loitering before their authority was established. Generally speaking, Negro policemen have the reputation of being stricter with Negro offenders than white policemen would be (Kephart, 1957, p. 115; Rudwick, 1962, pp. 11–12). Fears have often been expressed about the trouble which would ensue if Negro policemen were allowed to arrest Whites. In the North-eastern states it seems that there is rarely any difficulty and that the Negro officers authority as policemen is not questioned. In the South, Negro officers are sometimes allowed to arrest white offenders and sometimes required to call a white officer to make the arrest (Rudwick, 1962, pp. 9–14). In Carolina City and Georgia City, Negro officers had on numerous occasions arrested Whites without difficulty; perhaps they handled such cases very circumspectly, for certainly the Negro knows more about the white man and how to handle him than the white man knows about the Negro. I myself on one occasion went with Negro officers to investigate a family dispute in a ramshackle poor-white dwelling house, inhabited by people who looked to me like real hillbillies, and who had certainly been drinking, but I could detect nothing that suggested they resented having Negro officers attend the call.

The evidence concerning the policing of Negro neighbourhoods is scanty, but it would appear that in regions where segregation is traditional the situation is similar in some ways to the colonial one. There are few social controls built into police-public relations because the Negro citizen's defences against the illegal use of police powers are too weak. The white policeman may believe that he gets little co-operation from Negroes, and any common purpose is blotted out by mutual suspicion. The most effective control over the white officer is that of his own organization's discipline, but supervision is weak, selection of recruits is often inadequate, and men with sadistic tendencies get a policeman's badge. In country districts where the sheriff and judge are elected officials it is often impossible to overturn a local tyranny (*Justice*, 1962, pp. 6–13, 29–39, 41–55, and 69). In the gulf between the law's officials and the Negro community violence is bred. But when Negro urban neighbourhoods are policed by Negroes the moral consensus makes possible cooperation and mutual control.

The social separation of the police and the public is not, of course, the only factor giving rise to police brutality. Officers, both white and Negro, in an excellent Southern police department told me quite freely of occasions on which they had beaten prisoners. This was not a common occurrence. In one case the offender had tried to knife the officer, who had been behaving in a perfectly correct manner, and who felt quite shaken that anybody should try to do this to him when he had done nothing to provoke it. He lost control of himself. Another officer described how he, as a young policeman, had reacted similarly when prisoners had cursed him and spat on him. Illegal violence is apt to occur in this way when the police believe that the courts will not punish particular offences adequately and when senior officers fail to establish and enforce clear norms of what is expected of a police officer. In the Scottish city I have similarly heard stories from retired policemen and older officers of the use of illegal violence to punish offenders who the police thought would not receive a sufficiently severe sentence from the courts. Today, Scottish officers are inclined to insist that nowadays, and especially since the Waters case, illegal violence is never used.[1]

[1] Cf. p. 155, note 2, above. One aspect of this question which I have not seen mentioned is that offenders are more likely to try and goad policemen of shorter stature into a fight and, apparently, are more inclined to protest about any undue violence on their part – as if force from a big man were a fact of nature but from a small man an abuse of office.

The Policeman in the Community

If the policeman patrolling a neighbourhood populated by people of another race feels no identification with them and performs his duties less well, may not the same be expected where the residents are distant from the policeman in terms of social class? In Britain there is indeed a suspicion in some quarters that the police side with the propertied classes and are the enemy of the working classes. Whatever the police may feel, the public apparently do not think this. To judge by the results of the Social Survey poll there is no distinctive variation between social classes in their approval of the police. Of respondents in the Registrar-General's social classes I and II (professional and managerial) 85·2 per cent said that they had great respect for the police; among social class III respondents (clerical and skilled manual) 81·8 per cent gave a similar reply; as did 81·9 per cent of social classes IV and V (semi-skilled and labouring). The most significant variable seems to be age (older people expressing more respect for the police), though the distinction between motorists and non-motorists (79·7 per cent as against 84·1 per cent) merits some attention (*Royal Commission on the Police*, Appendix IV to the *Minutes of Evidence*).[1] But even though they may not affect generalized public attitudes, class differences may be significant for police-public relations in other ways.

SOCIAL CLASS AND SOCIAL ROLE

Every occupation brings its members into certain social relationships and teaches them how to conduct them, but occupations vary in their range. The miner spends much of his life in association with other miners. He can 'get on' with his mates in a way that no non-miner can, but he has little experience in dealing with other sorts of people. He may lack the social skills that would enable him to manage a relationship with, say, a librarian in a neighbouring town, and is apt to give offence where none is intended, for lack of *savoir faire*. The policeman's job brings him into many varied relationships. In the

[1] Geoffrey Gorer's survey, based on a self-selected sample of 4,983 readers of a popular newspaper, reported that three-quarters were in agreement in 'enthusiastic appreciation of the English police'. People earning less than £12 per week tended to be slightly more appreciative, but people who classed themselves as 'working class' were somewhat less favourable than those who considered themselves 'middle class'. Apart from the under 18s – who were enthusiastic – there was no association with respondents' age (Gorer, 1955, Table 80, p. 446).

176

short time the author spent with policemen on patrol when planning the inquiry on which Chapter 2 is based, officers had to deal with such different incidents as reprimanding schoolchildren for lighting a bonfire, quietening a matrimonial dispute between a couple almost old enough to be the young policeman's parents, and informing a woman that her husband had been drowned. One officer had to visit an old people's home because there had been a complaint of indecent behaviour. On arrival it transpired that an elderly mental defective had been lifting the skirts of two little girls who were daughters of someone on the staff. The officer admonished the man in language appropriate to a five-year-old, 'Tammy, you've been interfering wi' wee girls' clothing!' Tammy denied this: he said the girls had been calling him names while he gathered firewood. His own youth concealed by the uniform and cap, the stern-faced policeman asked, 'Do you want me to come back and take you to gaol?' 'No!' gasped the frightened Tammy. As a dramatic performance it was skilfully done and it was difficult to see how any other treatment could have been more effective. The man in question had a record of previous offences of the same kind though the last one had been five years earlier. After this interview with the policeman it seemed a reasonable bet that he would manage at least another five years before the next complaint. The policeman had never previously had to deal with mental defectives but his few years of experience with the range of characters that constitutes the public had clearly given him an impressive ability to respond to the individual. I remember another officer stressing how hard it may be to show a calm exterior when personally frightened. He recounted how once when on patrol he saw a group of people clustered round a tenement stair and went to see what was attracting their attention. There on the third step he saw a green snake with raised head gazing balefully around. The constable felt obliged to take charge. First he played for time, then he sent a small boy off to get a box with some straw. Then, when he could delay no longer, he had to advance, box in hand, upon the snake. Suddenly there was a sound of a door opening up the stair and a man came down. He saw the snake, said, 'So *that's* where you've got to, is it?', put it in his pocket and went back. The constable felt like a pricked balloon. Policemen frequently have to take charge of situations in which the other parties are emotionally aroused; they learn to handle such cases and to develop their social skills more than people in most occupations.

Experienced police officers develop very considerable skill in handling different sorts of people but because they acquire it unconsciously and are not given to examination of their own reactions, they usually cannot explain quite how they deal with awkward cases or why they employ one approach rather than another. In Britain the police officer's training in this respect, as has been noted earlier, is carried out primarily by putting a recruit to patrol with an experienced officer and allowing him to learn by demonstration. Formal training, in the sense of lectures, tends to be confined to generalities and exhortation. It is possible, therefore, that a close examination of the issues involved might in the end lead to some intermediate method of instruction which would be more economical of time and no less effective. One method would be to develop the analysis of suitable cases: this can reveal underlying general principles which are more than merely common sense and which do illuminate practical problems.[1] Because the policeman is faced with such a bewildering variety of situations, and the individual element in each is often so important, little attempt has hitherto been made to develop explicit techniques for training in the handling of police-public contacts, though the New York Police Department now has a major experimental programme on hand. The difficulties are considerable, but the police seem to have advanced less than the big industrial concerns in this respect.

Probationers in a series of discussion groups at the Scottish Police College were asked if they had found any kind of people more difficult to handle than they had expected: they were unanimous in replying that upper-class people were more difficult to deal with than any other. Many of them cited instances,[2] though none perhaps as

[1] To cite but one example, a driver who has his wife and children in the car with him will probably be more sensitive to reproof from a policeman than if he is alone. It might be worth pointing this out to trainees and suggesting to them that in such circumstances they might ask a driver if he would like to step out of the car to talk with the officer privately.

[2] An extreme case was reported in *The Guardian* (7 November 1961): 'Lady (Barbara) Beaumont yesterday paid to a detective and a policewoman a fine and costs totalling £16 6s. after the police had waited outside her flat in Beaconsfield, Buckinghamshire, for five and a half hours. They had called at her home in the

likely to draw a smile as that of the policeman who asked a woman driver for her licence, only to receive the reply:

'Don't you know who I am? I'm Lady So-and-so. You should stand to attention when you speak to me.'

Nothing daunted, the officer replied:

'Well I'm PC 99 and I'm booking you for a parking offence.'

It seems likely that a working-class offender hits back at an intruding policeman in ways that the constable is prepared for. If a man tells the policeman to go to hell, this shows disrespect for the law as well as for the individual officer, and if he cautions or charges the offender he must feel that he is vindicating standards of proper conduct. In this way he reinforces his conception of himself as an agent of the law. The upper-class offender – to judge from these discussions – hits back in a different way. He (or she) asserts that he is above the law (there is truth in this sometimes: not at all frequently, but often enough to appear as a threat to the young constable). Or he denies that the officer is really an independent agent of the law. 'I'm paying your wages', the offender says. 'You're not supposed to be doing this. You should be chasing criminals', etc. Such attacks are much more difficult for the constable to answer because they are more personal and tend to reduce any satisfaction he gets from doing his duty.

Quite apart, however, from any class differences in style of speech, the sorts of incident which bring together policemen and middle- or upper-class people tend to be different from those which give rise to contacts between police and working-class people. If policemen meet members of any one social category chiefly in situations which spell trouble for the officer, they are likely to react by expressing disapproval of the whole category. This happens in many United States cities, where a disproportionate amount of crime is committed by Negroes and where many white people build up unfavourable stereotypes of Negroes on this account. Practitioners of any occupation are

morning with a warrant for her arrest for non-payment of the fine, imposed on her in August, for failing to complete a census form. Soon after 11 a.m. Lady Beaumont called to the police officers through the locked door of her flat to say that she was dressing, but at midday they were still waiting outside. Three-quarters of an hour later, she called through the door again to say that she was having a bath. Finally, she opened the door and paid the fine.'

apt to be irritated by a group of people who give them extra trouble. However, 'trouble' requires definition. Most policemen would be acutely dissatisfied if they never had anything at all to do. Some tasks give them a sense of achievement and self-satisfaction, but if there were too many even of these they would lose their appeal. Beats or patrol areas in middle-class districts tend to be much larger, and there are fewer policemen compared with the number of residents than there are in the poorer districts; but while there are relatively fewer cases in which middle-class residents have to be charged or warned by the patrol officer, there are not so many cases from which he is able to get the satisfaction that comes from helping someone who looked to the police for aid. All too often the calls which the beat man in a middle-class area receives concern lost dogs, cats stuck up trees, or other trivialities. Many policemen dislike having to work in such districts for this reason. On the other hand, the average middle-class resident shares more nearly the policeman's ideas about law enforcement, and in some respects is more ready to cooperate than the average working-class man.

Many of the calls which a policeman on duty in a poor neighbourhood receives are fairly easily settled and do not count as 'trouble'. They provide the satisfaction that comes from a worth-while job well done without threatening the constable's person or involving him in difficulties with his superiors. Disputes between neighbours and minor requests for assistance can be settled without an officer's having to make detailed reports in writing about what action he took. There is less likelihood of these subjects going over his head to his superiors and causing them to put pressure on him in any way. So the beat man in such a locality can often establish a protective relationship with the law-abiding residents. One constable in a poor district asserted to the author that it was his responsibility to show particular consideration to people who had not had much opportunity in life, 'such as the people round here'. His attitude, though a little more vehement than most of his colleagues, was not atypical. A patrol officer in a poor district will probably get more tasks of an unpleasant character (e.g. searching bodies of persons several days dead, dealing with violent drunks or abusive juveniles) but he will also get more tasks that give his job meaning and may well advance his career. In a poor district the patrol officers have to give less attention to the protection of property and more to the supervision of the residents, because there is a much greater likelihood of breaches of the peace resulting from domestic disputes, drunkenness, etc., and probably less inclination on the part of the residents to report some kinds of offence to the police. The police become to a greater extent uniformed social workers as well as more active enforcers of the peace. Thus a constable patrolling a slum neighbourhood in the Scottish city observed that when on evening shift he always carried with him a card of fuse wire because he was so often asked for help by old people who could not get their lights to go on. In these neighbourhoods informal social controls are weak so that policemen get called in to settle matters that residents elsewhere would deal with by themselves. (For example, the woman in the tenement who complains that her neighbour deliberately arranges to have coal delivered when she has washing hanging to dry, or – and this is a true story – the woman who complained to the policeman that her husband did not treat her properly and then, to prove her point, telephoned him at 2 a.m. to complain that her husband would not let her have her share of the blankets!) In differing neighbourhoods the police provide different services.

FAMILIARITY AND IMPERSONALITY

To do his job properly the policeman, like the minister of religion, has to be to some extent a 'classless' figure. He has to deal with subjects of different class and his relationships with them must be determined by his office, not by his class position. But despite the powers conferred and the restrictions imposed upon him, the policeman is never completely separated from the class structure. At times – for example in dealing with a lawyer or a company director – an element of incongruity is present in the relation between the policeman and the subject: the policeman is in one sense the senior party in that he has a right to pose questions and expect answers, but both parties are conscious that out of uniform the subject enjoys a social status much superior to the policeman's. Knowledge of the parties' other roles may affect police-public interaction. The starting-point for a review of this question is the analysis by a social anthropologist, A. R. Radcliffe-Brown, of ambiguous social relations in tribal societies. A relation between a man and his wife's mother has, in most societies, an element of incongruity: he has to be friendly with her because of the close tie between her and his wife and yet at the same time he resents her claims upon her daughter if he perceives them as conflicting with his own – as they frequently do in some measure. Radcliffe-Brown argued that in such cases when incompatible elements were present in a relation between two parties of unequal status (the mother-in-law being entitled to deference) a custom would be found which required the two parties to avoid one another. In this way the conflicting pressures could be reduced. If, however, the two parties were of equal status (as husband and brother-in-law), custom was likely to prescribe a 'joking relationship' in which they would work out the tensions by abusing each other (Radcliffe-Brown, 1952, pp. 90–116, esp. p. 108).[1] Institutionalized joking enables one party to accept elements in a relationship he would otherwise consider demeaning by allowing him to enter reminders of another relationship between them. This question cannot, however, be properly considered or its relevance to police-public relations shown, without a somewhat technical analysis.

In the first few hours of his day a man will be involved in a considerable number of roles and relationships: he may pass quite rapidly from husband to father, pedestrian, employee, and colleague. But it should not be thought that a man changes his role only when the situation changes, or that when he interacts with some particular person he always does so as the incumbent of a particular role. It is frequently possible for relations between two people to be conducted in terms of several different alternative relationships. The same two men may be colleagues in one situation, rivals in another, associates in a club, but adversaries in political discussions. Moreover, two people who start a conversation on a basis of friendship may change over to a relationship of business and back again. Such shifts may be explicit, as when one says, 'Now let's get down to business', or they may be almost imperceptible.

Two people who are very intimate, husband and wife, for example, are involved with one another in many aspects of their social personalities and in many roles. They can interact on the basis of marital obligations, on the more generalized relationship of man to woman, or as senior to junior, motorist to non-motorist, comforter to

[1] Cf. Homans (1962, pp. 99 – 101).

bereaved, nurse to patient, and so on. On the other hand, two people who are parties to a strictly official relationship, say post-office clerk and purchaser of stamps, are involved in only one small aspect of their social personalities. The contrast suggests a general formulation: where the same two people can interact in many roles, this is a relationship of familiarity; where they can interact in very few roles, this is an impersonal relationship.

If two people have been interacting in a relatively impersonal way and they make a move towards familiarity, it is almost invariably the senior party who initiates the shift. For example, if two people who have been on last-name terms go over to addressing one another by first names, it is the senior who changes first. Similarly, a senior party sometimes has a right to ask questions about the private affairs of a junior without the latter's being able to pose comparable questions to the former. This general pattern is violated when a policeman has to deal with high-status subjects. The subject is apt to resent questions from a policeman if he regards him as his social inferior. The police-man's response when he encounters or anticipates such resentment is comparable to the avoidance behaviour of the African who must not dispute with his mother-in-law. The policeman cannot avoid inter-action altogether, so he attempts to make it highly impersonal, to convey the impression that he is acting purely as a policeman, and that he is not, as a citizen himself, passing any judgement upon the subject's statements. This approach, in turn, makes it easier for the subject to accept what might otherwise seem as subordination to someone beneath him. The policeman will be careful to give the subject no opportunity for a counter-attack. Scottish officers have told me that at times, when speaking to high-status motorists who have committed some offence, they have put their hand on the door or rested their notebook on some part of the vehicle and the motorist has promptly snapped, 'Take your hand off my car'. The policeman has had to obey; he has not risked making any reply but has confined himself to eliciting the information he is legally bound to obtain. Impersonal behaviour on the policeman's part prevents the motorist from bringing other roles into play.

Many policemen assert that in dealing with low-status offenders it is necessary to 'use their own language' if they are to be made to take notice. This also seems to be a case where different ways of managing the same social relations are possible, and the policeman's speech and manner serve as a way of indicating which one he proposes to adopt. If a policeman addresses a group of young roughs on a corner in the same impersonal fashion in which he might advise middle-class people to clear the pavement, he may well sound stilted to them and they would probably respond derisively, doing their best to insult the policeman, but in such a way that if he should charge them with insulting behaviour it would look as if he were being unduly sensitive and pompous. If the policeman then threatens them in some less ceremonious fashion he may well be more successful in obtaining compliance. By no means all policemen respond in this way. One supervising officer insisted to me that he never swore at even the most truculent subject. When asked if the socially correct mode of address did not make some people more angry and less cooperative, he replied that if they disliked the proper, impersonal mode of address this was an additional, if minor, punishment which he thought quite appropriate. If a policeman is putting an offender on a charge it may not make very much difference how he speaks to him, but if he wishes to obtain compliance without charging him, his mode of speech may decide what response he will get. If he speaks impersonally, the subject may well resent his claim to exercise police authority in a situation in which the subject thinks it is not justified, and the use of speech modes associated with another social class may prompt him to 'talk back'. To speak in a fashion that is officially incorrect indicates that the speaker is not handling the relation in the orthodox fashion. In the Royal Navy – and probably in the other services – a young officer was warned never to swear at a rating when taking any form of disciplinary action. If he were to do this, the rating could assert that he was not going to be sworn at and, by pressing a technically justified counter-claim, could blunt the criticism of himself. The same must apply in a modified degree in police-public contacts. A policeman is not supposed to use coarse language towards members of the public, and if he is reported for doing so he will probably be charged under the discipline regulations.

There is little likelihood of the police officer's swearing at subjects of middle- or upper-class status because such people would be likely to take offence and report him. They will be offended both because they are less accustomed to such language in general conversation and because they are more likely to object to it from someone like a policeman who in almost every other situation is their inferior in social status. This is not to say that swearing never occurs in these situations. A probationer related that he was on patrol one night with a more senior constable when the latter stopped a motorist for driving without lights and cursed him thoroughly. The probationer was surprised at this, but the other man explained that though not intending to put the motorist on a charge he did not want him to feel that such negligence could easily be overlooked. The verbal assault was in effect being used as a form of summary punishment because the offender, being vulnerable to a prosecution, was unlikely to complain. Supervising officers would not approve of such a tactic.

Coarse language will be used more frequently in dealings with lower-class subjects as a means of getting them to comply with police instructions without invoking legal sanctions. Out of uniform the policeman is socially superior to the subject, which gives him more claim to treat him in a familiar fashion; but by swearing at him the policeman is indicating both that he is not for the moment claiming social superiority and that he is not for the time being appealing to official police authority, but is putting himself on the man's own level and is threatening to treat him – extra-legally – with no more ceremony than one of his own associates. Swearing in this context, as in an African joking relationship, is therefore an indication of privileged familiarity: the two parties are not of equal status but the junior one (the subject) cannot employ avoidance behaviour or impersonality; it is therefore left to the policeman to indicate which roles are in play.[1] Such behaviour may also be undesirable in the eyes of senior

[1] Another and very different situation was encountered during the course of the research, which seemed to embody some elements of another variety of joking relationship, corresponding to joking relations between tribes in the African context. It may be argued that when a number of previously unrelated groups are brought together in a new context they have to elaborate some basis for interaction which will reduce the various particular characters and build a simpler social pattern. In African cities, previously antagonistic tribes come to feel solidarity with one another when they discover how much they have in common by comparison with some of the other groups. This combination of antagonism and solidarity in their relation is expressed in joking behaviour. At the Scottish Police College men from many different forces gather. The most obvious division is between the city forces and the county forces. The distinction between the two groups seems to be the basis for many jests and it was often reflected in the discussions held at the college. Thus the city-county distinction

police officers, but some men would defend it as the most economical way of obtaining compliance. To use legal sanctions when dealing with every loafer, they would say, would be to use an expensive steamhammer to crack a nut of little value.

It should be emphasized that though many of the policemen whom the author has observed on patrol, or with whom he has discussed the question of how to handle different subjects, in practice adopt an impersonal manner with socially superior offenders and a familiar one with socially inferior offenders, and though they can discuss their tactics in particular cases, they are not conscious of any significant difference in their manner. They are apt to say that everyone should be treated courteously and correctly, and to point out that each case is unique. As I have not been able to observe enough examples of police contacts with high- and low-status offenders (and in any case my presence might well influence the situation) I have been unable to test this theory. Discussions with British and American officers make me feel that there is some truth in it and that it might be worth further examination by the sociologist or by the police instructor interested in developing training techniques.

In Britain, middle-class status entitles a person to a greater measure of deference in most situations than does working-class status, so that the successful assumption of familiarity by someone lower in the scale (as with the policeman swearing at the motorist in the case quoted earlier) has more of the effect of punishment. However, deference is a privilege that must be earned, and people higher up the scale are expected to set an example in matters of conduct. They cannot afford to admit to a violation with the equanimity of the low-status offender. This gives the policeman an additional technique for controlling interpersonal relations: if his approach to a middle- or upper-class subject implies that it would be beneath the subject's dignity to respond in a certain way, the subject may be prevented from doing so. For example, a 'correct' impersonal and deferential approach will discourage the subject from arguing the point, where a more friendly, familiar, and egalitarian one would not. To recall the norms of middle-class conduct may also be a way of reasserting social control.

appears more important in the college than in other police contexts because of the tendency for small social units to coalesce in seeking a more general basis for group relations.

On one occasion in the Scottish city, for instance, an army officer was incensed by what he considered the dangerous driving of another car, and had his chauffeur pursue it so that he could give the other driver a piece of his mind. The other driver – who was a professional man – at first tried to escape, but after some hectic driving he was overtaken and a noisy altercation ensued. When a policeman came up and implied that this was not the sort of behaviour the police expected from people of their kind the dispute evaporated. Class factors can therefore be manipulated by police officers to assist in the maintenance of public order.

In the United States – so far as the author's observations go – class factors operate in a more restricted range of situations than in Britain and cannot be used by policemen to the same extent. Because the evaluation of class in America seems to be based more upon an individual's income and less upon his background (family, manner, accent) than in Britain, social mobility is to this extent easier. It seems probable that Americans are less inclined to expect middle- and upper-class people to maintain higher standards of general conduct so that the police officer does not feel the social inferior of a man driving a Cadillac. When the author suggested to American officers that they might be more deferential to the driver of a Cadillac they denied this; one reply was, 'I could have a Cadillac if I wanted to spend my money in that way'. Verbal responses are notoriously unreliable when dealing with questions of this kind, but at least they afford no support to the assumption. The officer may well treat such a subject with greater care, but this may be more from apprehension about his possible political influence than because of any moral claims his status gives him upon other members of society. Officers with whom this was discussed held that while middle-class complainants required more deferential behaviour from the police, their status did not make much difference when they had committed an offence. There might be a tendency to handle middle-class violators more impersonally, but the officers pointed out that there was considerable variation in the sort of approach used by different policemen: some were inclined to be gentler and others rougher with 'big shots'.

CHAPTER 7

The Segregation of the Police Officer's Role in Britain

If the policeman is too much involved in community affairs and loyalties, he lacks the impartiality required of an authority figure. If, on the other hand, he is detached too much from the community, he no longer has the understanding of people's feelings which he needs if he is to exercise his discretion effectively. If the policeman is too involved, he forfeits respect. If he is too detached, people resent his implied claim to be their moral superior. Indeed, it could be argued that this duality in the policeman's role is the logical starting-point for an analysis of police-public relations.

In Chapter 5 evidence was set forth to show how the police officer's membership of the society affected the way he policed it. This chapter will examine the way in which a man's privileges and obligations as a police officer affect his position as a member of the society.

If the public are to have confidence in the impartiality of the police it is essential that their exercise of the police role shall not be improperly influenced – or, perhaps almost as important, shall not *appear* to be improperly influenced – by their incumbency of private roles. This need to prevent a conflict of interests, or an apparent conflict of interests, is important in many occupations. A member of parliament is required to 'declare his interest' before speaking on any subject in which he has a financial concern. A scandal is aroused if a local council gives unduly favourable contracts to one of its own members who manages a building firm. To prevent this sort of conflict a policeman is forbidden to engage in any activity which might appear to compromise his role as a policeman. He may not identify himself with any controversial group in politics or religion. He must not be associated too clearly with any particular social class, for, like the clergyman, his occupation gives him direct access to persons of every class on an equal or superior footing. Because he has to take charge of criminals and at times has to obtain information about crimes, the policeman has to handle pitch and not be defiled. The public must be confident that he will not fall victim to the temptations with which his job is surrounded.

Wherever the incumbent of a role is given authority over others, some institution supports him. The tax official, the ticket inspector, the schoolmaster, the works manager, all have big organizations behind them which make it easier for them to require obedience. In most such cases the incumbent exercises the authority only when he is on duty or within the institution; when he goes home he is an ordinary citizen. But there are some roles, such as those of policeman and priest, which are hardly ever in abeyance. The policeman's powers and obligations are with him twenty-four hours a day and he is supposed to take official action at any time he sees a breach of the peace. When he meets an acquaintance on a sociable occasion it is difficult for either of them to forget that he is a policeman and that at some future time the policeman might have to take official action against the other. This leads to all sorts of problems. The policeman wonders whether, if such an occasion were to arise, the other man would embarrass him by expecting special treatment. For fear of such possibilities the policeman may be reserved and this may make the other man think he is being superior. Then again, the policeman frequently possesses confidential information about members of the public and could damage a few reputations if he were so minded. His occupation affects his leisure-time social relations in myriad ways and it is clearly important both for the performance of his official duty and for his own peace of mind that his public and private roles should be kept separate. This is more difficult for the policeman than for most authority figures because he is in a real sense always on duty although his organization cannot support him to the same extent when he is out of uniform. He has to rely upon his own social skills to convey to other people the appropriate balance between his public and private interests. The policeman's problem is greater also because he is lower down the social scale than other persons holding roles of comparable authority. The magistrate lives in a middle-class district and may have a servant who can be used as a buffer between him and importunate callers. The policeman sometimes has to live among the very people from whom he most wishes to dissociate himself.

The way in which a policeman's occupation follows him into sociable contacts has some complex consequences. The policeman, like the clergyman, is required to be a bit better than everyone else. His role puts him forward as someone more moral than others, as someone slightly sacred and at the same time dangerous. Quite apart from his powers of arrest, his presence may threaten people's social standing. In some districts people feel very much put out if they have a uniformed policeman come to the door. Thus the policeman's role has something of the quality of 'taboo' made famous by anthropological studies from Polynesia, strange though the comparison may sound. It is this suggestion which underlies an exchange of experiences between two Scottish police officers. One spoke of a conversation with his future wife when he was a young man:

'I spoke of my possibly joining the police and found she had fallen very silent. I had to ask her what she thought of it as an idea, and she hesitated quite some time. "I don't know", she said, "I'd never thought of policemen as human beings before".'

Then the other added:

'I can agree with that because my wife has said on a number of occasions that before she met me she had never thought of policemen as boyfriends. A policeman: that was something to be avoided – a race apart.'

It would be easy to exaggerate this aspect of the matter, but the association is not so very surprising. The more something is withdrawn from the ordinary mundane round of social and economic transactions, the more it is likely to have some 'special', 'sacred' quality to it, and it has been shown that policemen have to be withdrawn to some degree because of the power with which they are invested.

RESTRICTIONS

To protect the policeman's occupational role from appearing to be contaminated by unsuitable private obligations, the Scottish police officer is subject to a variety of restrictions. Similar restrictions are enforced in England and Wales. Some derive from formal limitations embodied in law; others stem from the nature of the tasks to be performed, from the discipline code enforced by chief constables, and from the informal expectations of public opinion. They will be considered in turn.

The Scottish policeman is subject to a number of legal disabilities, the most important of which are stated in the regulations in the following terms:

'No person shall be qualified for appointment, or shall be retained, as a member of a police force if:

(a) without the consent of the chief constable he carries on any business or holds any other office or employment for hire or gain, or

(b) without the consent of the chief constable he resides at any premises where any member of his family keeps a shop or carries on any like business, or

(c) he holds, or any member of his family living with him holds, any licence granted in pursuance of the liquor licensing laws or the laws regulating places of public entertainment in the area of the police force in which he seeks appointment or to which he has been appointed, as the case may be, or has any pecuniary interest in such licence, or

(d) without the consent of the chief constable, his wife keeps a shop or carries on any like business in the area of the police force in which he seeks appointment or to which he has been appointed, as the case may be.

For the purpose of this Regulation, the expression "member of his family" shall include parent, son or daughter, brother or sister, or wife' (*Police* (*Scotland*) *Regulations*, 1956, sec. 2).

The fourth schedule to the regulations adds:

'A member of a police force shall at all times abstain from any activity which is likely to interfere with the impartial discharge of his duties or which is likely to give rise to the impression amongst

191

members of the public that it may so interfere; and in particular a member of a police force shall not take any active part in politics' (ibid. sec. 1).

The schedule also states that the place at which a member of a police force resides shall be subject to the approval of the chief constable, and has provisions concerning policemen having lodgers in their houses or contracting debts. Further legislation prohibits membership of 'any association having for its object, or one of its objects, to control or influence the pay, pensions or conditions of service of any police force' other than the official Police Federation.

To this needs to be added a variety of material circumstances inherent in police work which reinforce the isolation of the policeman. In the cities, constables will always be needed for night shift and extra details on Saturday afternoon when the crowds assemble for football games. In the country districts, many officers have to be continuously on call; they are moved around from one village to another, which upsets their children's schooling and their social life. Such circumstances, of course, have their parallels in other occupations but they should not be overlooked just because they are so obvious a contingency of the work.

The *Police (Discipline) Regulations* is a statutory instrument which subordinates the constable to control by appointed superiors in specified respects. The regulations are wide-ranging in the matters they cover. The first of them defines as an offence:

'Discreditable conduct, that is to say, if he acts in a disorderly manner or any manner prejudicial to discipline or likely to bring discredit on the reputation of the force or of the police service.'

This clause is sometimes used by chief constables to exercise authority over matters that many policemen would consider are their private affairs, having no bearing upon their performance of their duties. Any group of police officers can provide a number of instances of what appears unjustified interference. Probably such stories lose nothing in the telling and they give a false impression of the frequency of very strict enforcement, but they do serve to remind the individual policeman that unless he is extremely circumspect such action could be taken against himself, and thus to make him more cautious than he otherwise might be. For example, in one force a young constable wished to sell a piano organ, and took it to a shop for this purpose. He was seen leaving without it and this was reported. This shop had a pawnbroker's licence and conducted a pawnbroking business from a side door. The person who reported the incident assumed that the officer had pawned the piano organ and he was put on a charge for discreditable conduct, transactions with pawnbrokers being considered unbecoming to a police officer. In the end the charge against the officer was dismissed but not before he had been put to much anxiety and embarrassment. Stories of this kind may not be representative but they can be influential nevertheless.

The policeman is expected to be circumspect in his choice of friends and though the discipline code only forbids him to 'place himself under pecuniary obligation to any publican, beer-retailer, spirit grocer or any person who holds a licence concerning the granting or renewal of which the police may have to report or give evidence', in practice, any close association with a publican, bookmaker, or money-lender would be disapproved. In such circumstances a man's superior would probably indicate to him that such relations were considered inadvisable. The code further penalizes any constable who 'directly or indirectly solicits or receives any gratuity, present, subscription or testimonial without the consent of the chief constable or police authority'.[1] It also specifies that:

> 'Any member of a police force commits an offence against discipline if he is guilty of . . . (4) Neglect of duty, that is to say if he (a) neglects, or without good and sufficient cause omits, promptly and diligently to attend to or carry out anything which is his duty as a constable.'

Such general phraseology permits considerable variation in interpretation, but since the regulations leave the question of interpretation to individual disciplinary authorities, the Scottish Home and Health Department does not intervene in this connection. For example, in one force the writing of occasional short stories for sale to magazines

---

[1] In some parts of the United States special police reward schemes are organized, and stores may display a little label in the window stating that they belong to the scheme; this is to encourage the police officer to guard the premises better than he otherwise might. In Scotland a rural policeman may be forbidden to accept a presentation which the villagers wish to make him on his retirement.

was construed as an 'office or employment for hire or gain' and declared impermissible under the code. Elsewhere, however, officers receive official permission to take on some kinds of employment (e.g. teaching shorthand at an evening school), or a blind eye is turned to their making extra money in less orthodox ways (e.g. trading cars).[1]

Once the British police were not allowed to vote, and the need to appear detached from political controversies still leads many of them to avoid discussion of political issues altogether. One group of five experienced officers at the Police College responded in this way to a question as to whether they would talk about politics in a boarding house on holiday:

A Police officers adapt themselves in such a way that they don't talk politics. They tend to avoid them. That applies to religion too.

B You tend to avoid the controversial topics that might lead up to trouble.

C I don't know. Provided I knew the people, I mean, on holiday and I was on a friendly basis with these people and they knew me to be a policeman, I could easily argue politics.

D Well you could, aye.

A Not vehemently, leisurely.

B It's a thing I never discuss.

C I don't normally argue politics at all, but I don't feel constrained not to.

D My wife 'phoned me last week. She said, 'I've been asked to sit on a committee. Have you any objections?' I said, 'What kind of committee is it?' 'Political.' 'Oh?' says I, 'I can't stop you from going, but I advise you against it. Go and attend a

[1] An indication how such matters are managed in London is unconsciously provided by the *Police Review* (8 March 1963) in noting that a member of parliament had asked the Home Secretary to look into the case of an officer who was a qualified football referee. For refereeing a first-division match he received a fee of £7 7s. He was allowed to keep £3 3s. of this for expenses; £2 2s. 9d. was set aside for tax; and the officer was required to give the balance to charity. *De minimis non curat lex?*

meeting if you like to but I strongly advise you not to go on any committee, love.' 'Oh.' So there you are . . .

Later E entered the argument saying:

E Can I answer the question this way, by saying that if I was pressed I would not hide my own politics – I wouldn't dodge my own politics and I have . . .

But D interrupted:

D You're no' supposed to have any!

and there the matter rested. Most Scottish policemen will give no indication of favouring a party political viewpoint except among people they know and consider discreet. This avoidance seems to cause some of them to lose interest in party politics and to feel detached from the controversies. It seems likely that the more senior officers feel a strong obligation to appear neutral and that city officers have more freedom than their counterparts in the country districts.

The policemen are required to avoid political controversies by the discipline code but there are other, vaguer, obligations imposed by popular expectations without any real legal backing. One sergeant spoke about a constable he knew in a 'quiet law-abiding village' and said:

'His wife felt that she had to go out properly dressed even if she was only going up the street. She could not just slip on a coat over a pair of slacks.'

'And she could do that in the city?'

'Well she could. I know a lot of people who do and it isn't terribly obvious, but in a village it would be talked about. They (the wives) are more conspicuous than the policemen actually.'

In the rural regions a policeman is not normally stationed in a village where he grew up, and if he becomes too familiar with the people round about he is posted elsewhere. Most officers with twenty years' service in a county force can remember the days when a policeman who proposed to marry was required first to submit the name of his fiancée to his superiors so that they could ascertain whether she was a fit and proper person for the role of policeman's wife. Then in addition there are the diffuse obligations imposed by public opinion which expects the policeman to be a bit better than his neighbours and causes him to be sure that his lawn is regularly mown and that his house and family display a respectable face to the world.

Popular expectations of the policeman cause him considerable inconvenience at times when he wishes to be at leisure. The village policeman probably works on 'discretionary hours'. He has no set hours, but turns to whenever there is a job to be done. If he leaves the village to go out with his wife he must have permission from his superior so that arrangements can be made for another officer to take any calls. The village policeman may have to leave in the middle of a meal or stop what he is doing at any time in order to attend a case, but since farmers and other members of the community are similarly exposed this does not seem so very strange. In the city, however, the pattern is different. Most men, when they leave their work of an evening, can put it out of their mind because it creates no obligations binding during their leisure time. As one man observed:

> 'Being a city policeman I've had them come to my house. I'm off duty. I hear a knock on the door and here's maybe someone from away along the crescent where I live. Possibly it's a fire, and they just think that although you're off duty you should come along in the capacity of policeman. Well, on these occasions I've referred them to a police box, or sent them down and told them to use the public 'phone or get in touch with the constable on the beat.'

Another added:

> 'Of course, it's only fair to point out that in a case of emergency or urgency you would do something.'

To the outsider such questions sound trivial and it is easy to point out other occupations that suffer from the same inconvenience, even if most of them are at a higher salary level. But the cumulative effect of these trivial calls can be considerable. Very many police officers would agree with their colleague who spoke thus:

> 'I have a very strong opinion that when my day's work is finished I want to be able to relax socially in the same way that a person

from another profession or occupation does. I think you're bound
to agree with me that you can hardly go into company, but someone will say some stupid remarks. He'll say, "Better watch what
you're saying, the bobby's here", or something to that effect. . . .'

And then the public identify all individual policemen with their
occupation to a degree that they seem not to do with doctors, clergymen, or representatives of any other occupation. As the policeman
continued:

'If a milkman goes on holiday and meets people, they don't start
telling him about their milkman having brought them sour milk.
But the minute we as policemen go away on holiday and it comes
out that we are policemen, we're immediately deluged with stories
"When we were given parking tickets", and so forth.'

It would seem therefore that the contamination of the policeman's
private roles by his occupation is accentuated by two factors. First,
in respect of income he lives at a class level which offers him less
protection. Second, the authority vested in the police role evokes a
distinctive response from the public such that they find it harder to
accept him as an ordinary sort of person.

Interference with the policeman's private life is accentuated by
the discipline regulation which requires him to take police action
whenever it is required even if such action will spoil the occasion for
the man himself or his family. One incident of this kind was embodied
in a questionnaire, the results of which are discussed in Chapter 9.
As might be expected, very many policemen try to guard against this
sort of interference by going well away from their own neighbourhood for entertainment. As one inspector remarked:

'As for taking my wife out in the town where I'm stationed, it is
the last thing I'll ever think of doing because you're never off
duty, and as soon as you're up the street with the good lady and
something happens you have to buzz off and leave her – as I've
had to do many a time, even on my day off when I've not been on
24-hour call. I've been seated in a picture house when I've had to
rise and come out and leave my wee lady sitting because somebody
was needed downstairs.'

197

Even in a new locality the policeman often feels visible:

> 'No matter where you go – into the best bars, hotel bars and lounges, wherever you care to go we can sense it. . . There's the height, there's the cut of your jib, there's just something they can recognize right away.'

A lot of Scottish police officers find the intrusiveness of their job so irritating that they attempt to conceal their occupation when on holiday. As one said:

> 'If someone asks my wife "What does your husband do?", I've told her to say "He's a clerk", and that's the way it went because she found that being a policeman's wife – well, it wasn't quite a stigma, she didn't feel cut off, but that a sort of invisible wall was up for conversation purposes when a policeman was there.'

Two-thirds of a sample of British officers interviewed in connection with the Royal Commission stated that they experienced difficulties in making friendships with people outside the force: 58 per cent of those interviewed thought that members of the public were reserved, suspicious, and constrained in conversation; 12 per cent thought that such difficulties should be attributed to the way policemen had to be selective in their associations and to behave circumspectly. The longer a man's period of service, the more likely he was to report this sort of experience (*Royal Commission on the Police*, Appendix IV to the *Minutes of Evidence*, p. 37). It would be difficult to consider separately these two aspects of the problem, public reserve and police circumspection, as for the policeman they are always intertwined. So the ways in which the problem impinges upon the man and his family will be discussed, and then an attempt will be made to outline and explain variations in its incidence.

A Scottish sergeant stated in a discussion among officers from city forces:

> 'I have lived in a middle-class area for twenty-one years and during that time I have made very few friends and it is purely because I am a police officer. My wife . . . is always referred to as being a policeman's wife and I am always introduced into company as a police officer. My children come home and tell me in a jocular manner

that one of the other children said, "Oh, I'd better not tell you. What does your dad do?", and if they say he's a law man, they say, "Oh, I'd better not tell you". So it does affect you. There *is* a difference. I feel that we are *shunned* and that we have difficulty in making friends. We are an exception. And our wives and children are shunned because we are police officers.'

His colleague added:

'As one who has also been born and reared in Glasgow itself, I agree with a great deal of what he says so far as my wife and myself are concerned in our treatment at the hands of neighbours.'

Men from Dundee and Aberdeen testified that these circumstances did not hold in their cities, and an Edinburgh man qualified his acceptance of the statement by saying that he would agree so far as the working class was concerned but that there was less difficulty in relations with middle-class people. The thesis that policemen suffer more social isolation in the denser urban areas receives some support from evidence to be examined later, but this does not appear to be the most important variable. Many officers who live in circumstances similar to the two Glasgow sergeants do not feel that their social life is constrained or restricted by their occupation.

A review of the sorts of social situation in which policemen experience this kind of difficulty reveals that the most common complaint concerns off-duty contacts with people that the officer might possibly want to be friendly with. Consider the following discussion:

A You can never get away from being a police officer. If you become a member, say, of a bowling club, invariably you'll get the remark 'Here, watch what you're saying. The police are here.' That always crops up. You can never walk in as John Citizen.

B Even last Saturday, well, I'd better explain first. I am quite interested in a certain breed of dog. I attended a championship show at the barracks in Edinburgh where I thought I was unknown. I spoke to a lady whose home is in Sale in Cheshire, and about the second thing she said to me was, 'Well, you're a policeman, aren't you?' I said, 'Who was

199

telling you this, Mrs Jones ?' 'Oh,' she said, 'I was told by some of the people from Scotland.' It just appeared to me that there was a tab – I don't know whether it was a good tab or a bad tab, but there's a tab attached to you. I was branded police-man.

c And you didn't like it?

B Well, I prefer to be, as Alan says, John Citizen. When I'm in Edinburgh I don't want to be a policeman. I want to be a visitor to Edinburgh. When I go into a dog show I want to be another competitor. I just want to be that, no more, no less. But before I go, the grape-vine whispers, the tom-toms beat out the message – the police are coming!

This theme repeats itself time and again. Another variation on it is contained in the following anecdote:

'I remember being in a boarding house up at Arbroath and it was nice and sociable until someone asked my wife what I did, and as soon as the police were mentioned you could sense the change of atmosphere. It took me until the next night to show that I was on holiday and that at least I'd forgotten for fourteen days that I was a policeman. I got on all right after that but I had to make a con-scious effort to overcome what happens to you then.'

But by no means all officers experience this sort of situation; some deny it and are willing to consider that the difficulty is largely of the policeman's own creation.

Because the policeman's occupational role is always with him, even if at times it lies passive, he cannot enter into certain other roles in the way a fireman, a schoolteacher, or a prison officer might, and even if he were prepared to drop his police obligations completely, the public would still be reserved. The distance they maintain in this respect is only partly one of personal caution; in part it is like the distance shown towards ministers of religion who are supposed to keep themselves undefiled by a whole range of associations. In parti-cular, both the policeman and the member of the public feel that the police role puts qualifications on a man's friendships. If it be agreed that the police must exercise personal discretion it must be accepted that they will sometimes modify their actions through considerations of friendship. Provided that this touches only minor matters there is no reason why it should not be regarded in the same light as schemes whereby miners get cheap coal. After all, the obligations of friendship are in all human societies felt as some of the most binding and sacred of all. (In one discussion group the participants were infuriated by one of their number who insisted that he would charge a neighbour for a burning chimney or an expired road fund licence. Referring to such officers, one man remarked, 'Some of them would do their grannies, just like Robertson here'; he thought such an attitude lacked a sense of proportion.) This question is referred to from another angle in the following extract from a discussion:

A I know a man who had a taxi business on my beat. I was very friendly with him and on cold days I used to go and get a cup of tea from him. Well, he was booked for speeding on one occasion and he asked me would I see the plain-clothes men who worked the speed trap; he said he'd be very happy if he didn't get a summons for it, you see. Now I went and saw the plain-clothes men and he was only two or three miles over the limit and so they scrapped it, see. He was protected because he knew the beat man; if he hadn't known me, I know I'd have looked at him and said, 'Sorry, I can't do that for you'.

B It depends on personalities. If I was operating a speed check and Dr Banton came along and we recognized each other, I don't know what Dr Banton's viewpoint would be, but he would say to himself, 'That's a queer so-and-so adopting all that red tape.'

A Yes, that's right, it's a matter of personal conduct.

B But if it was a strange policeman who saw Dr Banton and booked him he'd think nothing of it.

C Yes, but if Dr Banton was drunk in charge of a car you wouldn't . . .

Some discussions gave the impression that Scottish policemen avoided friendships with people who might ask for favours because they knew they would probably have to reject them and feared that this might poison their relations, but a more important factor is probably that referred to in B's last remark in the extract above. Many policemen feel rather guilty when they put anyone on a charge; if they have to charge a friend this is a disturbing situation even though they know their action to be correct. The desire to avoid any such conflicts leads some officers to restrict their social circles appreciably. When discussing the sort of persons with whom policemen would feel reluctant to strike up friendship, one Glasgow supervising officer added businessmen to the list. He explained how acute the parking problem was in the city; how businessmen were so easily forced into breaking the law and were resentful when they were prosecuted for parking offences. He had, indeed, a lot of sympathy for their viewpoint. But their resentment could make them prickly acquaintances and if they had a friend in the force they were liable to expect special consideration if reported for what they regarded as a trivial offence. This officer concluded that the path of discretion was to keep clear of businessmen as possible friends, at any rate in Glasgow. Officers who feel like this may be expected to seek the company of fellow policemen more. In a large force this is easier because there are more people of equivalent rank and because jealousy concerning promotion is less likely to intervene.

Even in smaller forces, probationers are often advised to restrict their friendships to fellow policemen. Some of their seniors, however, hold strong contrary views. They argue that they have had more than enough of police business during the day and wish to be free of it when they have finished. Or they hold that friendships within the force do not always fit in with the requirements of official duties and may cause others to suspect favouritism. Some officers dislike the recruitment of cadets, asserting that for a young man to have had no experience outside the police makes him too narrow-minded. This problem of just how separate the police should be can never be solved, for circumstances change and temperaments differ too much.[1]

[1] The secretary of the Scottish Police Federation comments: 'I think that the difficulties said to be experienced in connection with the social problems of police officers are overstated. The social position of police officers in Scotland

The Segregation of the Police Officer's Role in Britain

The personality of the police officer is, of course, an important factor influencing the solution any one man will adopt. Some men get unduly worried about the possibility of getting into trouble with their superiors or about the likelihood of an acquaintance's asking them to have a charge dropped. Yet it would appear as if the core of the problem lies not in personality so much as in the officer's skill in handling an ambiguous situation. A case in which one man has to deal with another who is angry, sick, under a misapprehension, or trying to exploit the situation to his personal advantage, is one that calls for social skills. Some men have such skills in high degree. They can jockey the other party into seeing things their way. They can indicate that they are acting in their official capacity while giving the impression of being personally friendly. They can make it easier for the other man to apologize or settle on some solution. These skills are learned, not inherited, and, as was shown in the

has never been better. Police officers in Scotland are probably more completely integrated with the public than in any other country in Europe. Many police officers in all ranks are house owners and these houses are located in every district in and around towns and cities. Police officers are to be found taking prominent parts in the affairs of many of our leading golf clubs, bowling clubs, swimming clubs, etc. A Glasgow policeman is the president of the Scottish Amateur Swimming Association while another Glasgow policeman is the secretary of the Scottish Amateur Boxing Association. Policemen are also to be found taking part in the affairs of local chess clubs, and photographic clubs, and are among the most successful youth club leaders. They are prominent in the lay activities of every known religious body in the country. They are connected with rotary clubs, round table, and almost every association of social importance. The work of individual police officers for deserving causes is well known. Many forces have concert parties, choirs, or other entertainers who give of their services freely for the needy, the aged, and the sick. A Glasgow police officer is a director of the Eastpark Home for Children and is a prominent member of an amateur film unit which produces films which are shown to patients in hospitals. Another Glasgow policeman will be the convener for a flag day in the greater Glasgow area for the National Childrens' Home and Orphanage.'

This constitutes a welcome gloss upon any discussion of the point, but it may well be that my account understates the social isolation of the policeman in some English urban areas. The National Council of Civil Liberties told the Royal Commission: 'In the towns and industrial areas the police tend to be housed together and encouraged to keep themselves to themselves . . . One of our speakers has been asking audiences throughout London at trade union meetings, church groups, etc., whether anyone present knew a policeman socially. In only one case was the answer in the affirmative. Most people have no social or personal contact with the police at all, certainly in the Metropolitan area' (*Royal Commission on the Police, Minutes of Evidence*, 13, p. 762).

previous chapter, policemen often develop them to a very high degree. Nevertheless, situations in which a policeman, out of uniform, is introduced into company are very difficult ones. Policemen agree that once they have got to know people well, the problems of potentially conflicting obligations do not arise. They are accepted as individuals and their police roles can slip into the background. Similarly, in country districts where peoples' personalities and reputations are well known, the pattern of expectations is relatively clear. The situations that are most apt to give trouble are the fairly informal gatherings when the policeman knows insufficient about the people he is meeting to tell whether or not he wants them as friends; he feels hampered by being typed as a policeman when he would sooner explore the situation as John Citizen. Some officers, apparently, have the manner to be able to carry off even the more delicate situations without feeling uneasy or making other people self-conscious. It remains an interesting question why officers of longer service should experience more social isolation (the Social Survey figures referred to show a response of 58·7 per cent for men of up to five years' service; 67·8 per cent for men of six to ten years' service; and 72·6 per cent for men of eleven or more years' service).

THE POLICEMAN'S FAMILY

One possibility is that a policeman's sense of social separateness grows as he comes to feel the effect his occupation can have upon his family. In a rural community the policeman's wife is strongly identified with her husband's occupation. She is referred to, not as Mrs McKenzie, but as 'the policeman's wife', just as people regularly say 'the minister's wife'. This happens to a lesser extent in the cities, but there criticism of the police is more frequent and the policeman's wife feels she must defend them. If there has been a newspaper report of a policeman's being convicted for some offence, another woman will bring it up or some other occasion will be utilized to put pressure on her. In some localities this sort of thing is carried to the point of outright hostility: for example, other women may use their perambulators to force the policeman's wife off the pavement. If the policeman knows this sort of thing is going on he can feel very disturbed whether his wife complains or not.

A similar situation may obtain with the children. In a few places police children may be victimized by the others, but this is unusual. Sometimes, too, youngsters who are up to mischief will try to get one of the policeman's children to accompany them because they think this may give them a measure of protection. The policeman is vulnerable through his dependents, and his authority in dealing with juvenile troubles will be reduced if his own boys get into trouble. One sergeant mentioned that some children near his house had been storing bonfire wood in an old, unused wash-house, and a window had been broken. He went and mended it. His own boy had not broken the window but he had been there when one of the others had, and the policeman thought it best to be on the safe side. Children may find some reflected glory in being a policeman's son but it has its reverse side in the way a mother may continually hammer home the reminder 'remember who your daddy is'. Some policemen are so careful to warn their children of the law that the children become inhibited and their fathers then wonder whether it would not have been better to let them go with their age-mates even if they might have stolen a few apples.

The detective officer's domestic life is often more disturbed by his occupation than is the patrol officer's. One detective officer remarked that he would never walk down the streets of his home town with his daughters because he did not want some of the shady characters with whom he had to deal to recognize them. He commented, as did another detective officer, on how unpleasant it was to have some of his less acceptable informants come up and greet him when he was out with his wife. Then the detective officer more frequently has to cancel his social engagements to go on a case, and often has to work many hours of overtime. One observed that where he was stationed the position was so bad that his wife had to be both father and mother to the children. On many occasions his daughter had asked him to help her with her studies or had arranged for him to go on an outing with her and he had been obliged to let her down. She had been grievously disappointed and he had been embittered over a job which prevented him from being a proper father to her and a proper husband to his wife.

The policeman's wife on a country station is in effect a valuable though unpaid member of the force; indeed, one sergeant said his wife had complained to him that family life was beginning to take too much of her time! But whereas her involvement in her husband's job helps the country force, it seems to work the other way in the city. As a Glasgow man said:

'I am definitely against putting, say, six or eight policemen all in two blocks congested together because I have seen from experience among my own constables that if one gets, say, a greenhouse, there's jealousy. Or one wife says, "How can he get made a sergeant? Why are you still a constable?" It can conjure up petty strife between the wives and their families.'

In one city at least the police found that other policemen made better neighbours than ordinary members of the public, but putting a whole group of police families together is another matter. Another Glasgow man added:

'In our city there are large housing schemes being built, and to me it seems to be the policy to allocate a particular close with perhaps six houses, at various points throughout that area. They're obviously selective in their sites for one purpose and one purpose only, as a steadying influence. It does have that effect, because I've visited these areas and noticed that in the vicinity of the police houses all was quiet. The road to come, there are noisy children and there are stone-throwers. I've also noticed the other effect on the children of police officers occupying these houses – a rougher effect, a deterioration. It's difficult for the families and heads of the families to keep those children in these conditions.'

Elsewhere when new estates are planned to receive tenants moved out under slum-clearance schemes, end flats in two or three of the blocks may be reserved for policemen. These are often places in which no policemen would willingly choose to live, and he may try to keep his children continuously indoors to counteract the influence of some of the neighbouring children. As one man put it:

'I had rented a house in a tenement – it was a reasonably good house, but I was on the fringe of a bad area where my children had to go to school with children from this bad area who were dirty. Their language was bad. Their habits were bad. And not because I was a policeman did I want to move, but because I wanted to do justice to my family. I mean, I didn't move because I was a police-man and because they were being set aside as policemen's children. I don't think they ever had that though of course they were very young at the time. Being a constable, I didn't have a good deal of money but I strained my finances quite considerably to put a deposit on a house elsewhere. But not because I was a policeman, I don't want that to come in. I wanted the kids to get a fair chance as anyone else would have done in similar circumstances although they weren't policemen.'

Given that these are very normal sentiments in modern Britain it points up one of the dilemmas in housing policy. If all the ambitious, middle-class sort of people avoid a neighbourhood, it is left without many of the people who might provide leadership in neighbourhood affairs and strengthen the social controls. The police officer living in some of the new estates may wish to send his children to a school in a better area, but he rarely has the extra money for this and it may only make the neighbours think him and his wife even more stuck up. In some of these estates the problem of the policeman's role, in requiring a man to be in the community and yet not defiled by any of its less worthy features, must be at its most acute. Most urban police authorities are now conscious of the social tensions that can derive from policies for police housing, but many policemen resent schemes which they see as designed to provide indirect policing at the expense of the officer's private life.[1]

Police officers are all aware of the social consequences of their job and try to counteract them. Those who have insight into their own reactions are often concerned about the psychological conse-quences. They suffer from what they call the 'police mind'. One man defined it thus: 'The police mind means that you suspect your grand-mother and that's about the strength of it.' Another referred to the police mind as 'a disease of the job'. He said that 'you come to view everything from a police angle so that, after many years in the police, to a degree you become a race apart'. This theme of the 'race apart' is a recurring one in Scotland. The chief characteristics of the

[1] On police housing in London, see the note by Leslie Smith in *New Society* (2 May 1963, p. 8).

'police mind' seem to stem from the way a policeman must examine critically every statement made to him. If Smith complains about Jones, Smith's account of what happened can quite well be false while Jones's is truthful. The policeman must not accept Smith's story because he tells it first or because he looks a more credible witness. Policemen must test any statement made to them to see if it has flaws; in their occupational role this is expected of them, but in sociable roles such suspiciousness counts as unfriendly behaviour. Probationers say that their parents or wives start to complain about such suspiciousness in leisure-time situations and insist that they leave police matters behind when they take off their uniforms. Some probationers at the college spoke thus:

A My wife is always getting on to me because when we travel home I've developed the habit of saying, 'That bloke's committed an offence', or 'That chap's doing something wrong'. Unconsciously you're doing that all the time after a while. . . .

B It's just the same with me. I've seen me out with my wife, maybe out for a walk past shops and that, the first thing you do is look at the shop door (i.e. to see if it has been properly secured).

A I'll tell you another thing that I noticed myself doing, is if there is something wrong in the house you begin to question your wife as if you were questioning a suspect. It's actually true. You ask a police sergeant – you begin to get into a routine.

C My wife says to me, 'You're not on duty now', when I get like that, questioning her.

I She doesn't like it?

C Oh, no! I find the wife gets angry, you know, whenever I start that. You don't actually mean to do it. . . .

Because of the special position they enjoy in the public confidence, some occupations have to maintain a front against laymen. The public expects near omniscience, in their respective spheres, from doctors and policemen, so both are careful never to criticize a colleague before laymen. Policemen are the recipients of a stream of questions, some silly, others requesting information which might be used to resist another officer's instructions; this tends to make them more conscious of the distinction between themselves and other members of the public. They usually feel obliged to support one another, even if it is only a question of countering criticisms of the police made on a social occasion. At times the contrary pulls of occupational and personal ties can be bewildering, as with the probationer who, with some colleagues, was clearing the pavement outside a dance hall one Saturday night. Among the crowd he saw a friend, a man who had been best man at his wedding; seeing him coming, this man started to come up to his friend and then hesitated, not knowing whether friendship would be acknowledged in such a situation. The policeman found it acutely embarrassing. Many policemen try not to discuss police matters with their wives, either for fear that they might let slip personal information or because they do not wish to discuss the rights and wrongs of what they have had to do in their occupational roles. However, to the extent to which policemen keep their occupational work separate from other social relations its aura of 'sacredness' is increased and the public's tendency to expect exemplary behaviour of policemen is heightened. Such expectations can hold even within the family and make the off-duty policeman toe the line more than he otherwise might. One constable spoke for many of his colleagues when he observed:

A We find now that my eldest boy, he's eight, when we're out in the car and going through a built-up area, he watches the speedometer like a hawk.

B Aye, 'Dad, you're speeding', I know!

A Yes, that's right. Constantly, 'Daddy's a policeman.'

In most of the aspects of police work considered above there are important variations between the position of the village policeman and that of the big city policeman. One officer, recounting how he had found a village post in comparison with the town, said:

A I moved from a burgh out to a mining village, a two-man station at which I was the senior constable. I found that after

209

you got to know the village you were being questioned by the doctor, the minister, the colliery managers, that's from the top level down to the worst individual you had in your village, and there were some tough men among them. Till one day you were walking them off and the next day you were giving them some family advice or something like that. I found that after being there for eighteen months or so you got into the social activities. Again you have to be very choosy how deep you get into certain activities, but I got interested in a boys' club and confined my off-duty time to them. I had no *real* off-duty time because of the suspicion caused by the uniform . . . In a mining community you must establish a few things. One of them is that you play fair. Secondly, you don't chase them, or chase their children. And thirdly, you use kindness, deliver messages . . .

B Aye, but let's take your village constable back into a town of any kind of size. It's a wee bit different there. Even the school kids are sometimes inclined to be sort of nasty with one another at the school, and that's something that still happens.

C Yes I can back that up . . .

I (*Later*) . . . what constitutes playing unfair?

A Well, if you sneak. You must catch them in the act, as it were. For instance, cycle lights. Give them a warning in the first place. On a number of occasions, particularly with lights, I've had it said in reply to the charge, 'Well you've warned me often enough'. Instead of making an enemy you make a friend, strangely enough. If you set a trap they may object to that very strongly.

TOWNS AND VILLAGES

In the villages the policeman is perceived as an individual known for his personal characteristics. In the bigger towns, policemen are seen more as members of a social category. In some working-class neighbourhoods they are identified with the propertied classes and at times viewed as enemies. Such feelings are more marked in the industrial regions of the west of Scotland, as the following remarks suggest:

'People were somewhat against the police at the time of the general strike in 1926. This was in Glasgow.'

'As far as the city we live in is concerned (Glasgow), I think that being a police officer amongst the average working class is a stigma.'

To which another man from the same force added:

'I agree with you there.'

And again:

'The average Glasgow youth knows the disrespect held for the police. He wouldn't like to be in the same category.'

Yet it would be a mistake to assume that people who prefer to keep clear of the police either dislike them personally or have something to hide. One officer commented:

'The ordinary working man is looked on with a certain amount of suspicion if he associates too closely with the police . . . When it came to entertainment . . . golf, whist, cards, going to a dance, you always found yourself pairing off with some baker, or somebody in a bank, a picture house manager, or somebody. There was always a company man. It wasn't a man who worked over a bench who felt that "my pal back up the street would say that lad was with a policeman the other night".'

This feeling that association with a policeman is somehow different from association with other people, and calls for some explanation, is probably much more widespread and complex than straightforward antipathy towards the police.

Suspicion of the police by the working classes in industrial areas is frequently countered by friendship from middle-class people. One man said:

'I have just been turning over in my mind all those people whom I can number as my friends, and most, in fact, practically all of them are of the higher or middle class rather than the working class. . . . When you get up into the realm of schoolteachers, bankers, businessmen with their own businesses, there is a different attitude altogether. They don't seem to care two hoots whether

P

they are suspected of anything or not. So that, frankly, the crowd I've always knocked about with, even as a constable and in the CID, have always been of that type.'

The same officer said later:

'If you go to a works dance where you are meeting every part of the employees it is only the management section that makes you feel at home.'

A county officer, who felt similarly, observed:

'You don't have any feeling of guilt with the upper structure.'

In a very few localities, resentment of the police passes into smouldering hostility. A sergeant who had worked in an industrial town on the outskirts of Glasgow reported that the police children were subject to so much victimization on the part of the other children that they had to arrange a roster to escort their children home from school. The hostility had made his son 'a bag of nerves'. Another officer from nearby said:

'There's a cooperative store in a housing scheme. Across the road is a police building used for living accommodation. Several policemen's wives have told me that if they suddenly discover they need something they nip across to the store. There'll be the usual huddle in the middle of the floor and a conversation going on. It dries up whenever they go in and everyone moves up to the counter to be served. After they (the police wives) have been able to get served they hear the hubbub break out again after they come out. I don't know if it's hostility or sheer suspicion.'

I Do you find women making anti-police remarks so that the police wives shall overhear them?

'Yes, that does happen. Not so much, I think, as this deathly hush. There's nobody speaking to nobody.'

Then there are a number of cases where the police authority has had to give up houses in slum-clearance estates because of hostility. One man, explaining that his wife had been on the verge of a nervous breakdown in one of these houses, said:

212

'I was perturbed about the conditions, certainly, but it wasn't affecting my mental fitness because I was away from it. My wife was getting it all the time I was away. As soon as I got on my bike to go up the hill they started on her. She couldn't go out to a local delivery van, she couldn't walk up the street without all these cat calls and leers.'

Such cases are extreme exceptions. Even so, they rarely pass into hostile actions (like cutting the police wife's clothes-line when she cannot see) but rely on indirect pressure. That it can, in these circumstances, be so acute (for policemen do not complain very readily of such things) is an instructive comment on the range of police-public relations in Scotland.

It seemed at first as if these variations in the social position of the policeman were due to his ambiguous position in the class structure, in being identified with the propertied classes but remunerated and housed on the same level as working-class people. In country districts this is countered by personal acquaintance, but city life tends to segregate the social classes and to sharpen the antagonisms. Closer inspection, however, showed that the cases of open hostility were not reported from the big city slums but from places in the industrial belt round Glasgow and from slum-clearance schemes in other localities. Hostility, it seems, is not experienced very much in the cities because policemen do not reside in the worst neighbourhoods; they and their families do not meet people from these areas in off-duty hours and are less likely to be recognized anyway. Pressure is brought to bear chiefly where policemen have to live in a locality ill-disposed towards them. This happens in some housing estates, and in industrial pockets within county police areas which are policed on the country pattern rather than the urban one. To quote once more:

A The policeman in Glasgow is quite distinct from the policeman in most places. He does his eight to four shift, then he's finished. He's never recalled. But the policemen in these places we're talking about are very often never off duty.

B I think that *is* the real point. There's the policeman who finishes his eight hours. Although he's in a different locality

213

the public accept him as being off duty, but in the village they never do.

This suggests that the social structure of the village is sufficiently differentiated for the policeman and his family to be members of the society socially, while he is to a degree separate from it occupationally. In the rougher urban areas the social pattern does not allow for such niceties, and though the policeman can display personal sympathy with many of the unsuccessful and reprobate, he cannot involve his family with them and still maintain the conception he has of himself as a husband and father in a society which encourages material advancement. As one policeman observed: 'It doesn't hit the man at all. We're immune to it. You've got a hide like a rhinoceros by the time you've done twenty years in the police.' But it does hit the policeman's dependents, and it hits him through them.

CHAPTER 8

The Social Definition of the Police Officer's Role

The previous chapter has shown that in Britain the policeman is enabled to do his job the more effectively for being set apart from society in a variety of respects. Because of the authority he exercises over members of the public he prefers to keep them at a distance and they prefer to keep him at a distance. How far might this same pattern be expected to occur in the United States also? Before my visit to the United States I thought that for a variety of reasons American police officers might well experience more social isolation than their British counterparts. I assumed that the heavier incidence of violent crime, the high proportion of 'cop-haters', the 'shoot first, ask afterwards' tactics American police have to use on occasion, and the lower prestige of police work, would cause policemen to feel more like outcasts or like troops in occupation of enemy territory. Such an expectation was in accordance with an impression to be gained from a study of Westley's dissertation, where it is said: 'The exigencies of the occupation form the police into a social group which tends to be in conflict with and isolated from the community; and in which the norms are independent of the community' (Westley, 1951, p. 294). The locality in which Westley's research was conducted turns out, however, to be far from representative of the present-day situation, and a reconsideration of his evidence from a comparative rather than a purely American perspective reveals a whole series of influences which operate in a contrary fashion. American police may seem isolated from the community to an American observer because he compares them with other occupational groups in the same society; they may at the same time seem to an outsider much less isolated than policemen in other societies. This possibility opens up a series of interesting questions, but before attempting to formulate and answer them, it will be necessary to adduce evidence as to the extent to which being a policeman in America does in practice affect a man's incumbency of other roles.

THE SEGREGATION OF THE POLICE OFFICER'S ROLE IN THE UNITED STATES

Where the British policeman is subject to disabilities deriving from laws enacted by the central government, the American police officer is completely free. Federal laws regulate the Federal Bureau of Investigation, not the state or local policemen who are subject simply to state legislation and local government laws; these do not define the policeman's position closely so that in practice the only formal disabilities derive from the discipline regulations of local police forces. In most places the police officer's tenure of office is based upon civil service procedures and imposes no restrictions more severe than those placed upon the clerks in City Hall. Every police department has its regulations, along lines similar to those enforced in Britain, which provide for the punishment or discharge of any officer found guilty of disobedience, neglect of duty, conduct unbecoming to a police officer, etc. In Georgia City these regulations prohibit officers from consuming alcoholic liquor even off duty (see p. 122). In practice, however, the Georgia City regulation is not rigidly enforced, and whatever the rule book says the American interpretation of such requirements tends to be much more permissive than the British. The American police officer is expected to be discreet off duty, not saintly. His chief will not mind his going off with a men's club for an afternoon by the river, to drink a little and have a few games of poker, provided no scandal is created. American officers are not usually expected to take official action out of uniform in other than exceptional circumstances, because the public frequently fail to recognize the authority of a man in civilian clothes claiming to be a police officer. His intervention often proves unavailing or actually leads to further trouble.

The American officer can take many kinds of off-duty employment without his chief's objecting. As was explained (pp. 96–7), he can work, in uniform, for a store which wants a policeman to walk around and discourage shoplifting, or for a firm which wants one to control

216

the squash at 5.30 p.m. when all the employees are trying to get their cars out of the parking lot. The policeman who wishes to get ahead socially can usually find other legitimate sources of income if he is prepared to do additional work. Because a man's wealth seems so often to decide how others will evaluate his position, he is motivated to take on additional employment. In Carolina and Georgia Cities, moreover, employment was generally available for women, and many policemen's wives had their own jobs: the availability of relatively cheap Negro domestic service facilitated this. In these circumstances, the idea that 'once a policeman has finished his shift his time is his own' was obviously stronger, and because of their extra commitments police officers had less time to associate together (e.g. at the Carolina City Police Club) than might otherwise be the case. Their outside jobs brought them into contact with members of the public in another fashion and meant that less of their lives circled round their police uniforms. Wives who had their own jobs were less apt to worry about their husbands' special position or their changing hours of work, though, of course, a man's having to work night shift is rarely popular with his family in any community. The lower density of American cities and the greater distances people travel in relatively anonymous automobiles also mean that people are less subject to neighbourhood surveillance.

American police officers, in my experience, rarely complain about the way their occupation affects their private lives. A group of Massachusetts officers, when asked about this, agreed with one of their number who responded: 'When you're off, you're just John Citizen', as if incredulous that it could be otherwise. The older police officers in all the cities visited emphasized that during their service the police had become appreciably less isolated. The assistant chief of Carolina City, for example, observed that twenty years previously people would have been surprised to see a policeman in church. In the South it was expected that the policeman would be 'the meanest man in town' and frequently a drunkard to boot. In recent years, however, police standards had been steadily rising and ever better recruits were enlisting, so that now many policemen took leading parts in church organizations and the occupation was becoming socially respectable. This draws attention to an aspect of the problem of role segregation that has not been mentioned hitherto:

217

the more the incumbents of a role differ as individuals from the normal range in that stratum of society (by being better, worse, or just different from the majority), the more the role itself is apt to be set apart. In that the American policeman has in most places been accorded relatively low prestige, however, this factor must have contributed more to the social isolation of policemen in America than in Britain.

American officers, like their British colleagues, say that their neighbours are apt to become more subdued when a policeman joins the party, and to regard him with some reserve. A policeman who sits on his porch to read the paper finds that the noisy children outside quickly disperse. One officer mentioned that while on patrol he had called on a friend who was mowing his lawn. The officer had not given a thought to the fact that he was wearing uniform until he noticed that the neighbours were looking on in curiosity, so, in order to demonstrate to them that this was not an official call, he picked up his friend's petrol can and went to the filling station with it for him. He resolved not to call again on friends while in uniform for fear it might embarrass them. American officers also complain about the frequency with which they are introduced into company as policemen, and the way people start talking to them about occasions in which they have been in trouble with the police, especially for driving and parking offences. The American policemen who spoke of this thought that members of the public brought up such topics on the assumption that people of any occupation like to talk 'shop'. This interpretation does not seem altogether convincing, but this response from the public is so common that it is interesting to wonder what causes it. In some cases, of course, the subject is complaining that he was unfairly treated and is seeking to put pressure on the policeman not to neglect the public's point of view. In other cases, the subject is probably suffering from wounded pride, for most drivers consider themselves good drivers; by giving their version to some policeman in the hope that he will say they were in the right they try to assuage their injured self-respect. By re-telling their story several times some drivers will come unconsciously to represent events in a way much more favourable to themselves and to believe their revised versions. If there is any truth in such an interpretation, it implies that carefully formulated appeals to drivers'

218

pride in their driving might play a greater part in highway safety campaigns. American officers, asked how they thought their own colleagues would react if given a citation for speeding while on a trip in another state, considered it quite likely that after their return they would mention it jokingly in the recreation room and would feel absolved by the laughter of their colleagues.

These observations notwithstanding, American officers seem to have much less difficulty than their British counterparts in getting away from their job, and it seemed unusual for a man's wife or children to be affected by it. Again, there was very little to suggest that American officers experienced 'the police mind' in the way British officers have described it. Nor is there so much chance that people may show distance or hostility towards a policeman's wife or children. In one Massachusetts town the officers made fun of any of their colleagues who showed undue enthusiasm and would, for example, ridicule anyone who carried a gun off duty as 'Dick Tracey'. All the evidence I was able to collect suggests that the American policeman in his public and private roles is less set apart from society than his British counterpart. The evidence, admittedly, is none too reliable, being largely based upon the subjective impressions of a single observer, but to assess people's feelings on such topics it is less important to get their answers to particular questions than to decide how important the topics are to them, and for this purpose the alternative to an impressionistic mode of inquiry would be a very complicated and laborious kind of attitude study. Anyway, the evidence for the conclusion seems internally consistent and in accord with the differences in the context of police work in the two countries.

Just as the American officer is less restricted by police requirements in his private roles, so also he has more liberty while acting in his official police role. In the first place, many American officers do not conceive their role as an exemplary one in the way their Scottish counterparts do. The Scottish officer stresses the features that set him apart from the general public whereas the American officer seems to stress the extent to which he is one of them. Often the American officer views his occupational role simply as a job and, either because of the national culture or because of frustrating elements in the way the department is run, he is not particularly dedicated to the duties of the role. Consequently he is apt to exploit such advantages as the job offers in order to compensate for its disadvantages. In the second place, there seems to be less agreement among the American population as to the limits of the policeman's role: it is less easy there to say whether it is proper or improper for a policeman to behave in a given way in a marginal situation. The role is less clear-cut, less sharply defined. For example, the author joined two American officers in a patrol car. Both made a hobby of collecting old coins and they had an arrangement with a few petrol pump attendants who used to put aside any old coins they received and exchange them for more modern coins given them by the officers. On this occasion they had just obtained a batch of coins and, as it was a quiet morning, they drove to a secluded spot and spent ten minutes going through their haul. Then they discovered they were fifty cents short; they drove back to the petrol station and asked the attendant if they had not given him a fifty-cent coin too many. The attendant went through his change and showed them that they could not possibly have done so but, because they did not give up at this point, he gave them fifty cents. One of the officers said that this was not really what they had come for, but they were grateful just the same; then they drove off. This a trivial anecdote, but the point of repeating it is that such behaviour would seem more irregular in Scotland than in the United States. Many Scottish officers, in a like situation, would be hesitant to go back lest the attendant should feel threatened by their making such an inquiry in uniform. One more senior Scottish officer, for example, related that once he led a raid on a brothel and found a certain lawyer among the clients. No charge was made against him, for frequenting a brothel is not an offence, but the lawyer knew he had been seen. Some time later the officer was looking round for a new house; he found one that appealed to him and was about to put in an offer when he discovered that the lawyer acting for the seller was the man he had found in the brothel. He reasoned that if he were to submit an offer the lawyer might feel constrained to try and persuade his client into accepting it, whether it was the best offer or not, for fear that if it were not accepted the policeman would get his own back by spreading the news about the circumstances in which he had discovered the lawyer. To avoid such a situation the policeman decided not to put in any offer though he really did want the house. This story may not be representative but people react differently to it. Scottish officers say the policeman was perhaps being more delicate than many would be, but Americans tend to regard it as virtue carried to the point of fastidiousness.

Where the Scottish officer acts more carefully lest members of the public should think he is using his role to obtain an unfair advantage, American officers claim that they are entitled to extra consideration from their fellow policemen. This is particularly evident in connection with driving offences. Almost everywhere in the United States upper speed limits, usually of 60, 65, or 70 m.p.h., are enforced even on big two-lane highways; very many drivers exceed these limits. All the American officers in the South whom I asked about this admitted to having been stopped at least once for speeding while off duty. When asked how they reacted, some – especially the more senior officers – said that it made them feel very foolish and even reluctant to mention that they were policemen, but some took a cold-blooded attitude and remarked that they promptly drew attention to the fact that they too were police officers. Usually, it seemed, officers of both kinds were able to avoid being given a ticket, for, as several of them put it, 'police officers don't usually take a strong line with one another because they feel they have enough to put up with from the public anyway'. A similar attitude is sometimes shown in respect of other regulations such as those governing parking: rather than keep strictly to the law, the police themselves decide when offences may be overlooked and they are ready to extend this licence to themselves and those associated with them.

A similar example of differences in the definition of the police role is found in respect of cheap meals provided by restaurant owners. At times this may be a matter of police officers' utilizing their occupation to obtain an advantage, and be therefore a form of extortion. Often, however, such practices are customary and are supported by restaurateurs for their own ends; they derive not from extortion but from the absence of any general social norm which labels such things as improper. The position is that in many American police departments patrol officers have no beat boxes or suitable premises in which to take their refreshments, and that the arrangement of shifts or watches often does not fit in with conventional hours for meals. Senior officers supervising patrol work may be permitted to lunch at home, and patrol men to eat in restaurants in their patrol area, provided that in both cases the dispatcher knows where they are and can telephone for them. In the author's experience in Carolina, Georgia, and Felsmere Cities, patrolmen were frequently given free meals or charged only a small sum because, as they put it, the proprietor liked to have them about the place since this discouraged troublemakers. Obtaining free or cheap services is referred to as 'mooching'. Chief Schrotel comments on it as follows:

'Most policemen recognize no wrong in accepting free admissions to public entertainment, discounts on their purchases, special favours and considerations from persons of influence, or tips and gratuities for services performed in the line of their regular duty. They choose to look upon these incidents as being strictly personal matters between themselves and the donors and are unwilling to recognize that moral obligations are involved. . . . No matter how much effort is expended in minimizing the derogatory effect of the acceptance of gratuities and favours by law enforcement officers, the practice has become so prevalent that the public generally concedes that policemen are the world's greatest 'moochers'. Aside from the question of the effect of the practice upon the officers' effectiveness in enforcing the law, it is a certainty that a reputation for 'mooching' does not elevate the standards of the profession in the public's mind' (Institute for Training in Municipal Administration, 1961, pp. 467–8).

Lest this give a false impression, it should be added that in many of the American departments with the highest standards the practices to which Chief Schrotel refers are probably as rare as anywhere in Britain. It should also be borne in mind that a reputation of this sort sometimes brings its own remedy. Some officers in the Northeast said they would on no account do any shopping on the way home or be seen with a parcel under their arm because of the popular readiness to assume that they had induced someone to present them with the contents. In Britain the idea of 'mooching' by policemen is regarded as intolerable and an officer should not enter a licensed restaurant except on duty. There are some constables who turn their office to private advantage: for example, they may in their leisure time visit public houses that lie on their beat, and since the publican is certain to recognize them they may get their beer on the cheap; then there are constables who, when they take their car to the garage, contrive to have an excuse for being in uniform as this, too, may get them cheaper service. Most constables disapprove of such behaviour and think the less of any of their colleagues who are known to act in this way. Moreover, it is never as flagrant as in the United States. Part of the difference in attitude is due to a real difference in the definition of roles. In Britain a constable who was given a free meal would probably feel under a definite obligation to the giver because such an action is exceptional. In the United States, ideas as to what may be expected of a restaurateur or a policeman are vaguer; the patrolman can accept a free meal without feeling under an obligation, and the dangers of impropriety or even apparent impropriety are much less.

These examples do suggest that there is a tendency for American officers to see themselves as representatives of the law rather than as public servants under the law, to a greater extent than occurs in Scotland. With the greater incidence of serious crime and the indifference shown by some sections of the community, this identification can be understood, but it is nevertheless a contributing factor to some of the weaknesses of current American police work. When Chief Schrotel says:

> 'In the preservation of the constitutional guarantees of civil liberty the police service has most certainly failed. False imprisonment, illegal search, 'the third degree', special privilege, and denial of due process of law are ... commonplace in many police organizations' (ibid. p. 463),

he refers to the evil results which can stem from police officers' seeing themselves as the sole agents of social control, and to the failure of the community both to define clearly the police officer's role and to enforce its definition. Little infractions lead to big ones.

This, however, is only one aspect of the complex differences between the British and American scenes, and it is necessary first to try and find any significant variations in underlying pattern before focusing on details, even if they are of importance from a political standpoint. The evidence indicates that the American officer is set apart from ordinary social relations to a lesser extent than his

223

counterpart in Britain. This can be noted in three respects: there are fewer laws and regulations segregating his role; his private roles are contaminated by his occupation to a lesser extent (though American officers complained of their low status they experienced much less difficulty in leaving their job behind them when they took off their uniform); his role on the job is less clearly defined and his conduct less narrowly confined to it. These conclusions are contrary to the expectations mentioned at the beginning of this chapter. If the reasons for this difference can be discovered they may illuminate some of the practical problems of raising standards in American police departments and point up problems that are likely to grow in Britain if present social trends continue.

SOCIAL DENSITY

A sociological approach to this question gives us a deeper understanding of the reasons for the difference, but it also opens up a more extensive prospect: analysis of the policeman's social position may tell us something about variations in the structure of societies. This possibility can be exploited better if the problem is seen in terms of sociologists' theories about how the transition from primitive production to industrialization affects the character of social relations. In his dissertation *The Division of Labor in Society*, Emile Durkheim (1947) depicted the simpler forms of society as congeries of many little self-sufficient communities; with economic development they were brought into relation with one another and then joined together as independent parts of a larger society. Individuals came to participate in a wider network of relations, and there was thus an increase in what Durkheim called 'dynamic or moral density'. This portion of the argument is incomplete or even false, for Durkheim views the process from the standpoint of the national society alone. Marx stated the same principle when, in a description of French peasant life in the middle of the nineteenth century, he spoke of the great mass of the French nation as 'formed by the simple addition of homologous magnitudes, much as potatoes in a sack form a sack of potatoes'. But Marx saw, more clearly than Durkheim, that while economic advance united people previously separated, at the same time it divided them up again in new ways. In industrial cities a man's livelihood may well depend upon thousands of others; if the workers specializing in just one stage of automobile production go on strike, it may hamstring the whole concern. But economic interdependence of this sort may have only an indirect effect upon personal relations. The automobile worker may believe that his interests are directly opposed to those of the managers and may feel no solidarity with them. Many blue-collar workers meet only people of their own class at work, and they live in residential districts populated by people of similar income to themselves. Class distinctions are widened; a gulf grows up between the spheres of work and leisure for which, of course, the automobile itself and the improved means of transport are in part responsible. Innovations which translate dependence upon people into dependence on machines inevitably loosen the network of social relations. Urban society, just as much as a region of peasant cultivators, is divided into segments, but instead of each one being like the others, the industrial segments are functionally different.

If social life in the relatively backward region and in the city is compared from the standpoint, not of economics or politics, but of the personal relations in which people are involved, it will be seen that there is in fact a decrease in what may be termed social density. The texture of social relations is denser in the village where the same two individuals may have to interact with one another in a greater variety of roles than is likely in the more fragmented social structure of the city. The village grocer may represent his district on the county council, and he may meet his neighbour the schoolteacher in his capacity as councillor, or as grocer, or as parent of a school child, or as neighbour, or in one of many other roles. There is only one doctor in the village, so everyone in the community has to go to him and he feels under an obligation to attend all the local people whether he really wants them as patients or not. The doctor has to join the local middle-class for social activities; he cannot avoid them out of the fear that such association may interfere with a professional relationship with them. People are vulnerable through their children; if children get involved with other members of the community this may have repercussions upon their parents' social relations. Because the range of social choice is restricted, people have to find ways of getting along with other residents regardless of personal feelings. One way in which they are helped, I suggest, is by a relatively clear definition of roles in such communities. People are aware that Mr Roberts is a councillor, a grocer, a parent, and so on; they are agreed upon what may be expected of him in each role and upon the interrelations between the roles. Similarly, in the village, differences of sex, age, and social class are considered relevant to conduct in a wider range of situations than in the city, and there is a greater measure of agreement about what is proper to a married woman, a juvenile, a labourer, etc. In the city a man's contacts are influenced to a greater extent by bureaucratic norms that respect neither sex nor age nor class, and there is less consensus on the definition of roles. This difference between patterns of social relations has been discussed by other writers in terms of the 'denseness of role texture', the tightness or looseness of the mesh of the social network, etc., and it is obviously related to differences in levels of social integration as discussed earlier.

Rapidly developing societies cannot afford high levels of social integration. Economic progress and the maintenance of a high standard of living require mobility of resources and persons, and this tends to reduce social density. Whereas the Scottish city has grown by about 6 per cent in the last twenty years, Carolina City and Georgia City have both doubled their population in this period. In these two cities there is a great social gulf between Whites and Negroes; to judge from the high figures for drunkenness among Whites (*Table 3*), which is predominantly a lower-class offence, class distinctions may also be greater than they appear on the surface. In such circumstances it is difficult for common understandings to grow about what constitutes proper behaviour for anyone who plays a particular role. The demands which technical progress makes upon social relations doubtless underlie the cultural tradition of the United States as a settler nation. Americans stress self-expression and deplore conformity in any sphere which is supposed to be indicative of individuality (this excludes basic political attitudes: anti-communist fervour and commitment to a free enterprise economy do not count as conformity). Where people in Europe might be inclined to ascribe someone's behaviour to the role he is playing, Americans are more likely to see it as an expression of his individuality, his likes and dislikes, or his psychological make-up. In their own country the Americans would probably be right, for, if my impressions are not misleading, social roles there both restrict the individual less and protect him less. The etiquette which enables Europeans to manage relations with persons while holding them at a distance is relatively little developed in the United States, and in that culture seems something cold and artificial.

The Scottish policeman can go up to someone knowing that he or she will almost certainly interpret his actions as being something he does because it is his job. He is impersonal in his approach to offenders, demonstrating that if he reproves them he does so as a policeman and not as an individual. This impersonality enables him to behave in a deferential manner to all sorts of people. An officer can come up to a woman who is trying to park her car in a stupid position, salute, inquire 'Can I help you madam?', and then persuade her to leave it elsewhere. He does not need to fear that because he behaves deferentially anyone will think the less of him, nor will he feel humiliated by behaving this way. Though this particular illustration is by no means representative – British policemen can respond in a very forthright manner to parking offenders – it is fair to set it in contrast with American police behaviour. In general, the chances of a British policeman's behaving in an impersonal and deferential manner – of acting solely as the incumbent of a role – are far higher than the chances of an American officer's doing so. The British constable often finds that he needs to do or say relatively little, the mere presence of a man in the blue uniform being sometimes sufficient to make people stop fighting, or to quiet down someone who was highly tensed. The American officer cannot rely upon the authority of his badge in this way and he develops his own techniques for handling people. The American officer in the North-east and the South seems to be much more familiar with members of the public than his British counterpart would be. This was particularly noticeable in two sorts of situation. First, in the use of 'kidding' and joking to persuade people to do things (e.g. in getting a rather anxious elderly woman to come to hospital so that a shoulder she had injured in a fall could be examined). One sergeant observed that his rule was to refer to all females of less than 25 years as ladies, and to all older ones as girls. Even if he did not always follow it, this 'rule' is indicative of an attitude many Scottish policemen would find strange. Second, when dealing with drunks and other

Q

arrested persons, American officers were inclined to be quite friendly, and nothing in their manner suggested any feeling of self-righteousness. Some superior officers who are concerned to improve the public image of their occupation are apt to complain that patrolmen are insufficiently dignified both on the street and in their dealings with citizens. They believe that the public will not consider the police officer important if he himself appears not to do so, but the officers would contend that the man who adopts a friendly approach can get the same work done with less resistance. The behaviour of American police, like their clothing and appearance, is less uniform than it is in Britain.

The American officer is less inclined to defer to members of the public: he is as good as they are and he sees no need to salute them.[1] If he were to show more respect to members of the public many of them would certainly misinterpret such behaviour and be less inclined to listen to him. The author remembers riding with a supervisor one evening when there was a heavy rainstorm and an underpass was flooded. A patrol car was stationed to stop cars trying to drive through from the one side, and the supervisor stationed himself on the other, placing his car across the road with its red light flashing. Many drivers still did not appreciate that there was a blockage; they drove up slowly, and shouted to ask what was wrong. The officer shouted 'You can't get through', but he did not attempt to stop the few cars that drove on, either determined to try it or merely out of curiosity. After a while the officer got irritated: he expected drivers to put two and two together and guess that the road was blocked, so when drivers did not take the alternative route but instead drove up to his car, he shouted, 'What do you think I'm here for?' and adopted an aggressive manner, commenting privately, 'They want me to get my butt wet'. Whether this would be sensible or not, a British policeman would have been more inclined to let himself get

[1] American police officers are less likely than Scottish ones to address members of the public as 'Sir'; when the term is used it often carries no connotations of superiority-inferiority. A judge in a Southern court room, having just found a Negro offender guilty and while questioning him in order to determine an appropriate sentence, failed to hear his reply. He asked interrogatively, 'Sir?' This was no slip of the tongue. The South has a reputation for courtesy and 'Mam' is regularly used by policemen and others, though not by white policemen to Negro women.

drenched redirecting traffic; he would probably not have expected drivers to guess what was wrong but would simply have instructed everyone to take the alternative route. Such differences in approach derive chiefly from differences in the people to be handled, and it is as well to assume that each policeman knows his subjects best.

A clearer example of how the American policeman gets less help from his role occurs in respect of domestic disputes, or 'house rows' as they are termed in Scotland. According to the Social Survey poll a small proportion of British officers dislike having to handle domestic disputes,[1] yet personal acquaintance would suggest that the great majority of officers find them a routine matter that causes them no particular worry. In some districts the night-shift patrolman regularly has a few cases each weekend and he is a recognized arbiter in such matters. My first acquaintance with this sort of case occurred while I was accompanying a probationer in the Scottish city one afternoon. When we were in the beat box at the refreshment time a knock was heard at the door. A woman of 32 stood outside and asked, 'Would you give me assistance please? My husband's lifted his hands to me.' She went on to say that while they had been walking along a certain road he had snatched her shopping bag and thrown it into a park; it contained £5. He had assaulted her before; only the previous week he had hit her in the back, and the year before he had given her a black eye; the doctor could testify to that. The constable inquired after witnesses to the action of which she complained and learned that there were none. The husband, who had been standing nearby, was a labourer of under average size, aged 37. He now spoke up, said he admitted to her accusations, and that now she had put him in charge she could pack her bags and get out of his house. The wife replied that she had nowhere to go and the policeman explained that there could be no charge because there were no witnesses. The wife said her man had shamed her before the neighbours but the husband said he was evicting her anyway. The woman then asked for the key to go and get her things but the husband said he would come and give her them himself. When he used the adjective 'bloody' the policeman promptly said

[1] The actual figure is not given but this is listed at the head of the miscellaneous dislikes (*Royal Commission on the Police*, Appendix IV to the *Minutes of Evidence*, p. 35).

229

'Let's cut out the swearing', and went on to obtain the man's address and that of the woman's father. The husband said she was always over there anyway and the wife responded by saying that her father had thrombosis; she wanted no policemen calling there and if she told her father she had been evicted the shock could be enough to cause his death. She would have to walk the streets that night. The constable told them to be quiet, to go home and make no disturbance, and said that a policeman would call later. Two minutes after they had left, the woman came back to say that he had shouted 'Go and sleep with your fancy man' in the street. Suspecting they were about to come to blows the constable warned the man about his behaviour, and the two of us followed them to their flat to see there was no breach of the peace. At the flat the parties gave further details of their respective versions of the dispute; he spoke of how she had once gone for him with a poker; she said he had had eighteen different women; once she thought he had given her a venereal disease and she had taken an overdose of sleeping tablets. It began to seem as if the wife was by far the stronger personality and won all the verbal battles. She probably had him fairly well under control and his assaults on her were all trivial; but he could hit back hard by his public demonstrations, for she was very concerned to appear respectable.

The interesting feature of this dispute for present purposes was that the officer was a young man of barely twenty years, and everyone was aware of it. Nevertheless, the two parties put their cases before him as if they were appealing to the popular morality and he were someone with full authority to pronounce upon the issues. The fact that he was such a young man made no difference: his uniform was a sufficient guarantee of his status.

In the United States, by contrast, policemen universally dislike dealing with domestic disputes, and this must be in part because they are so much more vulnerable in these situations than are their Scottish counterparts. Westley quotes one officer as saying:

'You know if there is one thing these men hate more than anything else it is to go out on a call for a family quarrel. You ought to see their faces when they hear the call come over the radio' (Westley, 1951, p. 115).

230

They are vulnerable both legally and physically. In very many cases they have no grounds to enter or stay inside the house, and if the house owner orders them to leave they must. Frequently the police do not get involved in such troubles until the parties are fairly desperate and it is by no means unusual for an irate husband to draw a gun on the interfering policeman. Of those policemen killed on duty during 1962 the largest category, 26 per cent, consisted of men 'responding to disturbance calls (family quarrels, man with gun, etc.)'. The role and authority of the policeman when he intervenes in a family dispute are unclear; as one man observed, 'You can't please everyone'. Though one party usually has cause for complaint the policemen can often do nothing effective. Sometimes, two people who have been fighting like cats join forces to attack the policeman. Again, American officers complained that in such circumstances – and because complainants are apt to withdraw charges – 'You cannot take police action'.

These comments support the contention that the British policeman's role is more clearly defined (in that the youth of the incumbent is less likely to invalidate his claims) and that it confers authority in a wider range of situations. The British officer who is called to a domestic dispute is normally listened to with respect; usually he is able to take some action which is socially constructive and seems to him proper to his office. The American policeman dislikes domestic calls because he is frequently accorded little authority in such situations and cannot take action that seems both constructive and in accordance with the other sorts of duties expected of a policeman.

Teachers and supervisors over a new group of pupils or subordinates are sometimes advised to be severe with them to begin with and only later to ease their grip. If they can first establish their authority and the demands of their role, when they later behave more moderately this is appreciated as a relaxation or as a sign of individual sympathy on the part of the person who has to play the role. The British policeman is in this sort of position: his role has been clearly established and, since he will not lose any authority by taking a generous view of a particular case, he can often afford to be tolerant. In such circumstances the policeman is under pressure to live up to public expectations of this role; this inhibits him in some ways, but the constable benefits from the respect that his office has accumulated. American policemen and citizens alike lack the protection of a well-understood relationship built up by years of relatively equable police-public relations.

The suggestion that the American police officer's role is less sharply defined fits with the earlier claim that social density is lower in most American communities. If this interpretation holds, then it provides an explanation of why the police role is not segregated so much in the United States. The more social roles are interrelated, the more necessary it is for them to be explicitly defined; indeed, complex interrelation depends upon sharpness of definition. The more roles are interrelated, the more necessary it is for potentially conflicting ones to be kept separate. The police role is more clearly segregated in Scotland because most other roles are more differentiated and the police role has to be kept apart from them. In the villages, the necessary separation has to be achieved by the constable's own social skill in mixing with the local people but not being compromised by his association with them. In the towns, segregation is obtained more by the requirements of discipline and the tendency of many officers to keep to one another's company when their shift is over. In the United States, on the other hand, with its heterogeneous population and rapidly changing social pattern, roles are not so clearly defined; people in service occupations cannot afford to defer to the public, and social behaviour is seen in more individual terms. As expectations of the police role are not so sharply defined, people are less apt to think that any potential conflicts can be avoided by the framing of regulations and more apt to believe that the difficulty can best be met by obtaining more trustworthy recruits. Most of the social segregation which officers in many American cities have experienced stems in fact not from any high public appreciation of the policeman's duties, but from the low prestige of their occupation. My impression was that officers in a large Massachusetts city seemed to experience more contamination of their private roles than did officers in the Southern cities visited; how far this was due to lower prestige and how far to higher social density is difficult to determine. But this aspect of the matter only strengthens the contention that the study of just one feature of one occupation can raise many interesting questions about differences in British and American social life.

SOME OTHER INFLUENCES OF THE WORK ROLE

This discussion of the effect of the policeman's job upon his private life has mostly centred upon complaints, because policemen are more aware of ways in which their private life is hindered by their office than of ways in which it is helped. Are there any compensating rewards? The work that is required of a policeman is in some respects more attractive than that which many factory workers have to perform, but it is not the nature of the tasks so much as their effect upon the man and his family that is here in question.

Where the factory worker often can get little personal satisfaction from his work and tends to regard it principally as a means of obtaining money, for most policemen work is a central life interest. They cannot stop when the hooter blows but must invest much of their personality in their duties. Helping citizens and checking crime give the policeman a sense that his contribution to society is worth while and he can usually take pride in belonging to an organization that has relatively high standards. If, as Durkheim (1947, p. 402) suggested, dilettantes are not sufficiently attached to society, then, by contrast, the British policeman is much more involved in society than are the people who follow most occupations.

The rewards of being a policeman are partly financial (pay and pension) and partly psychological, in terms of the satisfaction they get from their work. Policemen would say that the psychological rewards are the sense of making an important contribution to the life of the community, being able to take pride in their occupation, and the prestige that is often accorded to it. People who have been influenced by the psycho-analytic approach to social relations would say that such an answer is superficial. They would maintain that police work attracts certain kinds of personality because it offers psychological rewards of a kind less easily obtained in other occupations. Police work, they might say, attracts the sadist because it gives him an opportunity to exert power over others; equally it can attract the man with a very powerful superego, the type who is a slave to duty and unconsciously likes to be subject to harsh discipline because of his suppressed feelings of personal guilt. The validity of such hypotheses cannot be tested by sociological investigations and I can pass no comment on them, but it is perhaps relevant to record that when I became acquainted with Scottish policemen one of my

233

first impressions was that they represented a remarkable variety of personality types, from the tender-minded to the flinty and from the clown to the mandarin. The mode of recruitment to the police is obviously critical here. There can be few occupations which take in their men only at the age of nineteen (when most youngsters have made some progress in another occupation) and which require such general qualifications. This, of course, increases the possibility of psychological self-selection; but, after interviewing a sample of forty-one recruits immediately upon their arrival at the Scottish Police College, I am inclined to think that other factors may be more important. It is notable that of these men the great majority had been long attracted to the police: sixteen said that they had fixed on this career in childhood or while at school; thirty had first considered joining the police more than two years previously; in five cases the recruit's father was or had been a police officer; five others had close relatives or friends in the police and had been influenced by them in applying to join.[1] In the Scottish city there are about six applicants for every recruit who is accepted. It should also be added that even if unconscious desires influence a man's joining the police this does not necessarily mean that he will have much chance to satisfy them after he has joined. In most Scottish forces, I believe, the other constables would bring pressure to bear upon any one of their fellows who was over-inclined to exercise his authority.

The attractions of the police occupation and the psychological consequences of being a policeman have never been studied in any depth, so it may be of interest to quote the conclusions of a team of management consultants who were asked to appraise over one hundred senior members of the Chicago police department. These findings are of a rather subjective nature, but they parallel my own interpretation of the position:

'Police officers have seen the seamy side of life and a great deal of misery. While death on crime, they reveal clear feelings of sympathy and helpfulness toward the unfortunate. The men in the

[1] Information on the previous occupations and schooling of recruits to English and Welsh forces may be found in the *Royal Commission on the Police*, Appendix to the *Minutes of Evidence* (1–10), pp. 17–18.

study group did not conform at all to the popular stereotype of the tough, cynical hard-bitten police officer. Rather, all the evidence indicates that they are decent, kindly men, intent on doing their job, with marked social service values. . . .

. . . the lives of police officers are wrapped up, to an unusual degree, in their work . . . the reputation of the Department – which provides purpose and meaning for their own lives – is highly important to them. They are concerned with the public image of the police force and are sensitive to anything which brings it into disrepute. . . .

In many respects, police officers have the outlook and temperament of civil service employees or Army officers in peacetime. There is emphasis on seniority, security, conformity, and established methods and procedures. Many of the men joined the Force during the Depression when jobs were hard to get, and the Police Department represented security, respectability, and a professional-type career. Desirable attributes were sincerity, loyalty, ability to wear well over a period of time, and, "going by the book". These traits have many values, but can be limitations in terms of aggressive drive toward handling more responsibility and making decisions.'

Many of these remarks are applicable to British officers, as may be the following finding concerning the differences between above-average and average officers:

'The above-average police officer was adjudged to have somewhat better interpersonal skills. For one thing, he was less likely to be absorbed in his own problems so that, as a result, he was able to see more clearly the problems of others. Also, because his level of self-confidence was higher, he was less dependent on the acceptance and support of others' (Spencer & Jewell, 1963).[1]

SACREDNESS

In any organization some things can be changed relatively easily whereas others are so entrenched that it is difficult to get them altered. Stories abound of how bureaucracies emphasize the significance of customary procedures, the filing systems, the hierarchy of ranks, etc.; people who work in such institutions are apt to refer to such

---

[1] Quoted with the kind permission of the editor of *The Police Chief*.

235

things as 'sacred' and the expression is more than just a figure of speech. The more central a practice is to the structure of an organization, the more it is apt to be regarded as sacred; instead of being subject to rational secular control, it tends to become one of the points of departure from which other things are evaluated. This much will probably be within the experience of anyone who works in a large organization, but the phenomenon is not limited to procedures within such institutions: it applies also to the position of institutions themselves within the wider society. Institutions, like the monarchy and the church in Britain, which epitomize fundamental social values, are removed from the ordinary realm of secular evaluation. For example, satire of them or objective study of their effectiveness is often deprecated most strongly.[1] In British society, with its stress on order, the police seem to be one of these central institutions; in the United States, with its stress upon progress, private industry moves up in importance, while the police and the civil service move down. Indeed, it may be argued that because American society as a whole is less integrated and more pluralistic, all its institutions will appear more profane than those of a more traditional society. Among the factors which contribute to this general cultural secularity are, of course, the size of the nation; the rate of social change; the relative inefficiency of some of the social machinery, as reflected in crime and corruption, which discourages any traditionalistic acceptance of the existing order; the variety of minorities with different cultural values; the belief in economic liberalism; the depersonalized nature of many social relations in the big cities; and so forth. Then the relatively low prestige of police work, the fact that police chiefs have to persuade local government bodies of the need for funds, and other matters discussed earlier, contribute to the tendency for police departments to be seen as business organizations which must justify themselves in the public's eyes.

The extent to which the British police are regarded, and regard themselves, as different from other institutions is not fully apparent to anyone who knows only the position in Britain and has nothing with which to compare it. I came to feel that the police were a sacred sort of institution in British social life only after experiencing the very different situation in the United States. Police departments there are

[1] Cf. Shils & Young (1953).

much more open to sociological investigation, and police administrators are less concerned whether an observer gets his facts right: occasional errors even by someone who is regarded as impartial are not going to make much difference. What is said about the police in California does not have much effect upon the police in Connecticut and few investigations are regarded as authoritative. A journalist would probably experience a similar contrast. It is difficult to imagine any British chief constable echoing the Los Angeles chief in the remark quoted on p. 125 above: 'Every member of the department has the right to talk to the press about what he is doing. We make no attempt to muzzle our officers!' This comment is not introduced as a covert criticism of British police procedure but simply to point the contrast in outlook and the way it is related to circumstantial differences.

Not only are the British police as an institution somewhat sacred, but the British constable's role seems sacred compared with other occupational roles and compared with that of the patrolman across the Atlantic. I would emphasize again that here I speak of sacredness in sociological terms and that I refer to the way people behave towards policemen. Following Durkheim, I think of the socially sacred as that which is set apart and treated both as intrinsically good and as dangerous (Durkheim, 1953, pp. 48 and 69–70). That British policemen are set apart is evident from the regulations governing their private conduct and the other observations adduced earlier. That they are treated as intrinsically good derives from the way they symbolize social order. That they are treated as dangerous is evident from the way so many people – with or without justification – prefer to keep at a distance from policemen or feel slightly uneasy in their company. The comparison with the priest which has been made earlier several times is quite apposite, for while the role of priest is in a similar fashion set apart and sacralized, its incumbents are perceived as human beings. People like commenting upon the human characteristics and failings of priests as well as of policemen, as if they felt reassured by these signs that they were no different from anyone else. They are well aware that for a young lad from a humble home to become a minister of religion is for him a social promotion which gives a little reflected glory to his kinsfolk. For a role to appear sacred in respect of certain of its duties does not blind people to the secular aspects of the role and of its incumbents. These observations apply with less force to the role of police officer in the United States, but there too if a police officer or a priest falls from grace it is 'news'.

Some support may be found for this interpretation, I believe, in the way the British police reacted to the first performance of a BBC television programme called 'Z cars'. This show drew attention to the sometimes harsh discipline within the police, and featured the lives of a number of young policemen who were willing to use unorthodox methods and tricks to catch thieves. Policemen in the region where the film was made protested vigorously: 'Strong objection was taken to the portrayal of the home life of police officers, including the way in which they ate their meals and the fact that a constable had given his wife a black eye. Another complaint related to the obtaining of racing results from passing motorists.' A correspondent writing in his official capacity stated: 'Colleagues . . . have contacted me and expressed their views of dismay, disgust and annoyance at the type of person shown in the parts of police officers and of a police officer's wife'.[1] Since then the programme has become a popular favourite and policemen are doubtless more reconciled to this sort of presentation. My feeling at the time, however, was that police officers objected to the series because they thought it would reduce public respect for the police. They were claiming that because of the importance of their occupation in society it should not be shown in an unfavourable light, even if the unfavourable items were outnumbered by favourable ones. Other occupations and their practitioners – like dentists and plumbers – could be presented as ordinary or profane because they did not touch on fundamental values.

Interpretations of this kind are notoriously subjective and open to dispute, but one of the best police short stories to have come my way also conveys a suggestion that the police are a rather special body who are not obliged to account for all their actions. The story (by Donald Hesketh) is called 'The Ungrateful Kind' and it describes how a young man is before the court for assaulting a police officer and there are several off-duty constables in court interested to see that justice is done.[2] The chief inspector who is to conduct the prosecution picks up the files, and notices the name of the accused. It

[1] *Police Review*, 11 January 1962.   [2] Ibid. 3 November 1961.

reminds him of an occasion when as a young officer he had to serve as an emergency midwife in a poor home, and the mother gave the child one of the constable's names in gratitude for his help. The young man in the dock was once the child he had helped to bring into life. He is found guilty and asked if he has anything to say before sentence. He expresses no contrition but remarks that he's never had any help from the coppers and he hopes he never will have. Another officer observes to the chief inspector that fellows like him should be strangled at birth; the chief inspector wonders whether to reply that he once had that chance, but says nothing. This story underlines the way many British officers keep personal information to themselves even when they do not strictly need to do so. They build up a belief in the importance of police work such that they can get along without public appreciation, while believing that if all were known then the public would be truly grateful to them.

This sense of moral rectitude, of a certain invulnerability to public criticism, is much less characteristic of American policemen, who, as has been said, tend to see their work more as a job and less as an exemplary role. An officer in a large Massachusetts force, commenting on the need to help protect brother officers from injury, could add 'which is our principal concern most of the time', and go on to speak of some of the circumstances in which it was either dangerous or unrewarding for a policeman to do his duty, in as detached a way as if he were discussing the public transport service. American officers will frequently discuss frankly such questions as police corruption and brutality, the fixing of tickets, and the extent to which justice is denied. They do not feel identified with the whole system as Scottish officers do. The author has noticed many examples in which Scottish policemen have been much more reluctant to speak openly than American officers would, as if the subjects were not ones to be mentioned to any outsider even though the policemen probably had nothing to hide. In America he was often asked, 'What do you think of the department', by officers who were proud of their forces. In Britain outsiders are not thought to be in any position to pass judgement upon police efficiency. The reader who wishes to check on this difference in atmosphere might read Westley's (1953) article 'Violence and the Police' cited earlier; he will be surprised that such information could be obtained and printed; if he tries to discuss it with British officers he will probably find that his intention in bringing up this topic is easily misconstrued.

If it be true that the British policemen's role has a 'sacred' quality then it is obviously of interest to discover when and how it was acquired. When the first Metropolitan policemen walked the streets they were greeted with abuse, and when a ruffian stabbed one of them the jury returned a verdict of 'justifiable homicide'. Gradually this hostility declined, partly, perhaps, because of their success in reducing crime. Geoffrey Gorer has pointed to the big fall in criminal commitments in the middle of the nineteenth century and has suggested that 'the policeman . . . became for many Englishmen the ideal model of masculine strength and responsibility; as generations passed, aspects of this ideal figure became incorporated into the personality; and the English character became, to a very marked degree, "self-policing" ' (Gorer, 1955, p. 296). This is an intriguing hypothesis but it will be difficult to accept it until comparative studies are available of the development of the police services in other European countries. People often speak of a golden age one or two generations back when police-public relations were quite harmonious, but there seems to be no historical evidence of such a period. One chief constable asserts that 'the popular catch-phrase "if you want to know the time, ask a policeman" reflected not so much the confidence of the Victorians in the reliability of the police, as their assumption that any policeman who did not quickly "win" a watch from the pockets of a drunken reveller was unnaturally and abnormally honest or dull' (Rolph, 1962, pp. 52 and 187–9). His experience, and that of other officers, suggests that the London police have become more popular during the present century. It seems reasonable to suppose, however, that the range of citizens with whom policemen have to deal has grown considerably over this time. A hundred years ago they must have been chiefly concerned with lower-class crime; as they have come to oversee more middle- and upper-class persons they must have been forced into a more classless, separate, and 'sacred' position. This tendency, I suspect, is now being countered by another one. The increasing concentration of the population in cities means bigger and more costly police forces. Because of the general rise in living standards and the way legal regulations affect the town-dweller at every turn (especially if he is a motorist), police actions are increasingly

240

subject to interested scrutiny. Police organization and practice are more and more being examined by rational and commercial standards of efficiency, cost control, and personnel management. This movement regards the police like any other organization and denies its claims to a special position; it is almost certainly the stronger of the two tendencies.

Just how much the police should be set apart from the ordinary run of people is not a question that can ever be finally answered. Circumstances vary and the character of social relations is changing. A possible example of the presentation of the police as insufficiently separate and dignified is the American TV serial 'Car 54, where are you?' which presents two New York patrolmen as amiable numb-skulls. They are never shown doing any work, only as being involved – largely because they are so soft-hearted – in a series of scrapes with neighbourhood characters and with their own superiors. When I first saw this programme I could scarcely believe that it was supposed to be about policemen, and I have been assured that it is regarded with abhorrence by most American policemen. On the other hand it is argued that the presentation of police officers in this unflattering guise does not reduce respect for the uniform but actually improves the public image of the police. The technical adviser to the show is a retired New York detective who maintains contact with old colleagues still on the force. He insists that they all like it. 'The hardest part of a policeman's job', he explains, 'is to overcome the onus of meeting the public only in unpleasant situations, like giving out tickets. As they see it Toody and Muldoon help to overcome this impression with kindness and understanding, and they feel that, by being depicted on the screen as likeable human beings, Toody and Muldoon are putting over the message that other cops are "nice guys" too.'[1] Because of the many social divisions in American urban communities it is probably more important there for policemen to demonstrate their human qualities than it is in Britain.

Some British policemen would argue that they are forced to be too separate. In their evidence to the Royal Commission, the Police Federation of England and Wales emphasized that the policeman 'is a citizen and every encouragement must be given to enable him to live amongst his fellow men, for proper relations to unfold between himself

[1] *TV Guide*, 20 January 1962.

and his neighbour, and between his wife and children with adjoining families' (*Royal Commission on the Police, Minutes of Evidence,* 18, p. 1,035).[1] The Royal Commission endorsed this view but had little to say about ways in which the social isolation of policemen should be reduced (ibid. *Final Report,* p. 106, paras. 353–4). An American official of the International Association of Chiefs of Police, in the course of an analysis of factors underlying police scandals, similarly advises: 'Police workers should break out of their shells and participate more in community life' (Ingersoll, 1963). The Swedish commission of 1947 on police-public relations concluded that: 'The lack of understanding between the public and the police must be explained in part by the way the police have to a certain degree avoided close contact with the public in general. It is high time that this isolation was brought to an end and that policemen to the greatest possible extent participate in communal life' (*Polisen och Allmänheten,* S.O.U., 1947, 45, p. 73). Swedish policemen are allowed to join the democratic political parties; at least one of them has been elected to the Riksdag, and the relaxation of the restriction on political activities has not created any serious problems. In Britain, few policemen are irritated by this restriction; most prefer to stand aloof from political issues, but as more and more occupations are coming to do this too, the range from which local government representatives can be drawn is becoming narrow. There is widespread concern today that it is difficult to recruit people of suitable calibre for service on local councils. As organizational controls upon the use of discretion by policemen and other public servants become closer, there may be less reason in the future to prohibit them from some degree of open involvement in democratic politics.

[1] The National Council for Civil Liberties also thought it important that the police should become more integrated into the public than they are at the present moment (ibid. *Minutes of Evidence,* 13, p. 762).

CHAPTER 9

Conflict between Public and Private Roles

The comparison of the police role in Britain and America suggests that the more integrated a society is, the more clearly will roles be defined, and that because of the overriding importance attached to the policeman's occupational role, his private roles will be curtailed to prevent any appearance of conflicting obligations. If this is the case, the same relationships should be evident in a comparison of the role of the police constable in Scottish rural counties and in the cities.

As part of the study of the police role in Scotland, the author held a series of recorded group discussions with experienced officers on courses at the Scottish Police College. The initial purpose of these discussions was to explore variations in job satisfaction between town and country, and a series of hypotheses had been formulated for examination. However, the discussions took a different course from that intended. When the officers talked about factors in their job which reduced satisfaction, they tended to concentrate upon the way in which it interfered with their private lives, and in this connection the differences between town and country are not as great as they may be in other respects. There was the occasional officer who referred to what he did, or had done, in situations in which the obligations of his public and private roles were in conflict, but this was not a matter that could easily be explored in groups, so it was decided to draw up a questionnaire that individual officers could answer anonymously. This questionnaire was designed to find out which of several sorts of role conflict were more acute, and whether these conflicts were of higher incidence in the country than in the town. The general expectation, in fact, was that officers in the county forces would report more conflict, though it was open to question whether such conflict worried them any more than city officers.

In drawing up a questionnaire it was necessary first to decide whether the inquiry should be directed primarily to the advancement of our theoretical understanding of role conflict, or to the analysis of the police role. The first possibility would have entailed selecting a series of clear-cut conflict situations and applying some simple propositions designed to predict the ways in which people would resolve the conflicts in each case. The leading example then available was the study by Gross, Mason, and MacEachern (1958), which suggested that resolutions could best be predicted by the variables of legitimacy and sanctions: that is to say, if two courses of action were open, A and B, and A was perceived both as a legitimate expectation and as an action that would be rewarding, whereas B was illegitimate and unrewarding, ego would choose A. If the various possible combinations in this scheme are permuted, eight type cases result, two favouring A, two B, and four where the variables are mutually opposed and ego may be expected either to try and compromise or to withdraw from the situation altogether. Among subsequent studies a notable one is that by Ehrlich (1959),[1] who improved upon this procedure by asking subjects – in this case they were police officers – to specify the expectations that certain 'audiences' had of them (e.g. Post Commander, Patrolmen, Wife and Family, Personal Friends, Fraternal Organizations, the Press, etc.), before inquiring how the subjects would resolve any such conflicts. Ehrlich's examination of his own results and those of previous studies shows that it has not so far proved possible to predict resolutions with any high level of success.

On both theoretical and practical grounds it was decided to follow the second course. Propositions of the kind employed by Gross, Mason, and MacEachern seemed of limited applicability in a highly structured and integrated organization like that of the Scottish police, which minimizes illegitimate pressures and applies strong occupational sanctions. Moreover, it is extremely doubtful whether the verbal responses of Scots policemen, when asked what they would do in such situations, would correspond closely with how they would actually behave, for quite apart from any tendency to give the officially expected response, policemen's behaviour is strongly influenced

[1] See also Ehrlich, Rhinehart & Howell (1962).

by their own personal assessment of the concrete situation; when presented with a written description of a situation, no matter how long it is, they are apt to ask for more information, for they rely at times on very small behavioural cues as to people's character. They do not think in categorical terms but emphasize the uniqueness of every situation. Another difficulty is that so many conflicts are resolved by what have been termed 'expedient' solutions: when he is faced by a conflict between his occupation and his role as husband, a police-man's action is likely to depend not only upon the situation but upon what he did last time; if on the last three or four occasions he has stayed late to clear his desk, he may be less inclined to displease his wife this time than if he had put marital duties first on these previous occasions. A theoretically oriented study would entail over-simplify-ing some of these issues, and if the questions were to appear unreali-stic, then almost certainly police respondents would either ignore the questions or fail to treat them seriously. As this was the first study of its kind in Britain it seemed inadvisable to run the risk of appear-ing unrealistic, and preferable to keep as close as possible to what the police themselves could perceive as problems. This was also in line with my own interest, which lay not so much in the more psycho-logical considerations of how people resolve conflicts as in the socio-logical problem of how social structures precipitate or avoid such conflicts: Was the incidence of perceived conflict higher in the vil-lages? Was it higher for detectives than patrolmen? For men with children at primary school? All these possibilities seemed likely, and they posed questions about the articulation of roles and the integra-tion of social structures which were worth following up irrespective of whether police perceptions of role conflict corresponded closely with the actual incidence of role conflict as assessed by other mea-sures. The inquiry was not particularly successful and there were defects in the formulation of the questions, but the results may be worth summarizing for the benefit of other social scientists interested in these matters.

The administration of a questionnaire to officers at the college offered the opportunity to collect information on certain other points also. From the specimen reproduced (pp. 256–60 below) it will be seen that questions 1–6 follow up some questions of job satisfaction and role segregation that arose in the course of the discussions. Questions

7–14 relate to conflicts between the police role and the roles of friend (7 and 11), father (8 and 12), husband (9 and 13), and neighbour (10 and 14), though the incidents used do not all exemplify such conflicts as closely as might be desired. A straight question 'What would you do in this situation?' was not employed for the reasons given above, but the more general query 'How do you react to situations of this kind?' was added instead.

Questionnaires were distributed to classes at the Scottish Police College attended by sergeants and inspectors. With each one was an envelope addressed to myself; respondents put the completed form into this, sealed it, and handed it into the office at the college for forwarding. In all, 141 officers returned completed forms and two sent in blank ones. The great majority of respondents were of sergeant's rank. The composition of the sample is set out in *Tables 5* and *6*.

TABLE 5 OFFICERS RETURNING COMPLETED FORMS

	Patrol	*Detective*	*Married*	*Single*
City	21	23	42	2
Burgh	12	18	28	2
County	32	31	61	2
Not stated	—	4	3	1
Total	65	76	134	7

Note: Only officers from Glasgow and Edinburgh police forces have been included in the 'city' category; those from the smaller cities have been grouped with the burgh forces.

TABLE 6 RESPONDENTS' LENGTH OF SERVICE

	Years			
	5–9	*10–14*	*15–19*	*20–30*
Number of respondents	12	28	23	78

Note: Most of the officers in the last category had in fact between 20 and 25 years of service.

One of the first questions asked how subjects who had a son would feel if he were to join the police, and how their wives would feel, or

246

how, if they had no son, they thought they would feel in such circumstances. The answers are set out in *Table 7a*, which shows that policemen tend to be less disappointed over the prospect of their sons' entering their occupation than they believe their wives to be. This tendency should be regarded as suggestive, since it is statistically significant only at the ·10 level (chi-squared = 7·946, 4 df),

TABLE 7A REACTIONS TO SONS' JOINING POLICE FORCE

	Very pleased	Mildly pleased	Indifferent	Mildly disappointed	Very disappointed
Own reaction	18	25	14	25	11
Wife's reaction	9	28	11	23	14
Anticipated reaction if had son	8	8	13	11	3

TABLE 7B OFFICERS' REACTIONS BY TYPE OF FORCE

	Very pleased	Mildly pleased	Indifferent	Mildly disappointed	Very disappointed
City	2	5	6	11	6
Burgh	3	3	4	4	1
County	12	16	4	10	3

which is below the level conventionally regarded as indicating a statistically significant correlation. The next table (*7b*) shows men's reactions by type of force. The tendency of county officers to be more attracted to the idea of their sons' becoming policemen, by contrast with the views of city officers, is highly significant statistically (2 by *k*, chi-squared = 10·967, 2 df, *p* < ·01, grouping columns 1 and 2, 4 and 5). Policemen's reactions on this subject may be taken as a crude measure of the degree of their satisfaction with their jobs, but two cautions need to be remembered. In the first place, different sons show different aptitudes. One sergeant said he would be sorry if his elder boy were to join the police, because he was doing well at school and hoped to attend university, but he would be pleased if his other son, who was of a less intellectual disposition, were to become a policeman. This factor, however, is presumably constant for city, burgh, and county respondents. Second, a father who does not wish his boy to follow in his footsteps may nevertheless have accommodated himself satisfactorily to the demands of his job. Some sergeants seemed resigned to the incursions their occupation made into their private lives, and accepted them because of a high sense of duty, but they were positive that they would not wish their sons to let themselves in for the same troubles.

A topic which was frequently mentioned in the initial discussions was that of friendships with fellow policemen. Some men said that when they had finished the day's work the last person they wanted to see was another policeman. Others implied either that there were fewer occasions for embarrassment in associating with fellow policemen, or that it was safer to do so, or that they were ostracized by many non-police families. To explore this further, a question on the topic was included. While *Table 8* suggests a slightly greater social

TABLE 8 FRIENDSHIPS WITHIN THE FORCE

	None	Few	More than three
City	16	18	66
Burgh	30	13	57
County	37	13	50

Note: Figures are expressed as percentages for the type of force.

isolation of urban police officers—since more of their friends are within the force—it should be borne in mind (a) that county officers are frequently moved from station to station, making the formation of any sort of new friendship difficult; (b) that often several friends join the police together and remain friends, but that their ties have not been created after joining; (c) that as city officers work shifts it is easier to make up a foursome for golf or a party to go fishing from policemen working the same shift than from non-policemen. The results of this question cannot therefore be taken at face value, though it seems certain that the implication of the job for a man's friendships is a very important feature of the police occupation from a sociological viewpoint. A statistical test indicates that the correlation is significant at the ·10 level (chi-squared = 5·007, 2 df).

It was suggested in the earlier discussions that a police officer tended to form friendships more with people in salaried middle-class occupations that with people in working-class ones, and attention was drawn to the ambiguity of the policeman's class position. *Table 9* reveals a greater tendency on the part of city officers to associate with middle-class people. If the first two and the last three columns are grouped, and the reactions of city officers compared with those of burgh and county officers combined, this correlation is statistically significant (chi-squared = 5·274, 1 df, $p < ·05$).

TABLE 9 FRIENDSHIPS AND CLASS

	Practically all middle class	*Most middle class*	*Category of Friends* *Equal middle and working class*	*Most working class*	*Practically all working class*
City	8	14	18	0	3
Burgh	4	6	15	3	1
County	7	11	32	8	2

Another discussion topic was the desire to escape from identification with the police when on holiday. The fifth question attempted to measure this, and the results, set out in *Table 10*, suggest that the pressure to conceal his occupation is felt more sharply by the city policeman. If columns 1 and 2 are compared with 3, 4, and 5, and the views of city and county men contrasted, the correlation is significant only at the ·10 level and must also be regarded as only suggestive of a trend (2 by k, chi-squared = 5·035, 2 df).

One of the clearest examples in Scotland of a procedure designed to prevent police officers from appearing to be bound by loyalties that conflict with their police duty is the prohibition upon political

TABLE 10 CONCEALING OCCUPATION ON HOLIDAY

	Avoid revealing	Hope not discovered	Indifferent	Hope discovered	Tell people
City	11	22	9	2	0
Burgh	6	15	9	0	0
County	6	39	16	1	1

activity. In practice this causes many of them to refrain from identifying themselves with any party political policy or even to avoid any discussion of such issues. *Table 11* suggests that the city officer feels less inhibited in this respect than his county colleague, but the difference is not significant statistically.

TABLE 11 OCCUPATION AND POLITICAL OPINIONS

	Party view	Avoid party identification	Non-committal	Say not free	Say no politics
City	10	25	7	1	1
Burgh	5	19	0	2	3
County	9	35	8	4	5

Although some differences between city, burgh, and county forces are revealed in *Tables 8–11*, it is probably the general similarity of the responses that is most striking. This emphasizes the way in which the policeman's role shows fundamentally similar features whether he works in a highland village or in an industrial city.

The second half of the questionnaire consisted of eight anecdotes bearing upon possible role conflicts. Responses are classified in *Table 12*, which shows that – apart from question 12 – most officers perceived relatively few situations as posing any real conflict of loyalties. It is probable, however, that had Ehrlich's undoubtedly superior procedure of asking 'In this situation what would your wife expect you to do . . . your mates . . . your superintendent . . .?' been employed, this more sensitive measure might have indicated a higher

TABLE 12 RESPONSES TO CONFLICT SITUATIONS

Experience	Questions							
	7	8	9	10	11	12	13	14
Often and very disturbing	1	2	0	4	6	43	0	6
Often and mildly disturbing	2	4	1	2	5	19	1	2
Often but not disturbing	5	0	1	2	9	12	5	2
Seldom and very disturbing	11	23	20	15	11	11	2	9
Seldom and mildly disturbing	21	30	25	18	22	21	2	20
Seldom but not disturbing	37	27	12	12	42	4	16	8
No experience	64	55	82	88	46	31	115	94

level of conflict. *Table 13* gives a more detailed analysis of the responses to question 12, where conflict was most marked, about occasions on which police duty upsets a man's promise to take his son out; it shows that this conflict falls heavier on the county man, though here again the disparity is not as great as the author expected. This particular conflict also occurs more frequently for detective officers but, since some of the officers classified under patrol will at one time have been detective constables, the difference between patrol and detective work may be greater than the table suggests.

TABLE 13 WHEN DUTY UPSETS SON'S OUTING

	City	Burgh	County	Patrol	CID
Often and very disturbing	12	8	21	18	25
Often and mildly disturbing	5	6	8	7	12
Often but not disturbing	0	3	9	3	9
Seldom and very disturbing	5	2	4	6	5
Seldom and mildly disturbing	9	3	8	11	10
Seldom but not disturbing	2	0	2	2	2
No experience	11	8	11	18	13

In an attempt to summarize the experience reported in answers to questions 9–16 two simple codes were used. Each time a sergeant reported having experienced a similar situation often, this was scored 2; if he had experienced it seldom, it was scored 1; if never, then no score was given. These figures were added up to give the respondent's 'conflict score'; if he had a high figure this suggested that he had felt a conflict of loyalties more often than his colleagues. A similar score was used to total replies as to how disturbing these conflicts had been found. *Tables 14* and *15* have been constructed on this basis. By

TABLE 14 REPORTING OF ROLE CONFLICT

Conflict score	0	1	2	3	4	5	6	7	8	9	10	11	12
City	2	2	5	6	3	6	5	11	2	1	0	0	1
Burgh	2	2	3	6	5	3	3	2	0	2	1	1	0
County	3	2	6	5	10	9	9	8	4	5	1	1	0

TABLE 15 REPORTING DISTURBANCE CAUSED BY ROLE CONFLICT

Disturbance score	0	1	2	3	4	5	6	7	8	9	10	11	12
City	4	6	5	4	5	4	4	3	3	2	1	0	3
Burgh	8	1	6	3	3	5	0	1	1	1	1	0	0
County	11	6	10	6	7	9	6	4	2	2	0	0	0

similar means it is possible to see if any particular category of policemen is more exposed, or more vulnerable, to such conflicts than others. As a preliminary step simple averages were calculated of the conflict and disturbance scores of different categories (*Table 16*).

This comparison, combined with statistical tests on *Tables 14* and *15*, is interesting chiefly for showing that there is no significant difference between county and city officers in their levels of perceived conflict. There is, however, an appreciable and significant difference in their disturbance scores. (Comparing city with burgh and county combined, the difference is significant at the ·02 level, *t* 2·369.) City officers report that they are more disturbed by such conflicts as do occur, presumably because, in the city, workplace and leisure are separated much more than in the country; the city officer's

TABLE 16 CONFLICT AND DISTURBANCE SCORES

	Number of respondents	Average conflict score	Average disturbance score
City	44	4·9	4·6
Burgh	30	4·4	3·1
County	63	5·2	3·4
Patrol	65	5·0	4·0
Detective	76	4·8	3·4
Less than 20 years' service	63	4·6	3·7
More than 20 years' service	78	5·0	3·7
Youngest child 0–4 years	32	4·1	3·0
Youngest child 5–9 years	37	5·8	4·4
Youngest child 10–14 years	38	4·6	3·5
Youngest child over 15 years	17	5·1	4·1

neighbours can leave their work behind when they come home and he tends to be influenced by their style of life and expectations. In the country village, work and leisure are intertwined and the social structure has developed finer techniques whereby people allow for one another's incumbency of other roles in different situations (cf. Chapter 8 above). The incidence both of perceived conflict and of disturbance was highest for officers whose youngest child was between five and nine years, suggesting that the demands of home and neighbourhood are strongest at this stage of family growth.

A more interesting comparison is obtained if questions 8, 9, 12, and 13, concerning the domestic roles of father and husband, are contrasted with questions 7, 10, 11, and 14, relating to the community roles of friend and neighbour (*Table 17*). A superficial comparison suggests that for both city and county officers more conflict occurs between their police role and their domestic roles than between the police role and their community roles. This may be so, but it cannot be substantiated from this inquiry, for it is dependent upon the choice of questions, and it would be difficult to test the accuracy of question

TABLE 17 DOMESTIC AND COMMUNITY ROLES

	Question	Conflict scores		Disturbance scores	
		City	County	City	County
Father	8	64	67	66	60
	12	77	140	109	105
Husband	9	43	46	64	43
	13	18	25	7	5
Average domestic		51	70	63	53
Friend	7	55	67	37	30
	11	86	90	57	40
Neighbour	10	43	37	59	30
	14	59	35	55	32
Average community		61	50	52	33

Note: City $N=44$; County $N=63$; the two sets of figures have each been raised to a base of 100 so that they may be compared directly with each other; the maximum score on any item is 200.

7 as a measure compared with question 8, or of 12 compared with 14. Questions 10 and 14, for example, relate to an urban housing pattern, and the circumstances envisaged are less likely to arise in a village. Questions 7 and 11 both focus upon the visiting of friends' houses and are unlikely to occur when people are well acquainted with one another; here again the county officer might be expected to report less perceived conflict. However, valid comparisons can be made between the conflict and the disturbance scores. It will be noticed that county officers report less disturbance than conflict and that the fall is proportionately similar for both domestic and community roles. For city officers, the level of disturbance increases in respect of domestic roles, and though it declines for community roles it does

so proportionately less than either decline in the county officers' figures.

This conclusion is rather unexpected. It might be thought that conflicts with domestic roles would be fairly similar between country and town, for the character of the family does not change greatly from the one setting to the other, and that the county officer working on discretionary hours would report more disturbance than the city man on shifts. It might also be expected that the greater change would occur in community roles because there is an appreciable difference between rural and urban communities.

The comparison of the police role in Britain and the United States suggested that the American social structure was looser or less dense, and so it was easier for the policeman to separate his public and private roles. On this reasoning it might be expected, comparing the Scottish city with the country, that in the looser structure of the city the officer would also find it less difficult to keep these roles apart and would therefore experience less conflict. The present results throw doubt upon so simple an inference. They suggest in the first place that the city officer is less protected against such conflict as does occur, possibly because he derives his expectations from his neighbours in more orthodox occupations. This would not be in conflict with the original hypothesis, but indicates that it needs to be supplemented. In the second place, the city officer can more easily be involved in embarrassing social situations because he is more likely than the county man to meet new acquaintances socially, people whose background he does not know and who may be deviants in terms of conventional morality. His occupational role does not legitimize association with other members of the community to the extent to which the county officer's does; it exposes him to criticism and unwelcome requests for preferential treatment if he gets involved with unsuitable people. In the circumstances of urban life, formal segregation is less effective as a means of isolating policemen from undesirable influences, and the task of maintaining propriety falls more upon the individual officer. The expectations of the public and of the policeman's superior officers require the British constable to be more circumspect than his American counterpart, so although social density is lower, the city policeman in Britain does not find that his public and private roles can be any more easily dissociated.

The Policeman in the Community

QUESTIONNAIRE FOR A AND B COURSES

Dr M. P. Banton of Edinburgh University is making a study of certain aspects of the policeman's job, in particular of the way in which his occupation affects his private life. He would be grateful if you could answer the following questions. No information will be published without the approval of the police authorities, and care will be taken to see that no particular individual can be identified.

Your force

Length of service

Single, married, or widowed

Age of youngest child

Type of duty (e.g. CID, uniformed beat duties, traffic; state if on shift work)

Number of men on your station or in your unit

Note: if at any place you wish to expand upon your answer, please do so either on this form or on an additional sheet of paper.

1 If you have any sons over the age of 19 who are eligible for entry into the Police, have any of them joined?

2 If you have a son under the age of 19 who is likely to be eligible:
(i) If he were to join would you feel (a) very pleased; (b) mildly pleased; (c) indifferent; (d) disappointed; (e) very disappointed?
(ii) How would your wife feel?
(iii) Would the boy like to join?
If you do not have a son likely to be eligible, how do you think you would feel if you did? Please answer (a), (b), (c), (d), or (e) as for question 2.

3 It has been said that police officers count their acquaintances by the thousand but their friends only by the dozen. Would you say that you had made any close personal friendships with other police officers since joining the force?

4 Consider what are the occupations of your principal friends, and divide them between the 'middle-class' salaried occupations such as school-teachers, sanitary inspectors, businessmen, etc., and 'working-class' jobs such as electricians, machine operators, postmen, etc. Would you say that

(a) practically all your friends belong in the 'middle-class' category?
(b) most of your friends belong in the 'middle-class' category?

256

(c) you have roughly equal numbers of friends in both categories?

(d) most of your friends belong in the 'working-class' category?

(e) practically all your friends belong in the 'working-class' category?

Answer (a), (b), (c), (d), or (e)

5   If you are away on holiday staying in a boarding house, would you

(a) try to avoid revealing your occupation to your fellow residents?

(b) take no steps to avoid this, but prefer that it should not become known?

(c) feel indifferent?

(d) feel pleased if they discover your occupation?

(e) tell them your occupation as soon as opportunity offered?

Answer (a), (b), (c), (d), or (e)

6   Assume that you belong to an association of dog breeders that draws its members from a large region covering nearly half of Scotland. You are attending a gathering and sitting in the lounge that evening when a political argument develops. Someone appeals to you for your views concerning the de-nationalization of Richard Thomas and Baldwins the steel firm. Would you

(a) give your views indicating that on this particular issue you consider a particular party's policy superior?

(b) comment on the issue raised but refrain from identifying yourself with any party?

(c) make some non-committal reply and hope you will not be pressed further?

(d) state that as a police officer you do not feel free to reveal your views?

(e) say that as a police officer you have no politics?

Answer (a), (b), (c), (d), or (e)

7   At a social gathering you meet a man to whom you take a great liking. He seems a very respectable businessman and he is unusually good company. He invites you and your wife to come to a party at his house and you accept. Next day you learn that some years ago he was an active member of the Communist Party. You wonder whether you should offer an excuse for not going.

How frequently have you experienced incidents you feel to be in any way comparable (e.g. acquaintances who have several times been convicted of being drunk in charge of a vehicle, or have been convicted of some calculated offence)?

257

How disturbing do you find them?
How do you react to situations of this kind?

8 You are going away for the day with your children on a coach tour.
They have been looking forward to this outing for several weeks. You
take a corporation 'bus to the coach station and sit upstairs. There are
two or three other, ordinary-looking men on the upper deck. After a
while there are the sounds of a scuffle on the lower deck and shouts
from a man who sounds drunk. The conductress shouts up the stairs
'One of you men come and help me, will you?' She sounds anxious.
You know that if you go downstairs and take police action you will
miss the coach and the outing will be ruined.
How frequently have you experienced incidents you feel to be in any
way comparable?
How disturbing do you find them?
How do you react to situations of this kind?

9 You are sitting with your wife and friends in a licensed hotel having a
party to celebrate your wedding anniversary when the manager, in a
very excited state, rushes to the table. He has recognized you as a
police officer, although you do not know him, and he loudly requests
you to come and assist in quelling a disturbance that has broken out in
the bar premises in another part of the building. You know that this
will take some time and will spoil your wife's evening.
How frequently have you experienced incidents you feel to be in any
way comparable?
How disturbing do you find them?
How do you react to situations of this kind?

10 You live in a neighbourhood where there is no open space or playground for children. The children have been accustomed to play in the
street and no one has objected until a childless couple take up resi-
dence near your house. The new housewife orders the children away,
including your own seven-year-old son, and in view of the attitude of
this new neighbour you tell him not to take part in games there again.
Shortly afterwards the husband comes to your house one evening and
demands that you take action against the children playing in the street.
You warn them to stop it. You and your family afterwards meet with
coolness from your other neighbours (with whom you have previously
been on very good terms) because they think you did this only because
your own son did not happen to be present. You wonder whether you
should suffer in silence.

How frequently have you experienced incidents you feel to be in any way comparable?
How disturbing do you find them?
How do you react to situations of this kind?

11 You and your wife are attending a small social gathering in the home of a friend and among the company you find a man who was recently charged with a comparatively minor offence. You are introduced to those present as a police officer. Shortly afterwards the man in question relates the circumstances of the case, making out that he has been unfairly treated. You are sure that he is not telling the whole truth though you do not know the circumstances of the case. Everyone looks to you to explain why this 'innocent' man is being 'persecuted'. It seems to you that if you question him and show the company that the police have not acted unjustifiably this may well expose the individual and spoil your host's party; whereas if you change the subject of conversation everyone will get a wrong impression of the police, that they will think of you as 'one of them' and this will spoil the evening for your wife and yourself.
How frequently have you experienced incidents you feel to be in any way comparable?
How disturbing do you find them?
How do you react to situations of this kind?

12 You tell your small son that you will take him down to the seaside on Sunday afternoon, but just before lunch you are called out in connection with a crime and you don't get back until late in the afternoon. Your son, who is very distressed, insists 'But, daddy, you promised!'
How frequently have you experienced incidents you feel to be in any way comparable?
How disturbing do you find them?
How do you react to situations of this kind?

13 Your wife has been invited to join the committee of the local branch of a political party (it is the majority party in your district). She asks your advice, but expresses her own opinion that, as she is known to be of an independent turn of mind, people will not necessarily identify you with her opinion; she also adds that she puts up with the disabilities of being a policeman's wife when it is a question of detecting crime and preserving the peace but doesn't think her private life should be hamstrung because of trivial apprehensions.

T   259

How frequently have you experienced incidents you feel to be in any way comparable?
How disturbing do you find them?
How do you react to situations of this kind?

14 You have recently moved into a new neighbourhood. You want to get on reasonably well with your new neighbours for your family's sake as well as your own, and do not wish to be thought of all the time as a policeman. However, the occupant of the flat above yours is given to holding very noisy late-night parties. You have every cause to complain and wish to remonstrate with him as one neighbour to another, but you feel that if you do so your neighbours will not be able to dissociate your action from your position as a police officer. You wonder how long you ought to put up with the disturbance.
How frequently have you experienced incidents you feel to be in any way comparable?
How disturbing do you find them?
How do you react to situations of this kind?

Note: Question 7 by implication equates membership of the Communist Party with the commission of an offence. This stems from a culpable oversight in the construction of this questionnaire that has caused the author much irritation. Happily, it is not an offence to be a Communist in Britain. From the policeman's standpoint, however, such associations are highly controversial and best avoided.

CHAPTER 10

Conclusion

The preceding chapters may have given an unduly favourable picture of the present state of police-public relations. The comparison with the situation in the United States may lead the uncautious British reader to think that things are much better in his own country and that therefore it would be foolish to tamper with a system that is running relatively well. This would be short-sighted. One point that requires emphasis over and over again is that every social change has its costs, economic progress no less than any other. Great Britain is in the process of sloughing off a whole range of ideas about the proper ordering of the nation's life (declining industries, railway reorganization, obsolete work patterns of every kind) and moving into a phase in which none of the new ideas is assured of more than a temporary reign. People have to move about, change jobs, run risks. Young people cannot take their elders as exemplars to the same extent, and they assert themselves in new ways. In many respects our social organization is coming to resemble that of the United States and many of the problems that have appeared there may be expected in Britain.

Police work in the future is going to depend more upon public cooperation than it does at present. More and more of social life takes place in specialist organizations or in groups of limited membership. Less and less can be controlled by the routine patrolman. In many residential areas the police will soon be almost completely dependent upon telephone calls and messages from the public if they are to know about most of the offences that are committed. Then, within these specialist organizations, like work establishments and clubs, offences are often concealed because people do not like to call in the police, though their own methods of dealing with such cases

T*

are less effective. In today's circumstances, new methods are needed to inculcate social norms; there will have to be greater reliance upon the internal controls deriving from early socialization and schooling, and less reliance upon external controls such as punishment. Some social institutions will have to be overhauled to encourage citizen participation to a greater extent than they do at present. Much of modern life seems to stress anonymity and to make people unwilling to act independently of the crowd; private initiative is rewarded only in restricted fields.

These tendencies will necessitate a variety of readjustments on the part of the police. From my reading of the voluminous material that has been published in connection with police-public relations during the last three years I am inclined to feel that the British police services have become a little too much of a special institution, a little too much apart from the general community. Historically, this may stem from the independent position of the chief constable, who, according to the Royal Commission:

'. . . is accountable to no one, and subject to no one's orders, for the way in which, for example, he settles his policies in regard to law enforcement over the area covered by his force, the disposition of his force, the concentration of his resources on any particular type of crime or area, the manner in which he handles political demonstrations or processions and allocates and instructs his men when preventing breaches of the peace arising from industrial disputes, the methods he employs in dealing with an outbreak of violence or of passive resistance to authority, his policy in enforcing the traffic laws and in dealing with parked vehicles, and so on' (*Royal Commission on the Police 1962, Final Report*, p. 31).

Moreover, in most forces, chief constables have sole authority over the appointment, promotion, and discipline of subordinate ranks, and the Royal Commission has recommended that in English county boroughs where this is not the case, such powers be transferred to chief constables (ibid. *Final Report*, p. 61). The police have a special responsibility for the maintenance of public order but this mode of administration has, I submit, fostered among some policemen and some laymen the idea that public order is the responsibility of the police alone. The constitutional position of chief constables may be modified in the near future, but the problem of how to develop civic responsibility in an increasingly acquisitive society will long remain. It may therefore be well to ask whether, in some instances, the police do not do too much for the public and thus discourage them from doing for themselves things which are not necessarily a police responsibility? The decision by the chief constable of Southend to leave to the stores concerned the responsibility of prosecuting certain kinds of shoplifter raises this question, and I believe there may be other instances. The citizen should not be encouraged to regard the apprehension, trial, punishment, and treatment of offenders as something to be left to the police, the courts, the prison service, and the probation officers. The incidence of crime is increasing and will become more and more serious in the immediate future. The public will have to be better informed about what is involved in this problem, for many new measures cannot be introduced without the support of an educated public opinion.

In discussing police-public relations it is important not to regard the police as one homogeneous body and the public as another. To anyone acquainted with the police, divisions and tensions within their number usually seem more immediate than any division between them and the public. Like any large organization the police are divided internally into all sorts of factions, interest groups, and sections: new brooms versus old-timers, federationists versus traditionalists or Home Office men, town versus country, specialist officers versus patrolmen, secondary-modern boys versus grammar-school entrants, etc. These divisions are vital to any consideration of police efficiency, for it is from them that the strain to progress develops. Within the police forces support could be found for almost any kind of policy from the most die-hard traditionalism to madcap innovation. Rather than treat the police forces as being agreed on policy questions it is important to recognize these divisions, and to do more than is at present done to examine rationally the pros and cons of different plans, and then to see that the better ones are put into effect. It is widely felt that there is far too much veneration for established procedures in some quarters and that far too much paper work is thrust upon the patrolman. The police departments of Carolina City and Georgia City are well ahead of Scottish forces in this respect.

The Policeman in the Community

Despite these internal divisions there are, however, many occasions on which policemen tend to think in over-simplified terms of 'we, the police' and 'them, the public'. I remember, in 1958, speaking with a relatively senior policeman, when the question came up of the injuries sustained by a dangerous gunman called Podola when he was being arrested. (This was before the trial, when it was established – contrary to appearances – that there had been no unnecessary violence.) The police officer asserted quite confidently that the concern expressed over this incident was due to the approach of a general election. Hostility towards the police was being utilized, he implied, for party political ends. This sort of attempt to nullify any criticism of the police is not uncommon and it appears in various forms, though I believe that since the appointment of the Royal Commission the police have been much more willing to consider public criticism objectively. Even probationers, however, learn quite quickly to regard certain people as 'anti-police': for example, 'In our town there are two kinds of people. The one group think the police are grand. The others hate us.' This is a 'heads I win, tails you lose' kind of argument, for all too often any criticism is used to identify the speaker as being 'anti-police' and therefore someone who should not be listened to. There is substance too in the complaint of one writer that 'the police and their defenders, particularly those in Parliament, persist in trying to interpret any criticism as all-embracing condemnation' (Parker, 1963). He speaks of lack of frankness on the part of chief constables, and of an unwillingness to discuss police failings which undermines the very confidence they seek to maintain. Greater frankness in such matters might well be coupled with more forthright attempts by many chief constables to correct press reports that place their subordinates in an unfavourable light.

Unlike some organizations, the police cannot regard public relations as something separate from the way they do their everyday work. The internal efficiency of police departments in the long run affects public attitudes far more than press reporting or publicity campaigns. One critical factor in the operation of any organization is morale. The techniques exist for discovering whether high morale in a police force is associated with a favourable attitude on the part of the public, and if so, which one most tends to influence the other. The techniques also exist for uncovering the determinants of police morale: are the major factors in depressing morale material questions of pay and housing, organizational ones of discontent over selection for promotion and unnecessarily harsh discipline, or external ones depending on the attitudes of those members of the public with whom officers have to deal? I believe it would be of the greatest value to have reliable answers to such questions. The armed forces seem to think so, for they have commissioned investigations of morale, and the American services keep these matters under continuous review.

The flexibility of American police organization, as described in Chapters 3 and 4, cannot but impress the British observer and make him wonder whether we do not have too many policemen. Many officers spend a great deal of time standing by automatic traffic signals and doing little but answer the questions of passing pedestrians; many officers complete shift after shift walking round quiet streets without ever making an arrest.[1] It is said that a low arrest rate is a sign that the man is doing his job and preventing crime, but this argument is easily abused. A conscientious constable may indeed prevent crime but criminals soon discover if the man on the beat is lazy. Some senior officers complain bitterly of 'passengers' in their forces. It is said, too, that the public – who pay rates and taxes – like to see a policeman coming round. They might like it less if they appreciated how expensive policemen are nowadays and the high case load carried by many detective officers. There is a widespread nostalgia about the days when the man on the beat could keep order by personal influence, but those days are going. There is a case for reducing the number of men on foot patrol and for delegating more responsibility to them so that they will have more of the village constables' motivation to work.[2] This might entail improving entry and training standards, but the circumstances of the future will in any case make more demands upon the intelligence and education of the ordinary policeman. The police service is now getting a smaller proportion of the able and ambitious young men, for it is easier for

[1] In 1959, crimes known to the police in Scotland averaged 11·3 per police officer – 13·0 in the burghs and 8·9 in the counties (*Royal Commission on the Police*, Appendix to the *Minutes of Evidence* (1–10) p. 15).

[2] Cf. 'Super policemen: Mr B. N. Bebbington's proposals' (*Police Review*, 23 February 1962, p. 150) and L. K. Stewart, 'Abolish the beat' (ibid. 5 April 1963, p. 264).

them today to get scholarships to universities. The Royal Commission stated that they had come across no recent instance of a university graduate entering the service and expressed concern at the small proportion of recruits with a good school examination record. They continued with the warning that none of the measures they discussed 'will have any success in bringing men of high calibre into the service if they are not joined with a resolve on the part of those responsible for recruiting to use every available means to attract this kind of entrant' (*Royal Commission on the Police 1962, Final Report*, p. 95). The problem may be not only to attract this kind of entrant, but to retain him. One of the great characteristics of a university atmosphere is the freedom to pursue truth, and the right, at the proper time and place, to examine the propositions for which others claim authority. A graduate who was subjected to the old-fashioned ideas of discipline that linger in some police stations would have either to resign or to put his education into cold storage.

The efficiency of police forces cannot be improved in certain respects until reforms have been carried out in other institutions. The police have to spend far too much time locking up the same men, for the sentences administered by the courts often have little deterrent value. This problem will not be solved by the expensive procedure of locking offenders away for longer periods: it demands a more radical reappraisal. Then the procedure of many courts is certainly not devised for the convenience of the police. Cases may be postponed because the accused is due to go on holiday, but the same courtesy is not necessarily extended to the principal police witness; when he has to return from holiday for the hearing only to discover that the accused has since decided to plead guilty and that he will not be required to testify, this suggests that society places little value on his attempts to serve the public. Next year, possibly, he will try to avoid having to charge anyone in the weeks preceding his leave. In some parts of the United States a traffic officer who has to make many charges may put them all down for hearing on one particular day of the following week, and this reduces the time he has to spend waiting in court. In Britain matters are managed less expeditiously.

One further conclusion remains to be drawn. If my interpretation of police work is correct, and the job of the man on the beat is principally one of handling people so that they are more disposed to

266

keep the peace, then this has implications for the training curriculum. Recruits are apt to conclude that the importance attached to subjects in the curriculum is a measure of their importance on the job. This is not necessarily the case. Often, both in the police and in the universities, particular topics are taught because they are suited to systematic instruction or because they are easy to set examination questions upon. If the handling of members of the public is so important to the trainee policeman then he must be guided in the use of his discretion. New teaching aids are needed, such as the preparation of films concerning different kinds of encounter, and if the policeman is to develop his sense of judgement it would be appropriate for more emphasis to be placed in his training on the structure of modern society and the character of social trends.

This inquiry was not designed to provide answers to questions of public policy concerning police organization and practice. Nevertheless, it has brought together a certain amount of information which is relevant to discussions of policy. I would draw attention to two particular aspects.

Running through my analysis is one fundamental theme: that harmonious police-public relations depend to a significant extent upon the interrelation between the policeman's occupational role and his private roles. It is the policeman's participation in the society which most affects the way he exercises his powers. But his job prevents him from taking part in ordinary social relations with quite the freedom allowed to members of most occupational groups. If policemen are too detached, too much identified with criminal proceedings, relations with the public deteriorate. If they are insufficiently detached, they cannot do their work properly. If this is true it deserves to be taken seriously and its wider implications examined. On the one hand, the Scottish system whereby the Procurator Fiscal is responsible for prosecution seems superior on sociological grounds to the English practice of police prosecutions. The occasional headline in English newspapers 'Damages awarded against the police' exemplifies the way police prosecutions can convey a false image of the place of the police in society. Such damages are awarded against the community, in whose interest the police are acting. On the other hand, the over-identification of the police with responsibility for the maintenance of public order distracts attention from the public's responsibility. It would be advisable to investigate, more carefully than anyone has yet done, what the barriers are to increased public participation in the maintenance of order, and the ways in which other social institutions might be modified to facilitate such participation.

This study has also presented police forces as organizations that have to be administered just as have hospitals, industrial concerns, public services, and other organizations. The special character of police work should not conceal the fact that problems of the allocation of resources in terms of men and equipment are administrative problems requiring abilities that are not developed by pounding a beat. The arguments for making promotions to the top positions from within the police service are strong – perhaps decisive – but certain consequences follow inevitably from such a policy. The old-style English practice of appointing a retired army officer to the post of chief constable had its merits. Such a man was not dependent for social status upon his position in the police: he already had a military title of some prestige. As a result such a chief constable could afford (if he wished) to identify himself with his subordinates and to regard their failures as his failures. The chief constable who has come up through the ranks may be as good at his job, but his relationship to his police career is different and imposes other limitations. This is just one of the administrative problems of police organization which is more likely to be illuminated by a comparative approach than by one which stresses the uniqueness of police work. There is no shortage of good ideas within the police service. Scarcely a month passes without a newspaper's reporting a new scheme in some force. But because of a certain institutional rigidity the good ideas do not necessarily spread from one force or one section to another. Part of the reason for this insularity, I suspect, is that relatively few members of the public have taken an intelligent interest in the police. For information about police matters the recent Royal Commission had to draw very largely upon the police themselves and upon government bodies associated with them. Both the police and the public would benefit if there were more informed and independent opinion in the universities and among the public at large about the police and their duties.

References

ADLOW, Elijah (1947). *Policeman and people*. Boston: William J. Rochfort.

BANTON, Michael (1963). Social integration and police authority. *The Police Chief*, April, pp. 18–20.

CENTER FOR THE STUDY OF DEMOCRATIC INSTITUTIONS (1962). *The police: an interview with William H. Parker*. Santa Barbara, California.

CHAPMAN, Samuel G. (Ed.) (1963). *The police heritage in England and America*. East Lansing: Michigan State University.

DAVIES, Audrey M. (1954). Police, the law and the individual. *Annals of the American Academy of Political and Social Science*, 291.

DEL PESCO, Robert L. (1952). The municipal police department: more than an enforcement agency. M.A. thesis, Tufts College, Massachusetts.

DURKHEIM, Emile (1938). *The rules of sociological method*. Chicago: University of Chicago Press.

DURKHEIM, Emile (1947). *The division of labor in society*. Glencoe, Illinois: The Free Press.

DURKHEIM, Emile (1953). *Sociology and philosophy*. Glencoe, Illinois: The Free Press.

EHRLICH, Howard J. (1959). *The analysis of role conflicts in a complex organization: the police*. Ph.D. dissertation, Michigan State University. (Microfilmed.)

EHRLICH, Howard J., RHINEHART, James W. & HOWELL, John C. (1962). The study of role conflict: explorations in methodology. *Sociometry*, vol. 25, pp. 85–97.

ELMES, Frank (1963). *The police as a career*. London: Batsford.

GOFFMAN, Erving (1956). The nature of deference and demeanour. *American Anthropologist*, vol. 58, pp. 473–502.

GOFFMAN, Erving (1961). *Asylums*. New York: Doubleday.

269

GORER, Geoffrey (1955). *Exploring English character.* London: Cresset.

GOULDNER, Alvin W. (1954). *Patterns of industrial bureaucracy.* Glencoe, Illinois: The Free Press; London: Routledge & Kegan Paul, 1955.

GOURLEY, G. Douglas (1954). Police-public relations. *Annals of the American Academy of Political and Social Science*, 291.

GROSS, N. C., MASON, W. S. & MACEACHERN, A. W. (1958). *Explorations in role analysis.* New York: Wiley.

HALL, Oswald (1957). *Specialized occupations and industrial unrest.* A Lecture published by Tulane University, New Orleans.

HOLCOMB, R. D. (1950). *The Police and the public.* Springfield, Illinois: C. C. Thomas.

HOMANS, George C. (1950). *The human group.* New York: Harcourt, Brace.

HOMANS, George C. (1962). *Sentiments and activities.* New York: Free Press of Glencoe.

INBAU, Fred E. (1962). Public safety *v.* individual civil liberties: the prosecutors' stand. *Journal of Criminal Law, Criminology and Police Science*, vol. 53, pp. 85–9.

INGERSOLL, John E. (1963). The police scandal syndrome. *The Police Chief*, August, pp. 12–16.

INSTITUTE FOR TRAINING IN MUNICIPAL ADMINISTRATION (1961). *Municipal police administration.* (Fifth edition.) Chicago: International City Managers' Association.

JUSTICE (1962). U.S. Commission on Civil Rights, 1961. Report, Book 5. Washington D.C.

KEPHART, William M. (1957). *Racial factors and urban law enforcement.* Philadelphia: University of Pennsylvania Press.

LAFAVE, Wayne R. (1962). The police and nonenforcement of the law. *Wisconsin Law Review*, pp. 104–37 and 179–239.

MCMULLEN, M. (1961). A theory of corruption. *Sociological Review*, vol. 9, pp. 181–201, esp. 189–90.

MOYLAN, Sir John (1948). *The police of Britain.* London: Longmans.

MYRDAL, Gunnar *et al.* (1944). *An American dilemma.* New York: Harper.

PARKER, Tony (1963). From the other side of the fence. *New Society*, 29 August.

References

PARKER, William H. (1954). The police challenge in our great cities. *Annals of the American Academy of Political and Social Science*, 291.

POUND, Roscoe (1930). *Criminal justice in America.* (Quoted by LaFave, 1962, p. 116.)

RADCLIFFE-BROWN, A. R. (1952). *Structure and function in primitive society.* London: Cohen & West.

RODDENBURY, E. W. (1953). Achieving professionalism. *Journal of Criminal Law, Criminology and Police Science*, vol. 287, pp. 111–15.

ROLPH, C. H. (Ed.) (1962). *The police and the public.* London: Heinemann.

ROYAL COMMISSION ON THE POLICE 1962 (1962). *Final Report.* Cmnd. 1728. London: H.M.S.O.

ROYAL COMMISSION ON THE POLICE (1962). Appendix IV to the *Minutes of Evidence.* Relations between the police and the public, by R. Morton-Williams. London: H.M.S.O.

RUDWICK, Elliott M. (1962). *The unequal badge: Negro policemen in the South.* Southern Regional Council, Atlanta.

SHILS, Edward A. & YOUNG, Michael (1953). The meaning of the coronation. *Sociological Review*, n.s. vol. I, pp. 63–81.

SPENCER, Gilmour & JEWELL, Keith (1963). Police leadership: a research study. *The Police Chief*, March, pp. 40–5.

STERN, Mort (1962). What makes a policeman go wrong, by a former Denver Police Officer as told to Mort Stern. *Journal of Criminal Law, Criminology and Police Science*, vol. 53, pp. 97–101.

WARNER, W. Lloyd (1959). *The living and the dead.* New Haven: Yale University Press.

WESTLEY, William A. (1951). *The police: a sociological study of law, custom and morality.* Unpublished Ph.D. dissertation, University of Chicago. (Microfilmed.)

WESTLEY, William A. (1953). Violence and the police. *American Journal of Sociology*, vol. 59, pp. 34–41.

WESTLEY, William A. (1956). Secrecy and the police. *Social Forces*, vol. 34, pp. 254–7.

WHYTE, William Foote (1943). *Street corner society.* Chicago: University of Chicago Press.

WILLIAMS, Christopher (1954). Turning a blind eye. *Criminal Law Review.* (Reprinted in Rolph, 1962.)

271

WILSON, James Q. (1963). The police and their problems: a theory. *Public Policy*, vol. xii, pp. 189–216. Yearbook of the Graduate School of Public Administration, Harvard University.

Index

273

Date Due